DISEASES & PARASITES

of sheep and goats
in South Africa

PAMELA AND PETER OBEREM

Published by: *Landbouweekblad* and Afrivet

First edition, first impression, 2011

Text © Pamela and Peter Oberem
Photographs © Peter and Pamela Oberem, apart from those detailed in the photo credits
Copyright published edition © 2011

ISBN: 978-0-620-49561-5

DISCLAIMER

Although care has been taken to be as accurate as possible, neither the author nor the publisher makes any express or implied representation as to the accuracy of the information contained in this book and cannot be held legally responsible, or accept liability, for any errors or omissions.

Managing editor: Jacques Claassen
Copy-editor: Pat Barton
Proofreader: Pat Barton
Design and layout: Christina Botha
Cover design: Christina Botha
Photo editor: Gretchen Peiser
Retouching: Jason Wakefield
Indexing: Michel Cozien
Reproduction: Andre Beck
Printed and bound by: Unity Press, Airport Industria, Cape Town

Editorial director, Media24, Specialist Magazines: Jean du Preez

ACKNOWLEDGEMENTS

We would like to acknowledge the contribution of our many veterinary colleagues and friends to Diseases of Small Stock, either by providing information or photographic material, or reading the manuscript for accuracy. In particular, we would like to thank the staff of the Middleburg Veterinary Laboratory who trawled photographic archives in search of material and patiently copied the slides into digital form.

We would also like to thank Johan van Rensberg for his contribution, including proofreading the first draft, and giving useful advice and suggestions. Danie Odendaal gave us permission to use many of his own photographs and offered advice and encouragement throughout.

Dr Robin Taylor provided practical advice about the incidence and control of ticks and heartwater in small stock and Carol Enslin helped with tables. To these and the many others who contributed, our sincere thanks.

Peter and Pamela Oberem

PHOTO CREDITS

Afrivet Business management 7, 72, 87, 102, 117
Arno Moore Bioinsecta 105
Bertie Hugo 65
Danie Odendaal 5, 24, 25, 27, 28, 29, 38, 43, 50, 63, 67, 69, 81, 96, 113
Dorper Breeders' Association 73
Faculty of Veterinary Science, Onderstepoort (Pretoria University) 25, 26, 27, 40, 42, 43, 44, 45, 48, 51, 54, 60, 63, 65, 70, 77, 84, 88, 89, 90, 91, 106, 118, 123
Francois Malan 81
Gareth Bath 32, 34, 36
George Cadle 68, 106
Ian Southey 40
King Family 11
Landbouweekblad 2, 3
Leon Fourie, Clinvet 96, 97
Merino SA 2, 20
Middelburg Veterinary Laboratory 11, 32, 33, 34, 35, 39, 41, 50, 51, 52, 57, 58, 59, 62, 64, 65, 66, 67, 68, 71, 73, 74, 80, 112, 123,
Mike Picker and Charlie Griffiths 104
National Zoological Gardens 38
Sauer Merinos 13
Schering Plough Animal health 7, 13, 14, 59, 70, 71, 72, 97, 100, 102, 104, 105, 112
Wilna Vosloo 97
www.supiri.com (Steve Williams) 33

INTRODUCTION

After the publication of Mönnig and Veldman's handbook for farmers in 1957, no other comprehensive book of this sort was published until we compiled Diseases and Parasites of Livestock in South Africa, at the request of numerous farmers. To our surprise, it sold out rapidly, and had to be reprinted a number of times. This presented us with the opportunity to rewrite the original book, separating the conditions of small stock and cattle into individual volumes. Doing this allows for more comprehensive, coherent discussion of subjects such as parasite control, which differs radically between small stock and cattle. We have made a number of changes and additions to the original text, which we hope will make the book more complete and user friendly.

Pamela and Peter Oberem

Pretoria
January 2011

If you have any feedback/comments on this book,
e-mail us at: *lbw@landbou.com*

CONTENTS

1 GENERAL AND MANAGEMENT ASPECTS

2 CAUSES OF DISEASE AND DIAGNOSIS

3 DISEASES

4 INTERNAL PARASITES AND THEIR CONTROL

ROUNDWORMS

5 EXTERNAL PARASITES AND THEIR CONTROL

6 POISONING

PLAN A, BIBLIOGRAPHY and KEY TO DISEASES

INDEX

1

MANAGEMENT

General and management aspects

SMALL STOCK BREEDS IN SOUTH AFRICA

Sheep

Domestic sheep (*Ovis aries*) are descended from a species of wild sheep, possibly the mouflon (*Ovis musimon*); the only existing wild sheep species to have the same number of chromosomes. Selection of these wild sheep roughly 9 000 years ago caused the loss of horns, lengthening of the tail, shortening of the legs and the development of some more woolly variants. In Africa, two dominant varieties emerged: Thin-tailed, hairy sheep such as those that currently occur from Ethiopia to Damaraland; and the fat-tailed sheep which predominate in southern Africa because of their hardiness in hot, semi-arid conditions. The fat tail that characterises the southern African breeds is thought to be an evolutionary development to promote heat dispersal.

The breed called the Namaqua Ronderib, now almost extinct, is the descendant of the fat-tailed animal the Khoi Khoi brought from the central lakes area of Africa. This breed was long-legged and hardy, and could tolerate arid conditions. Nguni sheep were brought south by Iron Age migrants who initially journeyed into

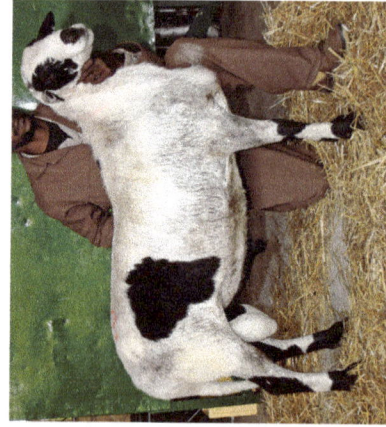

The Pedi is an indigenous sheep breed known for its disease resistance

The Meatmaster was produced by crossing fat-tailed sheep with European breeds to improve the musculature

Merino sheep are the breed of choice for wool production in South Africa

Natal and then spread into other areas. These breeds have a wide genetic base and a number of local variants are seen, namely the Zulu, the Swazi and the Pedi. The indigenous breeds are more resistant

to local diseases such as blue tongue, but may be susceptible to the tick-borne disease heartwater which occurs in the wetter, eastern parts of the country. They are also susceptible to introduced diseases.

Saanen goats are used for milk and cheese production

In 1789, European settlers imported the Merino from Spain. It was the first wooled breed that showed an ability to adapt to harsh South African conditions. Other breeds were subsequently imported from England, Germany and France. Breeds that originate from European countries are highly susceptible to blue tongue and other indigenous diseases.

Black-headed, fat-tailed sheep were imported from Ethiopia and used to cross breed with Dorset horn to produce the Dorper, now widely bred because they are well-adapted to South African conditions. Other composite breeds, such as Dohne-Merino, SA Mutton Merino, Dormer, Meatmaster and Afrino were developed to suit specific ecological conditions and production systems. These breeds are most commonly employed in commercial enterprises; indigenous sheep tend to be raised by rural peoples because of their hardiness to arid conditions, low maintenance requirements and disease resistance. For details of the history, breed characteristics and production statistics of the various breeds, see the SA Studbook website (www.studbook.co.za)

Goats

The ancestors of modern domestic goats originated in Asia and were present in Egypt in 5000 BC. The earliest evidence for the presence of goats in southern Africa is in sites dating from 500 AD, much later than the appearance of sheep. African indigenous goats are referred to generically as savannah goats, and specific names are given to those raised by the various tribes. Savannah goats vary tremendously

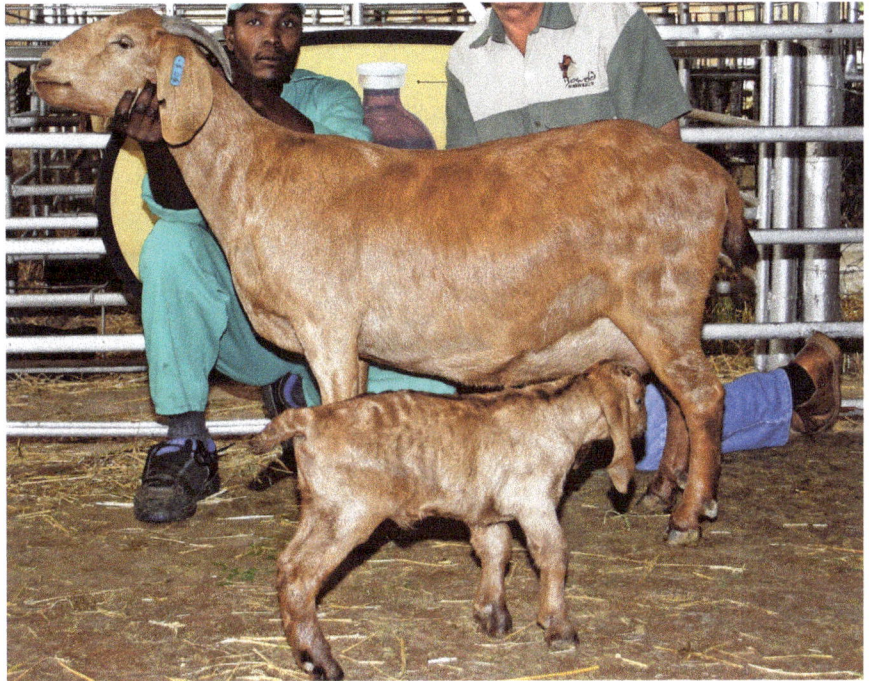

Kalahari red goats

Mohair is produced by Angora goats in South Africa

in horn size and presence, coat type, colour, ear length and size. They are almost unchanged by any artificial selection, but have been selected naturally for hardiness, and disease and parasite resistance.

The South African boer goat (*Capra hircus*) is a type that's been improved by selection of savannah goats crossed with Nubian/Indian goat genes. It was selected

for good conformation and size, growth, fertility and carcass traits.

A small group of Angora goats (*Capra aegagrus*) was imported into South Africa for mohair production and, because they originated from a small genetic base, they have some heritable problems such as habitual abortions. Milk-producing goats (milch goats), such as Saanen, Toggenberg

and British Alpine, were imported from Europe for the production of goat milk or cheese.

REPRODUCTION

The breeding period in sheep and (especially) in goats, is seasonal although the length of the season varies with the breed. British sheep breeds have a short breeding season, Merinos have a medium-length season and indigenous sheep can be bred almost all year round. Ewes come into oestrus under the influence of nutritional and seasonal effects, specifically the decrease in daylight length. The natural oestrus period in the southern hemisphere is therefore autumn (April/May), but in practice there can be two seasons if animals are managed and fed correctly. Grazing quality has to be good when stimulating animals to come into oestrus, and maintained during breeding (see Nutritional requirements for breeding, page 5 and 6).

The advantage of spring lambing in summer-rainfall areas is a good food supply at weaning, and high fertility when the animals are bred in autumn. Disadvantages are the occurrence of cold spells in spring and the prevalence of blue tongue when the colostral immunity of lambs is low. Autumn lambing avoids the blue tongue danger period in sheep, but ewes are less fertile when bred in the spring months. The hormonal synchronisation of the lambing period can be done by a veterinarian, in order to concentrate lambing at a particular time, which facilitates management.

All breeding stock has to be examined before the breeding season, to exclude ewes having damaged udders and vulvas. Bad mothers and infertile ewes have also to be removed from the breeding flock. Old ewes should be culled at roughly six years of age, depending on the state of their teeth. Rams should be checked for congenital problems of the penis, testes and sheath. If rams are overweight they should be forced to exercise by making them walk some distance to watering points. Sheep flocks showing signs of epididymitis should have their semen tested to determine the cause (see *Brucella ovis*,

Mothering ability is a genetic attribute

page 48 - 49 and Non-infectious causes of Epididymitis, page 49).

Breeding camps should preferably be small and the ground level and have multiple watering points. The size of breeding flocks has also to be considered; smaller flocks (a maximum of 250 animals) are easier to manage and better for mating.

The ideal ram to ewe ratio is two to three rams per 100 ewes; and ewes should be bred for the first time at 14 – 18 months of age (two- to four-tooth stage). The length of oestrus in ewes is 17 days and its duration is an average of 27 hours. The season is usually five to six weeks long. Ewes in oestrus will seek out the ram, showing wagging of the tail and permitting mounting.

Lambing usually occurs 147 days after mating. In the last month of pregnancy, the lamb grows rapidly and the ewe shows a firm, enlarged udder at roughly 10 days before birth. The decreasing space in the ewe's abdomen triggers the secretion of various hormones which prepare the ewe

for lambing by causing the contraction of the uterus, and the expansion of the cervix and the ligaments of the pelvis. This facilitates the lamb's passage out of the uterus.

Once the lamb passes through the cervix, the ewe begins to strain her abdominal muscles, propelling the lamb forward. The outer layer of placental membranes ruptures when the lamb passes into the vagina, and the inner waterbag then appears at the vulva. This bursts when the ewe gives the final push which ejects the lamb. After birth, the umbilical cord breaks off. The placental membranes usually come out soon afterwards, unless there is a problem. As soon as the lamb is able to stand it begins to suckle, which stimulates the ewe to let down her milk.

Ewes should be left to lamb without interference as far as possible, to prevent mismothering and failure to suckle. Observe a group of lambing ewes from a distance, and assist only under certain circumstances:

- when an ewe has been straining for more than an hour
- if the waterbag is still unbroken after an hour
- if the waterbag has burst and no lamb appears
- if there are signs of abnormal presentation (eg tail first).

If the ewe needs assistance, she must be restrained correctly for examination: she must be placed lying on her side on clean bags or newspaper, on a slope, with her head facing downhill. Wash your arms with soap and water and use a lubricant (liquid paraffin or KY jelly) before placing a hand or arm in the uterus. Failure to use a lubricant will cause damage such as a ruptured uterus, and lead to bleeding and death.

Try to establish the problem:
- if the cervix hasn't opened, the ewe won't be able to lamb normally and will need a caesarean
- if the cervix is open, check that the presentation is correct
- if the presentation is not normal, it will have to be corrected – i e head or legs will have to be straightened by manipulation using a hand or a calving rope.

Twins or triplets should be removed one at a time, and each must be identified and separated before this can take place. Dead, seriously deformed, or overlarge lambs usually need to be extracted by caesarean section.

Usually, a lamb begins to breathe as soon as it is born, but in assisted births lambs may have fluid accumulation in the airways. Ensure the nose is clear of membranes and gently swing the lamb upside down, supporting it under the chest so that fluid moves out of the nose under the force of gravity. Place the lamb on a towel and give it a good rub to stimulate breathing. Then leave the lamb and ewe alone to bond.

Lambs or kids may need to be fostered or artificially reared if mothers die or have no milk; sometimes they have to be destroyed if other options are impractical. Fostering is the method of choice, if possible. Bear in mind that the newborn needs colostrum on the first day of life so it should be placed with a newly-lambed

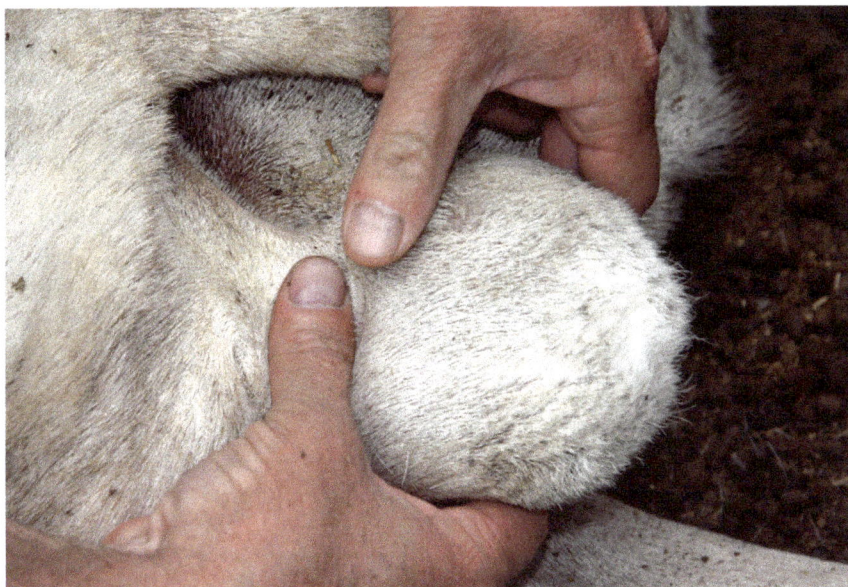

Stud rams have to be examined before the breeding season

ewe/doe or bottle-fed colostrum from a newly-lambed female. The colostrum contains essential antibodies and is highly nutritious, allowing the newborn to cope with cold stress.

Lambs and kids can be raised on full-cream cow's milk or calf replacer at a rate of 10% of body weight; for example, for a 4kg lamb give 150ml in four feeds, increasing the quantity as the lamb gains weight. For the first 14 days, warm the milk to body temperature (35 – 37°C). Thereafter, the milk can be fed by bucket at room temperature and the number of feeds per day can be reduced.

Note that calf replacer must be made up 20% more concentrated for lambs, since ewe's milk contains more fat. Good-quality replacers should be used to prevent abomasal bloat, which causes sudden abdominal distension, difficult breathing and sometimes rupture of the abdomen. Weak but otherwise normal lambs may be treated by injecting 20% glucose (10ml/kg body weight) through the abdominal wall. Colostrum should be given as soon as possible through a stomach tube. It can be stored in a freezer, thawed when required and dosed at a rate of 50ml/kg. Lambs have to be kept warm until they are strong enough to suckle, then they can be returned to the mother or placed with an ewe that's lost her lamb.

Nutritional requirements for breeding

Ewes and does require good nutrition at certain stages of the breeding cycle.

Since most small stock are raised on range (veld) conditions, their energy levels may be low and they may have to be supplemented at various crucial times. Flushing or raising the nutritional level by giving additional feeding two to three weeks before mating will stimulate ovulation. It is especially effective if the ewes' condition is poor.

If ewes are in good condition this will not be necessary and will make them too fat, which could lead to dystocias. Flushing can be done by feeding with concentrates or by simply moving the ewes to better pastures.

Nutrition should be supplemented – or at least improved – late in pregnancy when nutritional demands are high. Grazing on old lands is not suitable because of the low nutritional content and the presence of poisonous plants. Vitamin A should be supplemented to animals on dry feeds, poor forage and pelleted rations. Occasionally, selenium deficiency may cause infertility and supplementation may be necessary.

For ewes to produce sufficient milk for their lambs they must have adequate energy – if the grazing is inadequate, this can be supplemented using a protein source such as soya bean oil cake which stimulates feed intake and increases energy intake. Planted pastures such as barley are ideal as an energy source, but only for a few hours a day. Strip grazing is most economical and prevents trampling.

Creep feeding is strictly for lambs, and ewes shouldn't have access to this feed. It supplies energy to supplement the protein supplied by the ewes' milk, and can be given on demand to lambs from three weeks of age.

Increasing the protein above 12% in creep will not improve performance. Do not add urea, because an unweaned lamb doesn't yet have a functioning rumen. If lambs are on veld or pasture, roughage doesn't need to be added to the creep, but its addition at 15% or higher is recommended to limit acidosis.

NOTES

NUTRITION

Sheep and goats are ruminants, which means they are able to utilise the otherwise indigestible cellulose in plants by means of the micro-organisms in their rumens.

The microbes digest this fibrous plant material, and in the process, volatile fatty acids are formed which can be taken up directly through the rumen wall. This is the main energy source of ruminants. The micro-organisms also use the rest of the digested material as food and they are able to multiply. As their numbers increase, some of them will flow with the undigested plant material into the rest of the intestinal tract where they are digested in the abomasum and small intestine. The micro-organisms themselves become the main protein source of ruminants.

Small stock are able to eat a variety of fibrous foods such as forages (veld), planted pastures, crop residues in the form of silage and industrial byproducts, such as oil seed cake. Goats, in particular, are able to browse on the leaves and twigs of trees, sometimes standing on their hind legs to access branches which cannot be reached by sheep.

Digestion by ruminal organisms is disturbed by various factors:

- when the pH of the rumen becomes acidic as the result of a sudden increase in dietary carbohydrates
- when the pH becomes alkaline; for example, when excessive urea is ingested.

Under these conditions, the micro-organisms may die off and lead to indigestion (for treatment and prevention, see Part 3: Diseases). Certain drugs, plant poisons and folk remedies, such as old motor oil and disinfectants, may cause damage to the rumen organisms and also give rise to indigestion (see Part 3: Diseases).

The most important components of the ruminant diet are energy, protein, phosphate and calcium (macro-nutrients) and the micro-nutrients (vitamins and trace elements). All of these elements are contained in the dry matter component of plants. But because nutritional components of plant matter vary with the time

Even green pastures can be deficient in some nutrients

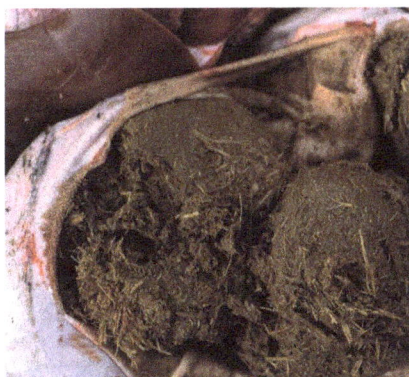

The rumen's micro-organisms are essential for good digestion in ruminant animals

Bowie is a calcium deficiency that occurs in young animals on green pastures such as lucerne

of year and the growing season, the diets of production animals are supplemented to optimise immunity, health, growth and production.

- **Energy**

Forage (veld) is essentially a low-energy feed and high-producing animals generally require additional feed in the form of planted pastures, grain supplements such as maize products or sorghum residue and molasses. The energy supplements are usually combined with protein supplementation for maximum effect.

An animal's energy requirements are expressed in megajoules (MJ), which is the most convenient unit. The energy supplied by rations is expressed as metabolisable energy (ME), which is the quantity of energy available to the animal after deducting the energy lost through the indigestible component and expended by the digestion process.

Energy deficiency symptoms are weight loss or reduced growth, reproductive failure, poor production and increased susceptibility to infections. Feeding an excess of energy is wasteful, and can cause reproductive problems (see Body condition evaluation, page 24, 27 - 29).

● Protein

Supplementation is needed when the quality of forage is low; for example, in winter (in summer-rainfall areas) or at the end of the plant growth season. Supplementation is usually in the form of a protein-rich industrial byproduct such as cottonseed oil cake, but it can also be a non-protein nitrogen (NPN) source such as urea, which can be utilised by the rumen microflora. A protein deficiency causes reduced appetite, poor growth or weight loss, and poor production, including wool shedding. More severe deficiencies cause anaemia, and swelling under the jaw (oedema). Feeding too much protein may cause alkalosis and diarrhoea.

● Calcium and phosphate

These are the minerals of greatest importance to ruminant livestock, and the balance between these components is extremely important. Supplementing one may upset the balance of the other, and it's essential to ensure that the ratio between them is maintained at 2:1. Phosphate deficiency occurs widely in SA on forage and pastures, particularly at the end of the growing season. A deficiency of phosphate on the veld leads to grazing animals developing "pica" or bone-chewing which can lead to botulism outbreaks. Supplements can prevent this and improve production. Calcium-phosphate imbalance in the diet may cause milk fever; this is precipitated by alkaline diets such as "chocolate mealies", so calcium has to be added to prevent this.

Lambs grazed exclusively on lush green pastures develop a severe calcium deficiency called bowie, which causes the outward bending of the legs as a result of poor bone formation.

● Vitamins

Ruminal microflora produce most of the vitamins required by ruminants. The only one that has to be supplemented, under normal farming conditions, is vitamin A. This vitamin is obtained in green feed, but as soon as it is cut for feeding, making hay or silage, the vitamin A content falls. Vitamin A levels are low in veld grass late in the growing season, as well as in nitrate-fertilised pastures. Since vitamin A deficiency may cause reproductive problems and eye infections, small stock should receive regular supplementation using drenches or injectable preparations, at the intervals prescribed by the manufacturers.

● Trace elements

These are minerals required in very small quantities which are nevertheless essential for good health. Deficiencies seldom arise in animals on planted pastures or complete rations, but may occur on forage in certain areas where deficiencies of iodine, copper, cobalt, manganese, selenium and molybdenum have been recorded. Most trace element deficiencies manifest in poor growth and reproduction. Supplements can be provided in licks or in injectable form, when necessary. This should be done on advice from a veterinarian or animal nutritionist, as some of them have a narrow safety margin and can be toxic given in excess.

USING GROWTH STIMULANTS

Growth stimulants have been used for decades in animal production, because they can improve weight gains by at least 10% and raise feed conversion by 15%. This is an important contribution, since feed is the most expensive input in all types of farming. Feed additives are used in small stock mainly in feedlot systems, but additives such as flavophospholipol can improve the performance of small stock on winter veld.

The advantage of growth stimulants is that they improve growth, and the feed conversion on specific rations. This can be an advantage, given the high cost of feed and the poor value of range and pastures during winter. Meat/wool therefore becomes cheaper and production is more cost-effective.

Developed countries are concerned that the use of antibiotics in animals promotes the spread of resistant organisms to humans. Most of the antimicrobial growth stimulants used in South Africa, however, aren't employed for therapeutic use in humans (e g ionophors or flavophospholipol).

In Europe, the use of antimicrobial growth stimulants in food animals is now banned. This EU ban is based on public perceptions and opinions, not on scientific principles. The promotion of animal products as "hormone free" is a sales gimmick, as all meat and milk contains hormones produced by the animals themselves, as do plants such as soya, peas and cabbage (phyto-oestrogen). Hormones are still used as growth stimulants in some developed countries, such as the USA, New Zealand, Australia and South Africa. Meat exporters should be aware that some of these products are banned in EU countries.

Most growth stimulants are added either in a feed concentrate or to the complete ration, depending on the type of animal being fed. Thorough mixing is essential to ensure good distribution and even feeding. Poor mixing results in some animals not receiving sufficient substance to effect a result. In some cases, poor mixing can cause overdosing and toxicity. Mixing should, therefore, be entrusted to reputable companies.

Zeranol and the hormones are implanted under the skin and slowly released into the bloodstream. They are delivered with special applicators, and good needle hygiene is essential for implantation. Some growth stimulants have a withdrawal period before animals are allowed to be slaughtered, and this has to be strictly observed.

Antimicrobial growth stimulants

The main effect of antimicrobials is the suppression of certain gut bacteria and the resultant dominance of others, with the result that there's better utilisation of feed, as well as prevention of certain diseases. Some antimicrobials are used for therapeutic effect in intensive systems.

● Tetracyclines (oxytetracycline and chlortetracycline)

These antimicrobials are used in feedlots to medicate ruminants for certain problems, such as feedlot pneumonia and liver

Small stock on dry winter veld can benefit from flavophospholipol supplementation

abscesses. The dosage prescribed have to be recommended by the consulting veterinarian for every prescription.

● **Ionophores**

Examples are monensin and salinomycin, which can be used to prevent coccidiosis and also to improve feed conversion. Ionophores change the bacterial flora of the rumen, which enhances propionic acid production, increases available dietary protein and reduces methane production, resulting in better food use. This group isn't used in human medicine, so it doesn't contribute to the problem of resistant bacteria in people, which is one of the concerns raised about antimicrobial growth promotants. Ionophores are widely used, especially in feedlots, because they im-prove starch, digestion and food use.

● **Flavophospholipol**

This antimicrobial is a growth stimulant, and its use is confined to animals. It produces its effect by suppressing certain rumen microflora. Flavophospholipol improves the performance of sheep and goats on veld as it aids the utilisation of poor-quality roughage. There's no withdrawal time for this product because it isn't absorbed into the bloodstream.

Non-antibiotic growth stimulants

This group has a direct influence on the protein metabolism of the animal.

● **Hormones**

Hormones are natural substances produced by animals. Sex hormones increase nitrogen retention, and enhance protein metabolism and feed conversion efficiency. Hormonal growth stimulants (male and female) are used chiefly for feedlot animals in SA, since they're not suitable for use in breeding animals.

● **Hormone mimics**

Zeranol is a synthetic molecule based on a substance initially isolated from a maize fungus. The molecule mimics the effect of oestrogen and stimulates animal growth by 10%. It can be used to round off sheep in feedlots, but is not suitable for use in animals intended for breeding.

NOTES
_____
_____
_____
_____
_____
_____
_____
_____
_____
_____
_____
_____
_____
_____

VELD MANAGEMENT

In South Africa, sheep and goats are raised mainly in range conditions, in the grasslands of the Free State and the High-veld areas of Gauteng and KwaZulu-Natal, in the Karoo and the Valley Bushveld or thicket of the Eastern Cape.

Veld management is therefore of the utmost importance, but experts estimate that an astonishing 90% of the veld in South Africa has low production potential as a result of bad management.

Overgrazing is the single most important reason for the degradation of the veld, and the main cause is the overstocking of veld, i e keeping too many animals per hectare. The carrying capacity of veld depends on the vegetation type (biome) – grassland, for example – as well as Karoo, or savannah. The correct stocking rates for small stock in a specific biome are available from local extension officers, range and forage experts at the Agricultural Research Council, and local agricultural colleges. Stock numbers should be reduced on veld in poor condition and during droughts. Keeping the same animal numbers during droughts as in good rainfall years, and sustaining them with additional feeding, contributes further to veld damage.

Overgrazing grassland and shrubs results in the gradual degradation of the veld. Although grass can regenerate after grazing, burning or cutting, it requires a period of rest in order to sprout again. If it isn't rested, the roots of the plant weaken and the grass plant dies off. This leads to exposure of the soil and gradual erosion of the nutrient topsoil, with the resultant exposure of less fertile soil. The exposed soil cannot be recolonised by plants, since it is compacted and poor in nutrients, and it's eroded by wind and water action, with the eventual development of dongas, leading to progressive desertification.

Undergrazing of grass pastures may also cause degradation, since the grass plants become choked and moribund.

The overgrazing of shrubs in the Karoo or valley bushveld results in loss of palatable bushes, the dominance of unpalatable shrubs and the invasion of poison-

Stoebe vulgaris, or bankrupt bush, is an unpalatable invader of overgrazed veld

The final stage of veld degradation is soil erosion

ous plants – with the result that the veld becomes less productive. Examples of poisonous plants that flourish with overgrazing in the Karoo are kaalsiektebos (*Chrysocoma ciliata*), kraalbos (*Galenia africana*) and scholtzbos (*Pteronia pallens*). Unpalatable plants increase, as their seeds or flowers are not eaten by livestock and dominate the veld.

These plants have to be thinned out to

1

MANAGEMENT

increase the productivity of the land.

Alien plants also increase in wetlands and rivers, contributing to the drying up of wetlands systems and springs. Blue gums, wattles, poplars, Spanish reeds, mesquite and oleanders drain valuable water sources and some species become very difficult to eradicate. The ecology and management of karoo areas is expansively covered in the excellent publication Karoo Veld (see Bibliography), which includes a photographic index of important Karoo bossies (bushes), and lists the palatability of the plants found in this area.

PREDATOR MANAGEMENT

Small stock, especially kids and lambs, are preyed on mainly by jackal, caracal and feral dogs. Experts who've studied the problem believe that losses from wild predators are exaggerated, mainly because farmers fail to distinguish between predation and scavenging. Bath (1994) reported in a study that lamb mortality on various farms was as high as 30%, and the major cause was starvation resulting from a low birth weight, poor nutrition and mismothering. These lambs die in the veld and are eaten by scavengers. The only way to distinguish between predation and scavenging is to do a thorough post-mortem (see Predators and Farmers, Bibliography).

Many farmers, convinced that predators are the main cause of lamb losses, resort to indiscriminate poisoning, trapping and hunting. In the process, many non-predators, such as bat-eared foxes and aardwolf, are killed as well as other non-target animals all of which are useful in the veld ecology. The threat posed by animals such as brown hyena is also greatly exaggerated, as they are predominantly scavengers which play an important ecological role. In addition, large predators such as leopards have been shown by various studies to prey on small predators like jackal, thus keeping their numbers down.

Predators such as jackal and caracal prey on lambs and kids, especially when they're unprotected, but destroying these animals has proved ineffective as a con-

King collars are used to protect lambs from predators

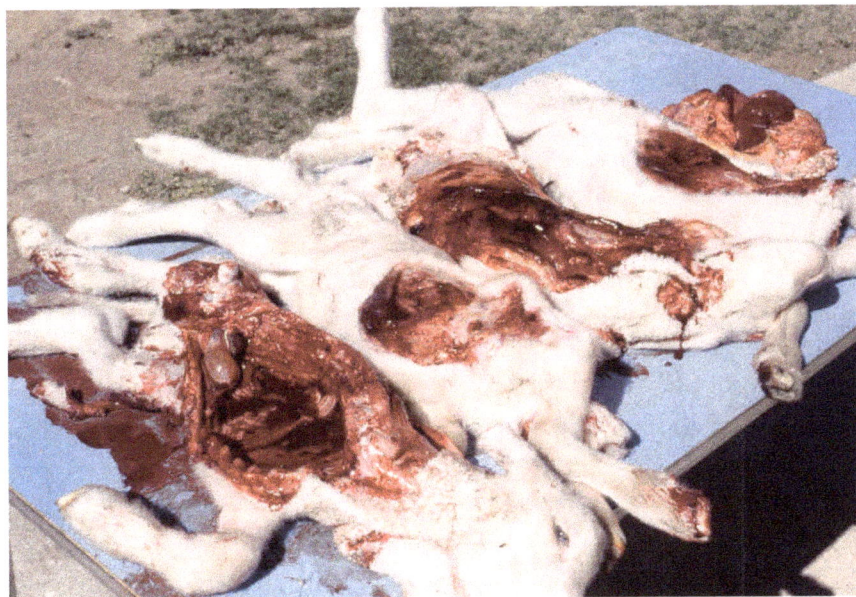

Predation can be confirmed by conducting a post-mortem examination. Note the bleeding into the carcass

trol measure, because it merely creates an ecological niche for other individuals of the same species. Experts recommend that stock be protected by the many available alternative measures. Predator fencing around lambing camps is a useful way to keep out predators, but it must be constructed correctly, complete with

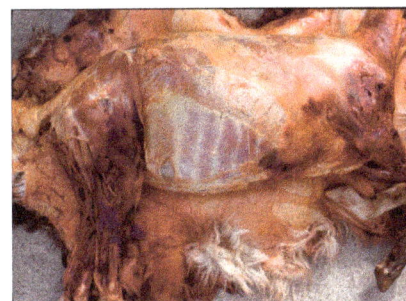

A sheep killed by a domestic dog. Note the bite marks

overhang, to prevent cats climbing over the fence. Other strategies include using guard animals such as donkeys, guard dogs (Anatolian sheep dogs), and shepherds. Deterrants to scare off predators include collars (King collars), bells (Steenkamp bells) and scent.

If a farmer's convinced that a particular animal is causing a problem, it can be removed using the correct strategy for the species – for example, traps or shooting, if really necessary. There are a number of problem animal specialists who can recommend the correct method, so the farmer doesn't have to waste time and resources on ineffective or incorrect methods. Note: It is currently illegal to use poison or gin traps for the control of problem animals.

NOTES

DISEASE AND PARASITE CONTROL

Prevention is better than cure

Controlling disease by prevention rather than treatment is more cost-effective, for a number of reasons:

- outbreaks of disease/parasites can affect many animals
- such outbreaks cause death or permanent damage
- outbreaks may not be treatable (if they are viruses) or are too acute to allow for treatment
- they cause production losses.

Selecting and buying animals

Many animal health problems can be prevented if specific precautionary guidelines are followed before animals are bought and brought onto the farm.

It's essential to purchase animals from reputable sources and to ask for a full history and proof of disease testing results of the flock; for example, for ovine brucellosis. Obtain from the owner a written declaration of the vaccination, dipping and dosing programmes followed.

If the animals being purchased are first examined by a veterinarian, it will prevent the buying of old, diseased, parasite-infested or infertile animals; as local veterinarians know which diseases are prevalent in a particular area, they're usually alert to potential problems being introduced onto a farm by new animals. The veterinarian may recommend laboratory tests before animals are purchased to prevent the introduction of new diseases; for example, Johne's disease, which is becoming more prevalent. Animals should be examined for signs of foot rot, eye infections and skin parasites or infections. The genitalia of rams and ewes should be carefully examined for any problems (see General examination, page 24, 27-29). The Animal Disease Act 35/1984 requires that farmers do not buy or sell animals that have diseases or parasites; this is not officiousness but a genuine attempt to prevent the spreading of disease and resistant parasites.

Once animals have been purchased,

New animals should be quarantined to prevent the introduction of diseases and resistant parasites

they should be quarantined on the new farm to prevent the introduction of parasites (e g worms, sheep scab, ticks or lice), especially resistant worms (see Internal parasites, page 76-91). Small stock should be dosed twice for worms, using two remedy groups, at two-week intervals, to ensure that parasites are not introduced onto the farm. Sheep should be given two macrocyclic lactone injections at a two- to three- week interval to ensure that they are free from sheep scab and blue (sucking) lice.

All animals should be identified by, for example, ear tags, tattooing or branding, and records should be kept when animals are vaccinated, dosed and dipped. On stud farms, mating group records should be kept to allow selection for breeding purposes and registration of offspring. Accurate record-keeping allows for precision in respect of preventing disease and controlling parasites.

VACCINATION

Using vaccines to prevent disease is a small investment with high returns, and

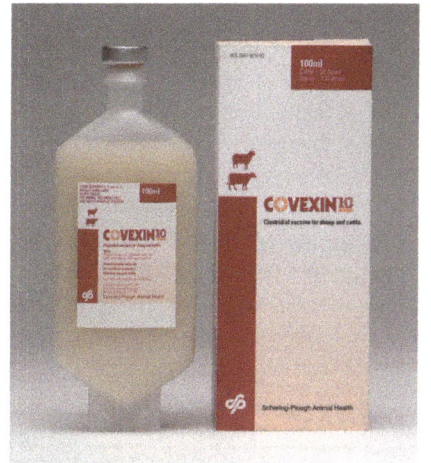

Vaccines are indispensable for the prevention of disease

as such could be considered an insurance policy. The cost of the vaccine is always low in relation to the cost of the animal, and as vaccines are tax-deductible, it's a curious fact that farmers are often happier to buy antibiotics for treatment than vaccines for disease prevention, even though they can't be used to treat viral diseases. Vaccines must be used correctly to give optimal protection. Using vaccines at the wrong time, or damaging them through

poor storage and handling, would negate their effects and be a waste of money.

All vaccines come with a package insert that details storage instructions, administrative route, the age and sex of animals to be inoculated, the time of year, and any contra-indications or precautions of use. Read the package insert carefully before using the vaccine.

Vaccines are given by specific routes for particular reasons. It's essential to administer them as recommended, because they may not be effective or may cause severe irritation if given by another route. The routes most commonly used for small stock are subcutaneous and intramuscular. The orf vaccine is administered by scarification, which involves scratching the skin with a sterile needle and dripping the vaccine organism onto the scratches. It's essential that all syringes and needles used for vaccination be sterilised by boiling for at least 20 minutes directly before use. Failure to sterilise needles sufficiently will cause abscesses and possibly death resulting from generalised infection. Don't use alcohol or disinfectants on needles and syringes used to administer vaccines.

To protect newborn animals against specific diseases, vaccines are given to the mothers and immunity is transferred via the colostrum. This is called maternal or passive (colostral) immunity. Newborns have to receive sufficient colostrum directly after birth if vaccines are to be successful against diseases such as colibacillosis, tetanus and lamb dysentery.

Young animals are usually vaccinated at about the time of weaning, when colostral immunity is at a low level. When it's done depends on the particular vaccine, so the recommendations have to be read carefully. Vaccination during outbreaks is usually a waste of time because the incubation period for a disease is invariably shorter than the time it takes to develop vaccine immunity, and the vaccination of animals during outbreaks always carries the risk of transmitting disease from one animal to another (Rift Valley fever, anthrax). Diseases associated with management practices, such as dipping (*Arcanobacterium ovis*), shearing sheep (quarter evil), and castration and docking (tetanus) need to

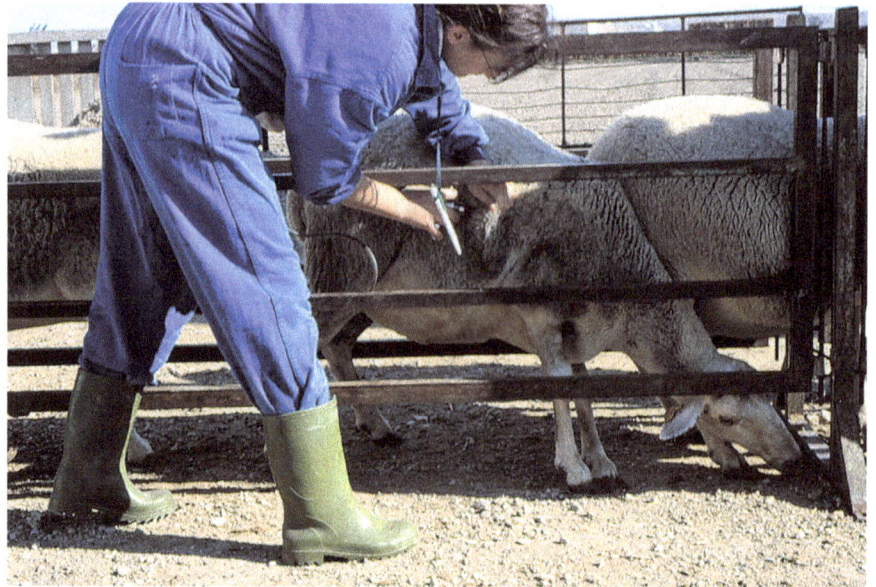

Vaccination must be carefully planned and implemented

be prevented by vaccinating before these procedures are undertaken.

Insect-borne diseases are seasonal and the vaccines used to prevent them should, therefore, be given in spring, before the danger period. Sufficient time must be allowed for the full course of immunisations; for example, blue tongue vaccination requires nine weeks to complete the full vaccination programme.

Vaccination is generally a harmless procedure, but occasionally there are side-effects. Anaphylactic shock is an immediate allergic reaction which may be triggered by any component in the vaccine. Such responses only occur in a small percentage of animals, but can be fatal in some cases, unless adrenalin is administered. Some live vaccines are contra-indicated for use in pregnant animals, because of the possibility of abortion. So study the package insert for contra-indications during pregnancy. Some vaccines may cause prominent swellings because they contain an adjuvant that stimulates immunisation. To avoid severe reactions, administer these vaccines strictly according to recommendations.

Vaccine failure
There are many reasons why vaccines might fail:

- **damaged vaccine (incorrect storage [heating or freezing] or exposure to direct sunlight)**
- **incorrect diagnosis**
- **failure to give boosters**
- **using the wrong route**
- **animal was incubating the disease**
- **under-dosing (wrong dilution or faulty calibration of automatic syringes)**
- **mixing vaccines with other products**
- **antibiotics given at the same time as live bacterial vaccine**
- **heavy challenge (not removing infected animals – *B ovis*)**
- **animals' immune systems are compromised (chronic diseases, heavy parasite infestations, malnutrition or genetically poor immune response).**

VACCINATION PROGRAMMES

Following a set vaccination programme ensures that vaccines are given timeously and boosters are not forgotten. The vaccination programmes given here are simply guidelines and should be adapted to local conditions with the help of a local veterinarian who knows the prevalence of local diseases. In Tables 1 and 2, the essential vaccines are indicated in bold type; those given in normal type are optional or only required in certain endemic

TABLE 1. Vaccination programme for sheep

GROUP	VACCINE	ADMINISTRATION
Lambs	Multicomponent clostridials including pulpy kidney	Weaning – booster 21 days later
	Anthrax	Weaning
	Blue tongue	Weaning (all 3 vaccines)
	Rift Valley fever (live)	Weaning
	Mannheimia (Pasteurella) haemolytica pneumonia	Weaning or as directed on package insert
	Corynebacterium ovis abscesses	Before weaning and give booster
	Orf	From day-old
	Botulism	Weaning (ram lambs for stud)
	Botulism	Weaning – give booster 3 – 4 weeks later
	Brucella Rev 1	Vaccinate ram lambs (stud) only, at weaning
Ewes	Multiclostridial, including pulpy kidney and tetanus	Last few weeks of pregnancy
	Anthrax	Annual – avoid late pregnancy
	Blue tongue	Annual booster in spring, but avoid first third of pregnancy
	Enzootic abortion *Chlamydiophilia* (Chlamydia)	Before breeding (see differences for live and killed vaccines)
	Orf	When required
	C. ovis abscesses	Annual booster before shearing
	M. haemolytica pneumonia	Before danger period, eg winter
	Botulism	Annual booster
Rams	Multiclostridial with pulpy kidney	Annual revaccination
	Blue tongue	Annual revaccination
	M. haemolytica (*pasteurella*)	Before danger period, e.g. winter
	Anthrax	Annual booster

TABLE 2. Vaccination programme for goats

GROUP	VACCINE	ADMINISTRATION
Kids	Multiclostridial with pulpy kidney	Weaning (repeat 21 days later)
	Anthrax	Weaning
	Rift Valley fever (live)	Weaning
	Mannheimia (*Pasteurella*) *haemolytica* pneumonia (sheep vaccine)	Weaning or as directed on label
	Orf	From day-old
Does	Multiclostridial with pulpy kidney	Last few weeks of pregnancy
	Anthrax	Annual booster (avoid late pregnancy)
	Chlamydiophilia (Chlamydia)	Before breeding (see differences for live and killed vaccines)
	Mannheimia (*Pasteurella*) *haemolytica* pneumonia	Before danger period, such as winter
	Orf	When required
Rams	Multiclostridial with pulpy kidney	Annual revaccination
	M. haemolytica	Before danger period
	Anthrax	Annual booster

areas. The term multiclostridial refers to vaccines which offer protection against a broad range of clostridial diseases. These are more convenient and cost-effective to use than single component clostridial vaccines. For more details about a specific vaccine, see the discussion in Part 3: Diseases. Note that the vaccination programmes for sheep and goats differ slightly.

Parasite control

Dosing programmes for internal parasites are given in chapter 4 (page 76 – 91).

Although these are generic programmes given for specific rainfall areas, they should be fine-tuned in consultation with a veterinarian, as there may be unique local circumstances that warrant additional control measures.

The control of external parasites is discussed in chapter 5 (page 94 – 113).

Use your vet

The veterinarian is a highly qualified graduate who studies animal anatomy, physiology, reproduction, behaviour, medicine, surgery, parasitology, infectious diseases, nutrition, pathology and pharmacology – to name just a few subjects – over a period of six years. Veterinarians are therefore qualified to help farmers plan disease control and breeding programmes on their farms; sadly, many farmers only use veterinarians when they have an individual animal that has a problem, such as needing a caesarean – the so-called "fire-engine" practice. Because of this, veterinarians find it difficult to make a living in country districts. Good farmers use veterinarians

to prevent problems as well as solving them. The veterinarian should become a valued partner on the farm, if one is serious about good management. Nowadays, many veterinarians are specialists in specific fields; e g feedlot management, nutrition, dairy and reproduction.

First-aid kit

Most rural veterinarians are located some distance from their clients, so keeping a small stock of first-aid remedies for minor animal health problems is a practical solution to handling minor incidents. What such a first-aid kit contains will naturally depend on the area, the type of farming and the types of animals involved, but the basics can be expanded to accommodate the specific problems of the region or the particular farm.

The basic first-aid kit contains:

- injectable oxytetracycline
- injectable and/or oral sulphur remedy (dimethoxine)
- wound oil or spray, containing insecticide if screwworm or blowflies are a problem
- tick pour-on for spot treatment
- gloves and liquid paraffin/KY jelly to assist with lambing problems
- activated charcoal for plant poisoning (where necessary)
- cotton wool or gauze dressing to control bleeding
- sterile needles and syringes
- thermometer.

Buying animal health products

Stock remedies – animal medicines sold directly to the public – are controlled by the National Department of Agriculture in terms of Act 36 of 1947, which requires that the manufacturers prove the product is safe for the animal, the handler, the consumer, and the environment, before the product can be sold. Remedies deemed safe and efficacious by the authorities are registered and obtain a "G" number which identifies the product as officially acceptable.

The product is identified by a label which states clearly the nature of the remedy (eg dip or dewormer), the animal species for which it is registered, the claims (which parasites/conditions), the chemical group to which it belongs, and its potential toxicity. Most remedies have a package insert which gives more detailed information about the application (dosage and route), the precautions and side-effects. It is essential before purchasing remedies to read the label and the package insert. The details should be read again before applying the remedy.

The safety and efficacy of remedies are approved, based on the specified usage in a specific way, and cannot be guaranteed by registration authorities and manufacturers if this isn't adhered to. Some animal medicines are controlled by the Department of Health in terms of Act 101 of 1967; these remedies are only available to farmers on prescription.

When buying stock remedies, check that containers are in good condition, with no broken seals, leakages or bloating of the container. Don't buy vaccines that haven't been stored in a refrigerator or those that have been frozen by accident. No animal product should be purchased or used if it has expired or has a homemade label. Don't buy animal health products at auctions, because they are often expired or damaged, or products that have been brought into the country illegally.

Always record dosing, dipping and vaccination, noting the date, the remedy and the batch number. The batch number is an important reference if there are problems, as manufacturers keep archive material of all product batches for examination or testing in case of complaints.

From a scientific point of view, using home-made, herbal and homeopathic remedies is pointless and can be harmful. Poisoning still occurs because materials such as lamp paraffin and old motor oil – both of them highly toxic – are used. Home-made pour-ons for ectoparasites can cause severe burns and promote parasite resistance.

Equally dangerous are remedies containing plant extracts such as garlic, aloe or khakibos, which claim to control external or internal parasites. They are totally ineffective for this purpose and using them often results in an outbreak of tick-borne disease or losses from worm infestations.

Homeopathic medicines can be said to be completely safe because they contain nothing except an inert diluent, usually water or alcohol. They are diluted millions of times so the initial substance is, scientifically speaking, diluted out. The resulting preparation will therefore have no toxic effect but will also have no therapeutic effect.

It's widely accepted in human medicine that homeopathic medicine has some effect in some people for certain non-fatal, chronic conditions because of the placebo effect. This is caused by the belief that the remedy or procedure will be effective.

The impression that homeopathic remedies work is created by some conditions clearing up spontaneously because of the body's ability to overcome infection, or because chronic conditions are undergoing a temporary remission.

Controlling veterinary products

Although regulatory authorities control the registration of stock remedies, the manufacturers themselves have formed a body which regulates their industry by endorsing a code of conduct.

Reputable veterinary companies are members of The South African Animal Health Association (SAAHA) which has drawn up a code of conduct governing research and development standards, advertising standards, training of sales staff, warehousing standards, transport standards and after-sales service by staff. SAAHA sales staff are required to do an intensive training course in veterinary subjects, which qualifies them for accreditation.

Qualified sales staff receive an ID card which shows that they have sufficient background to sell stock remedies.

Farmers should ask to see these ID cards to ensure they are buying from accredited agents. Companies registered with SAAHA provide the client with back-up service, whether from salespeople or from company veterinarians.

Problems encountered with remedies should be reported to sales staff who will then contact technical support staff. In this way the industry aims to prevent "sell and run" tactics by sales staff.

SAAHA is the animal health arm of the larger Agricultural Veterinary Chemicals Association of South Africa (AVCASA), an organisation of manufacturers and distributors of agricultural chemicals. This is an industry organisation that, among other services, provides training to farmers and farm workers on the handling of agricultural chemicals.

The law and stock farming

Act 36 of 1947 governs stock remedies, and the Animal Diseases Act 35 of 1984 specifies the responsibilities of the Department of Agriculture and of farmers with regard to disease control. The full act can be accessed on the internet, but the main issue pertinent to farmers is their responsibility in preventing the spread of diseases not under government control, and preventing the dissemination of resistant parasites.

NOTES

SAFETY ON THE FARM

Although the veterinary remedies used nowadays are much safer than those used decades ago, such as the old arsenic dips, some of them are toxic to humans and the environment if not handled correctly. The remedies currently registered under Act 36 of 1947 are classified, for the convenience of users, to indicate precautions with respect to storage, handling and impact on the environment.

The ectoparasite remedies, in particular, are of concern here. On the label of registered remedies is a "HAZARD" classification to indicate the toxicity in increasing order: "Versigtig/Caution", "Skadelik/Harmful", "Toksies/Toxic" and "Baie toksies/Very toxic".

The HAZARD CLASSIFICATION pictograms indicate how the product should be handled; for example, "Store under lock and key, wear boots, wear eye protection, use a respirator, wear gloves when handling a concentrate."

If you are transporting remedies from a depot or co-operative, follow these basic safety guidelines: don't load products in the front of the vehicle, make sure that containers are upright and do not pack other objects on top of them, as this could damage the neck of the container and cause leakage. Don't transport remedies along with people, feed or food. If there is a spillage, avoid contact with the chemical.

The basic guidelines for personal protection are to avoid eating, drinking and smoking when handling the chemicals, and washing the hands thoroughly after use. If the chemical is spilt on clothes, remove them immediately and wash the skin thoroughly. The highest risk of poisoning is when concentrates are handled; ie when opening, measuring and cleaning up spillages.

Follow the advice on the label which may specify the use of more advanced protection such as respirators, boots and gloves. Gloves should be made of PVC, neoprene or butyl rubber, which prevents the product's penetrating them. Disposable polyethylene gloves or plastic bags can be used as a temporary measure. After using gloves, wash them thoroughly using soap and water. Wearing gloves is recommended when administering pyrethoid-containing pour-ons because these can potentially cause skin irritation. Also use gloves when mixing and applying organophosphates.

Wear gloves when you dilute products, and follow the directions on the label carefully. The quality of water used for dilution is also important as hard, acid and alkaline water prevent thorough mixing. Rain water is a suitable replacement for poor-quality borehole water.

If someone accidentally comes into contact with a poisonous chemical, he or she should be taken for medical treatment if one or more of the following symptoms are present: nausea, headache, light-headedness, salivation, cramps, vomiting, sweating, muscle weakness and anxiety. Ensure that the person can breathe normally and remove them from the contaminated area, remove clothing and wash the skin with water for 10 minutes. If the chemical splashed into the eyes, wash them with water for five minutes. Keep the person warm. Contact a doctor and make the label of the product available for reference.

If the remedy has been swallowed, don't induce vomiting unless advised to do so on the label.

Empty dip containers should never be used for any other purpose because of the danger of poisoning. To make sure the containers are safe before you dispose of them, use the triple rinse method: quarter-fill the container, shake vigorously and empty the contents into the dip tank. Do this three times (e g for the first rinse 4 000 ppm is diluted to 40 ppm, and with the third rinse to 0 ppm). Make holes in the container to make sure it cannot be used and bury it in a refuse pit dug specially for the purpose. The pit should be fenced off and be located away from water sources. Alternatively, recycle the containers.

It's dangerous – and an offence – to dump chemicals by the roadside, in bodies of water or on municipal dumps, as this can cause poisoning and environmental contamination. Irresponsible disposal of poisons can cause devastation of wildlife/livestock and the impact can be extensive.

Another safety aspect is the disposal of carcases on farms. In general, animals that have died from any condition should not be eaten by humans: in the case of death from anthrax, the carcass presents a risk to the person cutting up the meat and – to a lesser extent – the person eating it. Animals that have died of krimpsiekte can cause secondary poisoning if fed to humans, or dogs.

Carcases that pose a risk to human or animal health should be placed in a pit, covered with quicklime and buried. This area should be fenced off in the case of a disease such as anthrax to prevent carcases being disturbed (see Anthrax, page 70).

PRODUCT SAFETY

There is increasing public concern about chemical residues in animal products. For remedies or drugs administered to animals, the authorities have determined a minimum residue level (MRL) based on the risk posed by consuming these very low levels of chemicals over long periods of time.

A broad safety factor has been built into this calculation. Withdrawal times have been determined for all products used for human consumption to achieve levels below the MRL. (The withdrawal time is the period from when the drug is applied or administered until the animal is slaughtered or its milk is used for human consumption. At this point the level of the chemical will be below the MRL.) Note that export markets may require compliance with an export slaughter interval (ESI) which may be more stringent than local requirements.

Milk used to make microbial-based products such as yoghurt or buttermilk may be affected by trace amounts of anti-microbials, even those below MRLs. To prevent chemical residues remaining in animal products intended for the market, stock owners should clearly adhere strictly to the directions on the product label regarding dosage, route, and time before slaughter or product use for human consumption. Always keep records of any treatments and dispose of chemicals

strict about chemical residues in wool.

Wool Withholding Period (WHP) values are not yet available for products sold in South Africa, but the following values used by the Australian authorities may be used as a guideline. In general, long wool residues for insect growth regulators and macrocyclic lactones remain for two to three months; although the period for organophosphates is two to three months, a voluntary WHP of six months is recommended for residue-sensitive markets. Spinosyn has no WWP (Department of Agriculture, Australia, Fact Sheet 6/2003). Note that the kind of formulation and method of application may cause some variation in WHPs.

Contact the manufacturers for more details. The quantity of chemicals used for the control of parasites can be reduced if management practices are improved; in cases such as blowfly strike, see Integrated pest management (page 106). See also Parts 4 and 5 for further discussion of the various groups of chemicals used for dipping/application.

ABOVE: Chemical dips that bind to the wool fat are not dangerous to health but may contribute to environmental contamination

LEFT: The withdrawal period of a product must be observed to rule out residues in meat and milk

ANIMAL WELFARE

In terms of the Animal Protection Act, No 71 of 1962, farmers have to provide the following for animals in their care: sufficient suitable feed and water, protection from extreme weather, protection from disease, injury and pain; and the opportunity to socialise with other members of their species. The basic principles of animal welfare – food, water and shelter – may seem obvious, but it's surprising how few farmers provide shade or wind shelter for animals experiencing extreme conditions. There's little sense in acquiring improved stock and then exposing the animals to poor conditions under which they cannot maximise their genetic potential. The same principle applies to animals kept under intensive conditions; failing to provide them with comfortable and hygienic accommodation will lead to stress and predispose them to disease.

The stock owner also has a responsibility to prevent and treat disease. It is unlawful to use unregistered home-made

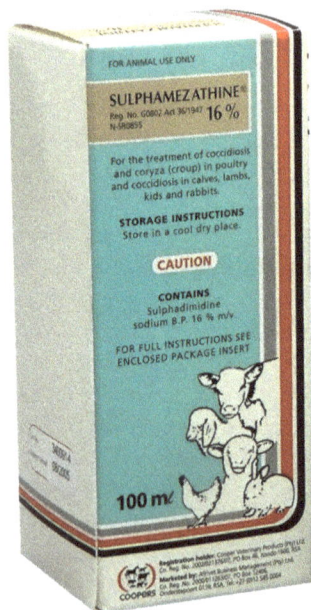

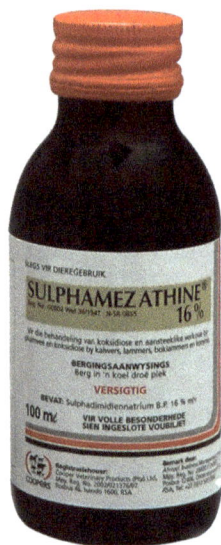

responsibly (see section on safety, page 19). Meat can also become contaminated by the presence of organochlorines and substances, such as arsenic, used as crop chemicals.

Chemicals used for sheep dipping can potentially bind to the wool fat – the most important being the synthetic pyrethroids

that have a high binding ability; organophosphates and insect growth regulators (IGRs) bind to a lesser degree. The residues are not a direct threat to the consumer, but when the wool is washed the chemicals in the fleece can cause environmental contamination. For this reason, authorities in developed countries are becoming more

remedies such as old motor oil and aloe extracts, which are at best ineffective but can also be toxic. The most commonly misused remedies in small stock farming are disinfectants which contain coal tar/phenol; they are corrosive and toxic, but farmers use them as parasite dips or worm remedies, even though they have no effect on external or internal parasites.

Under the Animal Protection Act, it's an offence to cause suffering to animals, either by failing to provide for their needs or by active cruelty. The law makes provision for the prosecution of farmers guilty of any contraventions. Farmers should also be aware of the Animal Slaughter, Meat and Animal Production Hygiene Act, No 87 of 1967, which governs the transporting and handling of animals to be slaughtered. This Act spells out clearly that animals must be transported and handled in a manner that will not cause them excessive stress, injury or death.

Slaughter for emergencies or for consumption must be done humanely. The recommended method of killing small stock is using a captive bolt pistol. For hornless animals, it's best to aim behind the poll in the direction of the muzzle, as the animal is less likely to move around. (It's also the best method for goats, since the brain is further back in the skull.) Alternatively, aim for the crown of the head, in the direction of the throat. The point to aim for in horned sheep is the centre of the forehead, in the direction of the spine.

Indigenous sheep, such as the Pedi, are ideal breeds for organic farming

If you don't have a captive bolt pistol, use a .22 calibre firearm, at close quarters (a few centimetres); bear in mind the potential danger of the bullet's exiting the skull and injuring or killing someone.

Cutting the throat is less humane but is used in emergencies. Lay the animal down, hold the head back and, using a sharp knife, cut cleanly along the throat up to the spine.

ORGANIC (NATURAL) FARMING

Although the word organic has been abused by marketers, it is generally accepted in farming terms to imply adopting a more natural approach to farming, by moving away from intensive systems, utilising veld in a sustainable fashion and minimising the use of chemicals.

Organic farming can be assisted by selecting breeds more resistant to disease, such as indigenous types that require less veterinary intervention and therefore minimal use of chemicals like antibiotics, dewormers and dips.

Organic farmers can be helped to achieve these goals by using vaccines, which will reduce the need for antibiotic treatment.

The need to control internal parasites using chemicals can be reduced by selecting animals for worm resistance; for example, using the FAMACHA© system (see Internal parasite control, page 83, 84, 85).

External parasite control can be reduced through integrated pest management, which uses management factors to reduce the use of insecticides (see the example under Blowfly control, page 104 - 105). General disease management principles, such as preliminary examination and using a quarantine system, may be employed to avoid buying in diseases, to cut down on the need for disease control measures, and also to reduce stock losses.

NOTES

MANAGEMENT

1

2

DIAGNOSIS

Causes of disease and diagnosis

CAUSES OF DISEASE

Disease in animals can be caused by a variety of factors, which can be divided into the following categories:

• **Physical** These factors include exposure to excess heat or cold, injuries such as fractures or laceration, and exposure to radiation – usually the ultra-violet rays of sunlight which can damage skin and predispose animals to cancer.

• **Genetic causes** Animals born with defective genes that affect their ability to function normally may become ill or die from the condition. They may also pass these defective genes on to their offspring, if they are able to breed.

• **Infections** These are caused by micro-organisms including bacteria (e g anthrax), viruses (e g blue tongue), fungi (e g ringworm) and protozoa (e g *coccidia*).

• **Parasites** Heavy infestations of internal parasites can cause severe damage to animals and could end in death. External parasites such as ticks could carry fatal blood-borne diseases (heartwater), or cause toxicosis, paralysis, or damage to the skin or organs.

• **Nutritional factors** Animals may become ill as a result of an excess of certain food types (acidosis) or a deficiency of energy or protein (starvation). The micro-nutrients, vitamins and minerals, may also cause problems, either of excess or deficiency.

• **Poisons** Many plants, minerals and chemical compounds may cause illness and death in animals.

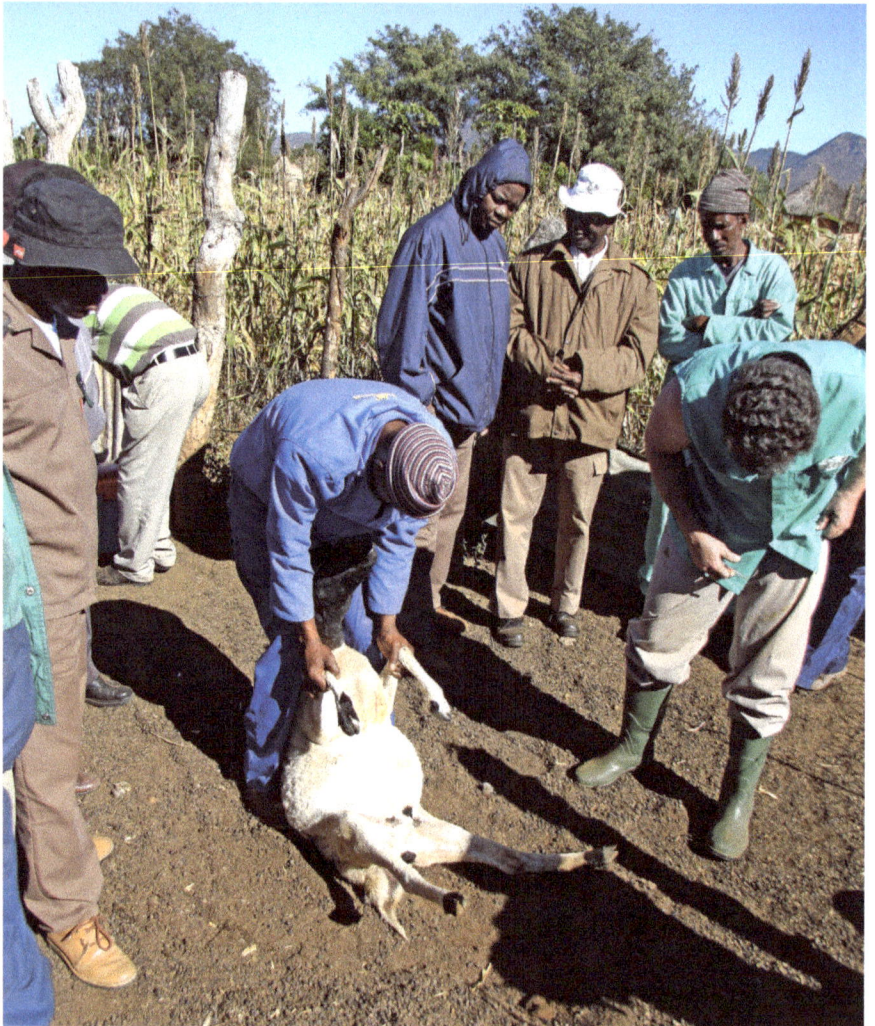

DIAGNOSIS OF DISEASE

Diagnosing the specific cause of illness is possible but requires a number of important steps.

Taking a history

The history is the summary of all information that could have bearing on the condition, including the age and species of

Examination of the live animal is the first step in the process of making a diagnosis of disease

the animals affected, grazing/feed, recent management practices such as castrations or dipping, treatments, vaccinations, deworming schedules, etc. It helps the veterinarian exclude certain causes and focus on other, more likely, ones.

Examining the live animal

The symptoms or clinical signs seen in the live animal on examination can give useful information about the cause of the disease. It's not always possible, however, since animals may die rapidly without showing any signs of acute disease. In addition, a symptom (e g lameness) may be part of more than one disease syndrome,

so more information is required to eliminate other causes.

Examining the dead animal (post-mortem)

A veterinarian or other trained person should conduct a post-mortem to detect such signs of changes or damages to the tissues as may be seen with the naked eye. These changes can be evaluated more closely by taking tissues for microscopic examination (histology).

Laboratory tests

On the basis of the history, symptoms and post-mortem signs, the veterinarian se-

lects samples from the live animal or the carcass for laboratory tests such as serology (antibody detection), the culture of micro-organisms, toxicology and histology. These tests help the veterinarian to make a definitive (proven) diagnosis. Some tests may be costly and add to the expense of services, so a veterinarian often makes a presumptive diagnosis; the most likely cause given the history, live animal examination and post-mortem findings. An example of how a definitive diagnosis is made is given below.

DIAGNOSTIC PROCEDURE

History (as given by the farmer)
Date of outbreak: March 2008 (late summer – autumn)
- **Description of problem:** abortions in 50% of the pregnant ewes and 30% of the cows in all stages of pregnancy; acute deaths were seen in 20 newborn lambs and older lambs died after showing general signs of illness; some calves also showed signs of illness; influenza-like symptoms suffered by farmer and two farm workers.

The ewes had been regularly vaccinated against blue tongue and clostridial organisms, and had recently been dewormed, using a broad-spectrum product.

Physical signs or symptoms
Young lambs were found dead. Older lambs showed general signs of illness before they died (not examined by veterinarian).
- **Ewes:** No illness was noticed apart from abortions.
- **Calves:** Showed general signs of illness; on examination they showed jaundice and a few had diarrhhoea.

Post-mortem examinations
A consistent finding on the post-mortem carried out by the veterinarian was a marked orange discoloration of the liver, particularly in young animals, indicating liver damage. Haemorrhages were seen in the gut of some of the young animals on which post-mortems were done. Haemorrhages were also seen under the skin and

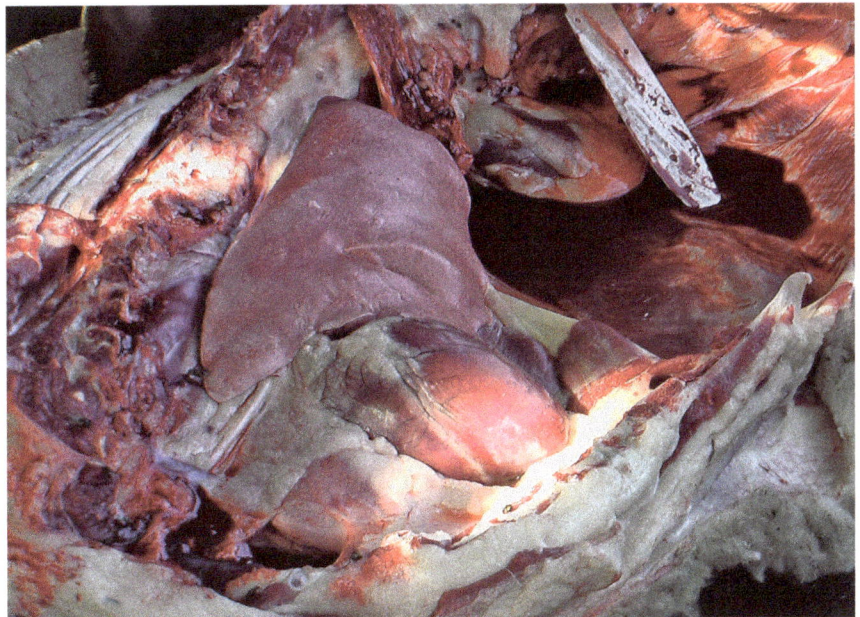

Post-mortem examinations provide useful information for diagnosis and about parasite infestation

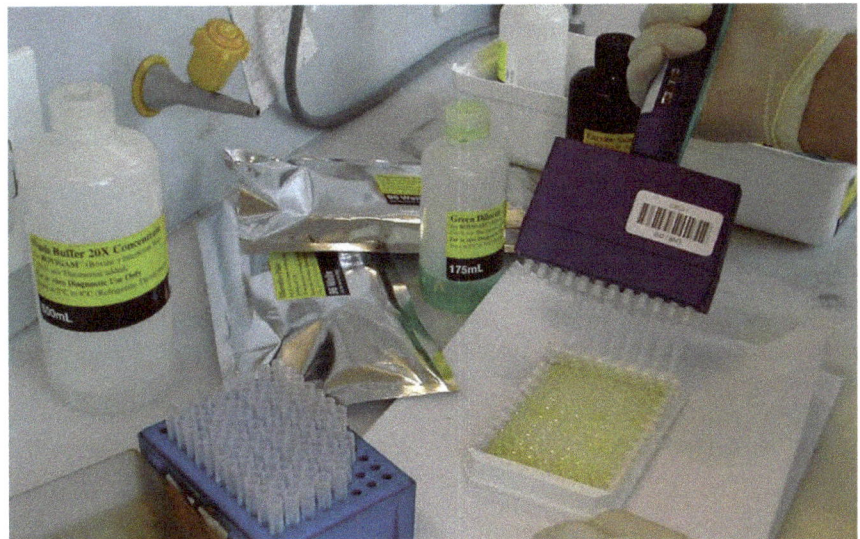

Laboratory tests can be used to confirm a diagnosis

in some of the organs, such as the kidneys.

Laboratory tests
Histology Microscopic examination of the liver samples from some of the dead lambs showed signs of severe damage to almost all the cells of the liver (pan-necrosis).
Serology Antibody testing of animals which aborted requested by veterinarian indicates positive antibody to Rift Valley fever (RVF).
Virus isolation Rift Valley fever virus

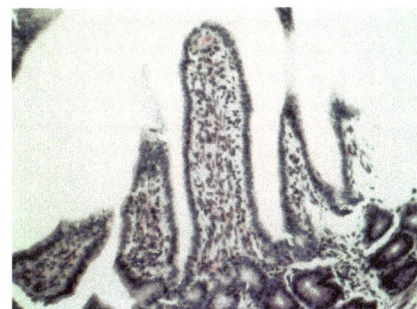

The microscopic examination of tissues is known as histopathology

was detected on culture of liver, spleen of two dead lambs submitted and the dead sample of one of the aborted fetuses, by culturing the tissue on tissue culture, embryonated eggs and laboratory mice.

Final diagnosis

Based on the time of year, the history of abortions in sheep, the deaths of lambs and calves, as well as the evidence of flu-like symptoms suffered by the people handling the aborting ewes, the veterinarian made a presumptive diagnosis of Rift Valley fever. This is a mosquito-borne viral disease which occurs during wet years. The post-mortem findings of severe liver damage in both foetuses and young animals were typical for RVF infection. The serology, which showed the presence of antibodies to the virus in aborting sheep, is additional evidence since, according to the history, the animals had never been vaccinated against the disease (ie the antibody was not caused by vaccination but by exposure to the wild virus). The isolation of the virus from foetal and lamb tissues is definitive (deciding) because this does not occur under normal circumstances. Even if no virus had been detected from the tissues, it wouldn't have eliminated the cause as RVF because this can be difficult from autolysed tissue. In this case, the veterinarian would have made a presumptive diagnosis based on all the other findings and the typical history.

A differential (alternative) diagnosis would have been enzootic abortion (Chla-

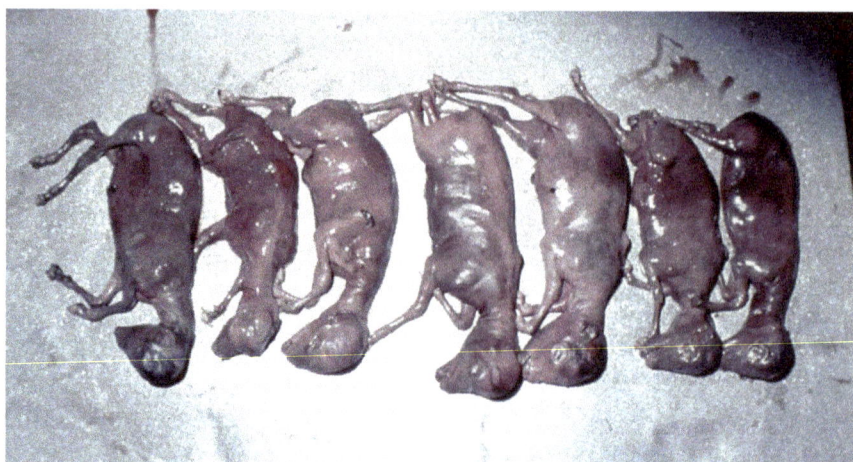

Rift Valley fever causes abortion storms

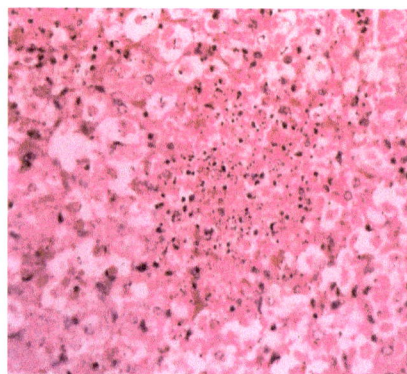

The liver necrosis seen here confirms the diagnosis of Rift Valley fever

Liver pathology caused by Rift Valley fever

mydiophilia) which causes abortion storms and deaths in lambs. This organism would, however, have been eliminated as a cause by the post-mortem since this disease doesn't cause liver damage in either the lambs or the foetuses. Note that making a diagnosis can be more complicated than in this example, especially at beginning of an outbreak, when only a single case of death, abortion or clinical disease is seen.

NOTES

_____

_____

_____

_____

_____

_____

_____

_____

_____

_____

2 DIAGNOSIS

GENERAL EXAMINATION OF THE LIVE ANIMAL

A general examination of an animal should be made to assess its health; when buying animals, for instance, when animals are held in quarantine or when they become ill. Stock owners should familiarise themselves with the normal appearance, behaviour and temperature of a an animal by regular examinations as described here:

Behaviour

Normal animals are alert, and interested in their surroundings. When animals at rest are approached they rise, stretch and then walk away. Observe whether the animal is eating, drinking, ruminating (chewing the cud) and defecating. Sick animals often stand with their heads hanging down, and show lack of interest in eating or drinking, or human activity. Excessive tail wagging or stamping is often a sign of pain in small stock.

Body condition

A healthy animal should have well-developed muscles and sufficient body fat, if on

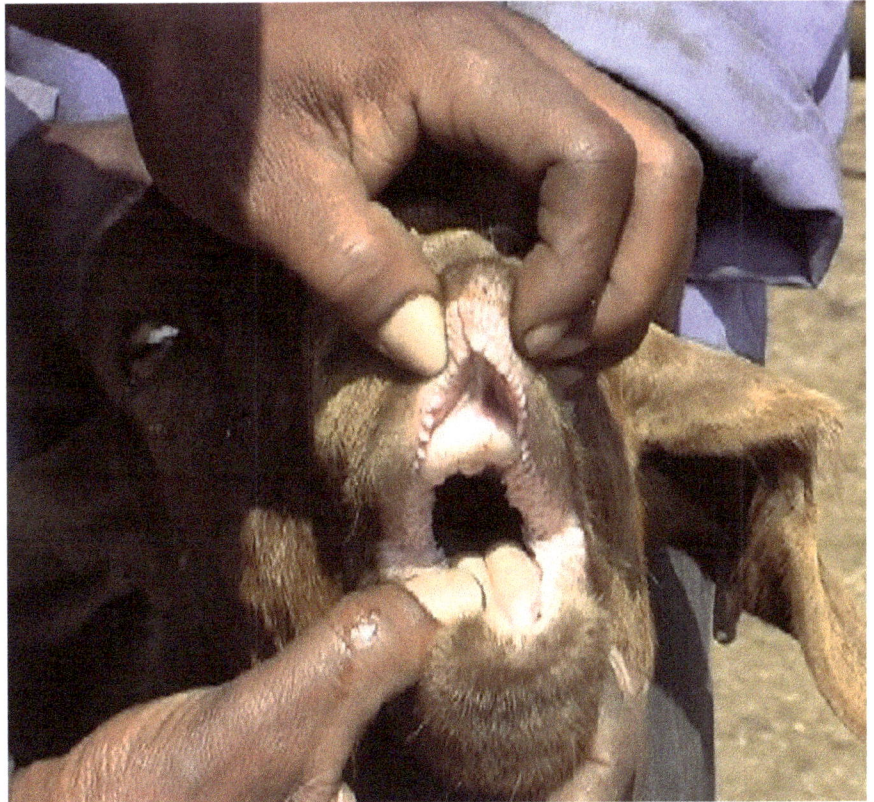

Examining the mouth

Examination of the mucosa of the eye

Deviation of the neck resulting from muscle damage caused by blue tongue

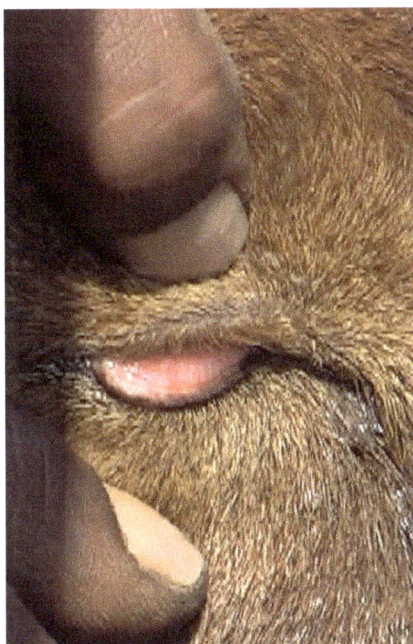

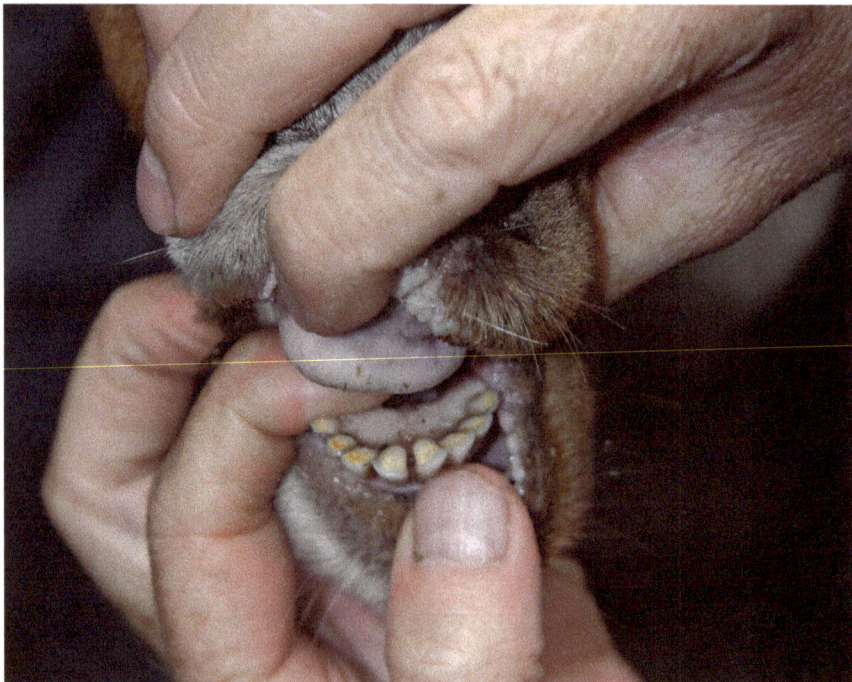

Examining the teeth

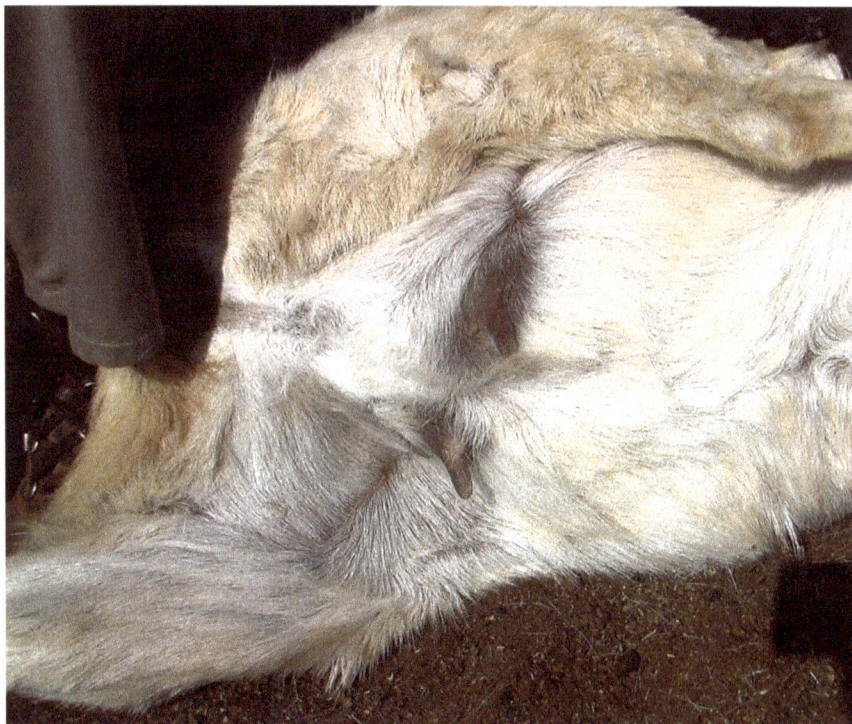

Examining the udder

a good level of nutrition. Body condition evaluation (see **Table 3**, page 29) allows one to assess the efficiency of feeding, and whether the animal is in the right condition for breeding or slaughter.

Body temperature

The animal's temperature should be taken using a standard mercury or digital thermometer. Mercury thermometers should be shaken down before taking the reading.

Insert the thermometer in the rectum and keep it in place for two minutes. Remove the thermometer and clean it off with a tissue so that it's easy to read. The normal temperature range in sheep is 38,5 – 39,5ºC. The normal temperature range in goats is 38,6 – 40,2ºC. One degree over the normal range can be considered to be a fever but it should be noted that the body temperature can increase as a result of high ambient temperature, chasing the animals or muscular spasms.

Mucous membranes

These are the wet "linings" of the body. They can be examined by looking inside the mouth or by turning out (everting) the eyelid. The normal colour of the mucous membranes is a light pink. Dark red, blue, brown or white mucous membranes indicate some abnormality.

Ears

The ears should be erect, pink and clean with no swellings, discharge or parasites.

Eyes

The eyes should be clear and moist and shouldn't have any discharge from the inner corner.

Nose

In sheep and goats the nose should be pale, smooth, velvety and dry. A runny nose or any ulcers on the nose indicate some problem. Rumen content seen around the nose is seen with conditions such as vermeersiekte.

Skin/coat

In wooled sheep the coat should be even without clumping or bare patches. Hairy sheep and goats should show a smooth, regular hair coat. Any signs of ragged wool, scratching or biting the coat should be investigated.

Mouth

Examine the lips, outside and inside. Open the mouth and check the mucous membranes of the mouth, the teeth and the tongue. The mucous membranes of the mouth should be smooth and pink. The teeth should be even, regular and clean.

2

DIAGNOSIS

There should be no saliva dripping from the mouth.

Neck

Run hands over the neck to detect any lumps or swellings of the local lymph nodes. Deviation of the neck indicates some problem with the muscles or nerves.

Front and hind limbs

The animal should move around with a normal, even gait. The legs should be straight and smooth with no swellings, pain or heat over the joints. Examine the coronet (the junction between hoof and skin). Lift the hoof and examine the underside. The sole must be intact with no separation of the hoof material and the underlying tissues.

Chest

Run hands between the front legs. Observe the breathing which should be steady and regular at rest, without wheezing or coughing sounds. Check the prescapular lymph node which lies in front of the shoulder.

Abdomen

Examine the outline of the abdomen from behind. It should have a regular outline,

Evaluating the body condition of an animal

without distension. Feel the activity of the rumen in the paralumbar fossa (the cavity seen on the left side).

Genitalia

In the ewe, the vulva must be pink with no wounds, ulcers or discharge. The udder must be firm with no lumps and both teats must be intact. If the ewe is lactating, the milk must be normal without clots or any discoloration, such as blood.

In the ram, feel the testicles for any thickening or lumps. The penis can be pulled out from the sheath to be examined for any injuries or blockages. Examine the process at the tip of the penis.

TABLE 3. Body condition evaluation
This evaluation is done by examining the muscle and fat cover over the lower backbone and the "short ribs" which are the lateral spines of the vertebrae of the back

OBSERVATIONS	CONDITION	SCORE
No muscle or fat along the backbone. The spine sticks out and the short ribs are easily felt	emaciated	0
The backbone is still prominent and short ribs can be felt	very thin	1
The backbone and short ribs can just be felt	thin	2
The backbone and short ribs can only be felt with very firm pressure	medium (ideal)	3
The backbone can be felt but not the short ribs	fat	4
The backbone can't be felt without firm pressure; the short ribs can't be felt at all	very fat	5

NOTES

DIAGNOSIS

2

3

Diseases of small stock

LAMBS AND KIDS

Surveys of deaths of newborn lambs in South Africa have shown that 50% of cases resulted from starvation due to low birth weight, and mismothering; 25% were the result of difficult births (dystocia). All these problems can be solved by improving management (see Reproduction, page 4 - 6). The remaining 25% of cases were found to be the result of infectious diseases, nutritional deficiencies and predation. The specific causes of lamb diseases and deaths are discussed below.

Arthritis (polyarthritis)

Lambs and kids contract a form of arthritis when bacteria invade th)e body through the umbilical stump or wounds caused by eartagging, docking or castration.

The bacteria, usually *Arcanobacterium pyogenes*, enter the blood stream and lodge in one or more joints (polyarthritis), usually the knee or hock joints. The first signs of infection are heat and swelling around the affected joint, with lameness resulting from pain, and restriction of movement.

The swelling usually subsides after a few days, but often a mild lameness persists. The infection results in poor lubrication of the joint with eventual damage to the bone surface. The condition becomes chronic and as a result the animals do not do well.

Injecting long-acting tetracycline early in the course of the disease may prevent permanent bone damage, but after a number of weeks of infection, therapy will not be of any use and the condition will become chronic.

Prevent the condition by improving hygiene in lambing camps. If possible, disinfect the umbilical stump with wound disinfectants such as iodine preparations. Use wound disinfectants when tagging, docking and castrating to prevent wound infection. Prevent excessive wound damage by using sharp knives for docking and castration.

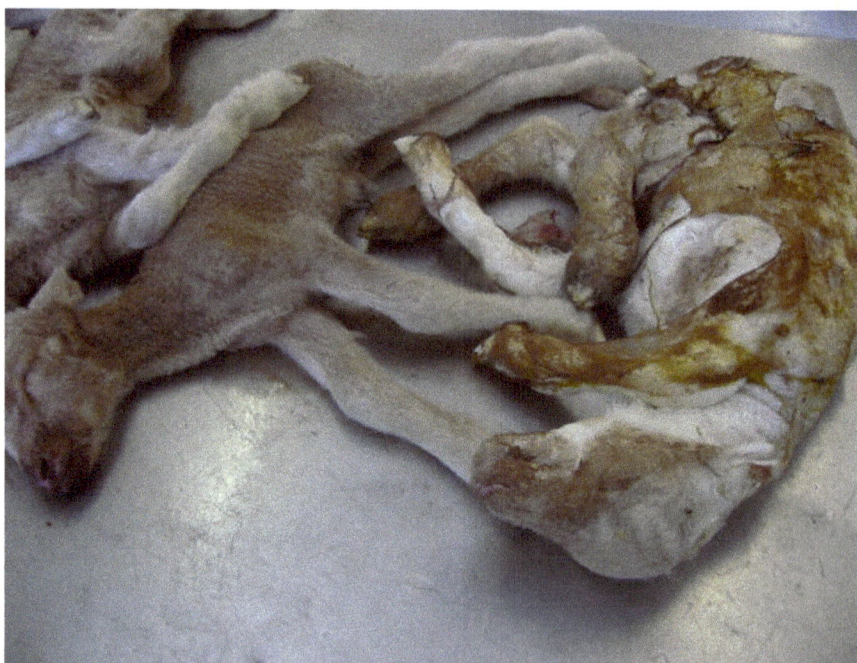

Enzootic abortion causes abortion storms

Lameness in a young lamb caused by bacterial arthritis

Weak lambs can be born during outbreaks of enzootic abortion

Enzootic abortion (*Chlamydiophilia abortus*)

Flocks infected with *Chlamydiophila abortus* will initially experience abortion storms but also the birth of weak, premature lambs. These lambs are often too weak to suckle after birth and they die of starvation. The diagnosis of enzootic abortion is made on the basis of the history of abortions and weak lambs, the examination of aborted foetuses, post-mortems on weak or dead lambs and the testing of the ewes' blood samples. The main control measure for this condition is vaccinating ewes before the breeding season. During abortion storms, ewes can be treated with long-acting oxytetracycline injections to prevent further abortions (see also Enzootic abortion, page 48).

Coccidiosis

Coccidia are protozoa which colonise the intestines of normal animals. A number of coccidian species can affect small stock

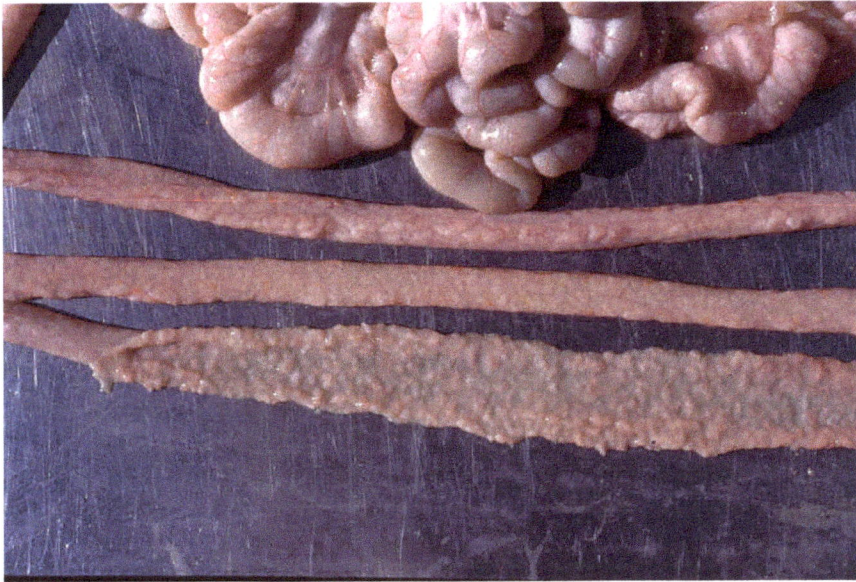

In coccidiosis cases, white foci are typically seen on the mucosa of the small intestine

A severe case of coccidiosis in an Angora lamb

(Isospora, Eimeria) but all have the same general life cycle and cause similar symptoms. The eggs or oocysts of coccidia are excreted in the faeces of infected animals and mature under warm, moist conditions. When susceptible animals ingest the coccidial organism, it (the organism) invades the gut and in the process causes damage to the intestinal epithelium. Animals develop immunity to these organisms on exposure, so clinical disease is rarely seen in adult animals.

Coccidiosis develops in young lambs or kids raised on cultivated pastures which favour the maturing of the organism, or those crowded together in intensive systems. The young animals pick up the infection from older, immune animals that shed the organism in faeces. Unhygienic conditions, crowding and stress can be predisposing factors to coccidial infections. The symptoms of coccidiosis are a loss of appetite, diarrhoea and weight loss. Severely affected animals may die after a few days; less severe chronic infections may last a few weeks. Angora goats may show severe cases, often dying without showing marked symptoms.

On post-mortem, the small intestine is inflamed and small; white, raised foci may be seen. The diagnosis can be confirmed by laboratory examination of intestinal smears in which the parasites will be seen,

or by taking faecal samples from live animals for microscopic examination.

Sick animals can be treated with oral sulpha remedies such as sulphamethazine or sulphonamide (Kalftabs); sulfadimethoxine (Ecosulf/Disulfox) is an injectable sulpha which is active in the gut. Repeat the treatment in severe cases. Severely dehydrated animals will also need

fluid administration.

In intensive systems, coccidiostats such as monensin, salinomycin and lasolacid can be added to the feed to prevent outbreaks. These remedies suppress coccidial development but aren't suitable for the treatment of clinical cases. General hygiene, such as removing manure and avoiding overcrowding of animals, are important in preventing outbreaks of coccidiosis. Other stressors – such as worm infestations, poor nutrition and cold stress – also need to be corrected.

Congenital malformations

Congential (hereditary) malformations of lambs or kids are primarily the result

A rare genetic defect (polydactyly) causes a lamb to develop three additional limbs

of genetic factors, such as gene mutations. These usually occur at a very low frequency. The most common congenital conditions of small stock are underdevelopment of the skin, the absence of a lower jaw, a short lower jaw, a cleft palate, and deformation or amputation of the limbs.

A high incidence of malformations indicates the involvement of infectious agents, particularly viruses. During the summer months, insect-transmitted viruses such as Akabane and Wesselsbron viruses, may infect pregnant ewes causing foetal malformations. Certain viral vaccines, such as some Rift Valley fever vaccines, blue tongue vaccine and the Wesselsbron vaccine (no longer produced), can cause a small percentage of malformations when given in the first third of pregnancy. A history and post-mortem examination of the foetuses by veterinary pathologists will give an indication of the cause.

Diarrhoea

There are various causes of diarrhoea in young lambs and kids, including *E coli*, the lamb dysentery organism *C perfringens* B and coccidiosis. These conditions are discussed separately. Other causes are worm infestation (see Parasites, page ??, for more details).

Dystocia

The term dystocia means "difficult birth". It is most commonly caused by overfeeding ewes in late pregnancy, which results in the development of large lambs. Large lambs are more difficult to expel, leading to a prolonged birth process, with the result that the lamb is deprived of oxygen for considerable periods. These lambs are usually born dead, with a swollen head, and the fleece is often discoloured by placental fluids. A post-mortem can confirm that a lamb was born dead, as the lungs won't be inflated and the stomach will be empty.

Another specific cause of dystocia is big lamb disease (grootlamsiekte) which occurs in the Karoo when ewes graze on *Salsola tuberculatiformis* (the cauliflower saltwort).

The plant contains a substance which delays the hormonal triggering of the nor-

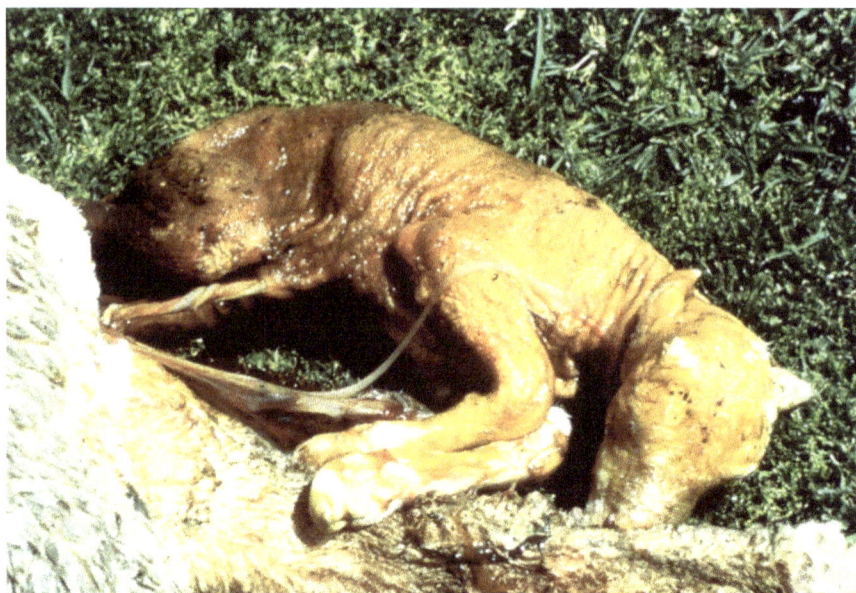

Lambs born after prolonged or difficult labour (dystocia) show a brownish discoloration in foetal faeces

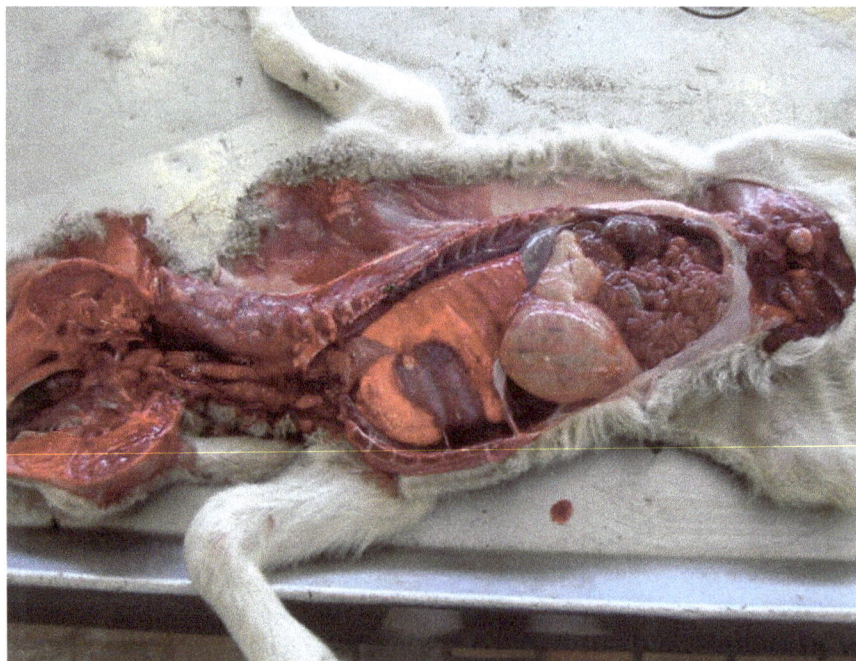

A case of septicaemic colibacillosis in a lamb

mal birth process. The lamb continues to grow in the uterus and the ewe's abdomen becomes massively swollen. These lambs usually have to be removed by caesarean section.

To prevent the problem, avoid grazing ewes on the plant for the last 50 days of pregnancy (see the section on reproductive conditions in Diseases, page 46).

Escherichia coli scours (Colibacillosis)

E coli bacteria are found in the gut of all healthy animals. Young animals pick them up shortly after birth from contact with feaces. Although most *E coli* bacteria are harmless, a few strains are able to cause disease in young animals, either septicaemia (blood poisoning) or severe diarohhea.

In small stock, *E coli* infections in individual animals result if the newborn doesn't receive sufficient colostrum, because the ewe has swollen or damaged teats, or mastitis. Outbreaks of colibacillosis occur if ewes or does lamb in camps where there is a build-up of fecal material.

Colibacillosis occurs in lambs or kids in the first week of life, causing diarrhoea, dehydration and death. There is also a septicaemic form from which lambs die rapidly without showing any symptoms of diarrhoea.

Colibacillosis is possible when lambs/kids between the ages of one or seven days are dying of diarrhoea orthere are acute deaths due to septicaemia. The diagnosis can be confirmed if pathogenic *E coli* strains are isolated from the organs or from the intestine.

Lambs or kids that have diarrhoea must be given electrolytes as soon as possible, either by mouth or intravenously, if they are too weak to drink. A wide variety of these preparations is available from co-ops.

To prevent colibacillosis under intensive conditions, pregnant stock may be vaccinated with vaccine registered for sheep and cattle.

Goitre

The term goitre refers to the swelling of the thyroid gland, sometimes seen in newborn lambs and kids. This occurs because of an iodine deficiency in the diet of the ewe causing the enlargement of the thyroid gland in the foetus. Iodine deficiency can arise as a result of a deficiency in pasture, the action of plants which inhibit the metabolising of iodine (goitrogenic plants) or − in very rare cases − a genetic inability to process iodine.

Pastures on the southern Cape coast, in Natal, Lesotho, Swaziland and northern Namibia can be deficient in iodine. Lucerne pastures, certain Cynodon grass species and the cabbage family (*Brassica* spp) are known to be goitrogenic. Goitre has been reported in Angora lambs whose mothers were grazed entirely on lucerne pastures and the lambs of ewes raised on star grass (*Cynodon* spp) pastures during pregnancy.

Goitre (enlarged thyroid) in a lamb

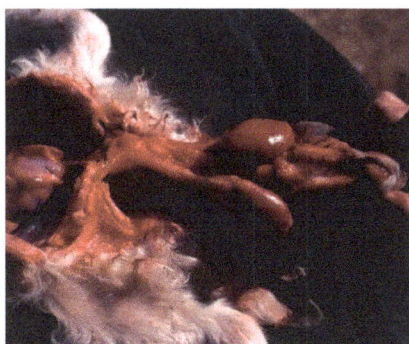

The enlarged thyroid seen on post-mortem

A case of lamb dysentery

Goitres are seen in lambs and kids at birth as an enlargement under the throat, sometimes as large as an orange. These animals also have a poor hair/coat, are weak, prone to cold stress and die early. Abortions may also be seen in flocks suffering from an iodine deficiency.

The diagnosis of goitre is made on clinical examination and can be confirmed on post-mortem histopathology. The exact cause has to be determined if the problem is to be treated successfully. Iodine deficiency of the pasture can be addressed by providing iodated salt licks, or giving potassium iodate drenches. But supplementing iodine will not address the problem of goitres caused by goitrogenic plants; in such cases, pregnant animals should only be grazed on these plants for limited periods.

Lamb dysentery (bloedpens)

This disease occurs sporadically in some areas of South Africa, and affects lambs one to seven days old. The disease is caused by *Clostridium perfringens* type B bacteria, which the lambs pick up via soil and faeces on certain farms. Typically, these lambs refuse to drink, show pain and bloody diarrhoea, dehydration and death. If cases are identified early enough, injectable sulpha preparations (sulphadimethoxine) which are active in the gut should be given, but usually the diagnosis is too late and lambs die rapidly. At post-mortem, these lambs show blood and ulcerations in the small intestine.

The only effective control measure is vaccination. Pregnant ewes on affected farms should be vaccinated with a vaccine containing *C perfringens* B or C, since

there is cross-protection between the two types.

Mismothering

Mismothering is the behavioural tendency of some ewes which leads to the rejection of lambs or the failure to allow their lambs to suckle. These lambs then die of starvation if not raised by hand or adopted by other ewes. Mothering in sheep is a genetic characteristic; certain breeds have better mothering abilities and individual ewes should be selected for their mothering capabilities.

Rejected ewe lambs should therefore not be used for breeding. The crowding of ewes into camps can also cause ewes to reject their lambs, and so does the disturbance and unnecessary handling of ewes with lambs. Lambing camps need shelter from sun and wind, accessible clean water and sufficient feed. Supervision by a professional shepherd is extremely valuable as lambing problems can be handled timeously.

Starvation/Underweight newborns

The normal birth weight of lambs varies with the breed, but should be 3,5 – 4,5kg. Underweight lambs are the result of poor nutrition of ewes during the last stages of pregnancy. For example, ewes grazing on old lands during late preganancy usually give birth to underweight lambs. These lambs are born with low fat reserves and as a result are weak, unable to suckle and are very susceptible to chilling. They die a few days after birth, and are often

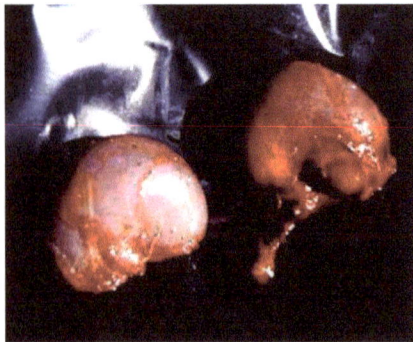

On post-mortem, lambs that died of starvation show no fat reserves around the kidneys

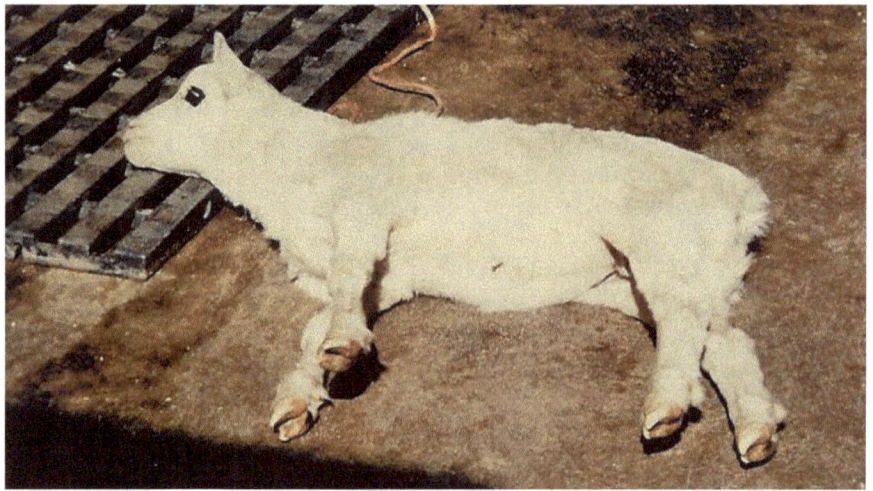

A lamb suffering from tetanus shows typical stiff spasms of the limbs

only found once scavengers have had a go. Death is usually attributed to predation. Lambs born alive show inflated lungs; the presence of the soft "slippers" on the lamb's hooves will indicate whether it has walked or not.

At post-mortem, underweight lambs have no fat reserves around the kidneys and have empty stomachs. Losses due to low birth weight can be prevented by ensuring the pregnant ewes get good nutrition, especially during the last six weeks of pregnancy. Ewes carrying twins or triplets will need more feed than single lamb ewes.

Tetanus

Tetanus is chiefly a condition seen in lambs and kids although sheep and goats of all ages are potentially susceptible. The disease results from the infection of certain types of wounds with the spores of *Clostridium tetani* bacteria, particularly those caused by docking and castrating.

C tetani is widespread in the soil because it produces resistant spores which are shed in the faeces of livestock. Because they're common in the soil around farmyards, they often contaminate wounds, but they usually only cause problems when they contaminate deep wounds in which oxygen levels are low. In small stock, this occurs particularly with castration or docking when using elastrators (rekkies) since this causes crushing and bruising of the tissues. Animals docked using knives can also develop tetanus, if the procedure

is carried out unhygienically.

Tetanus spores germinate under such conditions and the bacteria produce a powerful toxin which affects the nerves, causing spastic, or stiff, paralysis.

Lambs and kids will develop signs of the disease seven to 10 days after docking/castration. The first signs of the disease are a stiff gait. Eventually, as the disease progresses, animals lie down and are unable to rise. They show convulsions typically a stiff extension of the legs (tetanic spasms). Other signs are dilating of the nostrils and holding the ears stiffly. The animals are hypersensitive to noise and movement, which can trigger convulsions.

Animals having tetanus die within three to four days, when the toxin affects the muscles used for breathing.

The diagnosis of tetanus is made based on the typical symptoms and a history of docking/castration. There are no specific pathological signs which can be used for diagnosis. Treatment with antibiotics or specific tetanus antiserum is almost always ineffective once the symptoms appear.

Vaccination is the only cost-effective control measure; a clostridial vaccine containing the tetanus component is given to the pregnant ewe and the lamb receives protection through the colostrums. It can then be safely docked and castrated at three weeks of age (see Acute (sudden) deaths, page 73, for a discussion of effective clostridial vaccination).

DISEASES

3

NOTES

GASTROINTESTINAL DISEASES

The gastrointestinal (GIT) system in ruminants includes, in order of progression, the mouth, pharynx (throat), oesophagus, the forestomachs (rumen, reticulum and omasum), the abomasum or true stomach, the small intestine, and the colon or large intestine which terminates in the rectum. GIT disorders can be caused by obstructions, incorrect feeding, poisoning, infections or parasite infestations.

Acidosis (grain overload)

This condition results from the sudden intake of a large quantity of carbohydrate-rich feed, such as grain. This can be accidental, or the result of feedlot managers failing to allow sufficient time for animals to adapt to a high carbohydrate diet. Feeding a large quantity of carbohydrates to ruminants causes an increase in the gram-positive bacteria, specifically *Streptococcus bovis*. These bacteria break down the carbohydrates, releasing vast quantities of lactic acid. In the initial stages, acidity in the rumen causes movement of water into the rumen, resulting in dehydration of the rest of the body and a watery rumen content. The presence of high concentrations of acid in the rumen also cause damage to the lining, leading to inflammation, but other organs are affected as well.

Animals that survive severe attacks may have complications such as fungal or bacterial rumenitis and laminitis or show blindness, because there's been brain damage. Liver abscesses occur in animals that survive, resulting directly from the invasion of bacteria through the rumen wall.

Depending on the quantity of carbohydrates eaten, animals show a variety of symptoms, ranging from temporary loss of appetite and mild diarrhoea to more serious cases which show staggering and collapse. If acidosis is severe, it will result in renal failure, collapse and death. In less severe cases, animals will become listless and stop eating. Diagnosis of the condition is usually obvious since there will be a history of accidental gorging on grain or a sudden introduction of a high concentra-

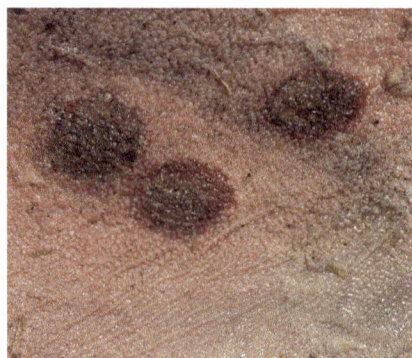

Lesions in the rumen caused by acidosis

tion of grain into the diet.

On post-mortem, the animals show watery diarrhoea; a lot of grain is often visible in the rumen. The rumen lining shows severe inflammation. The rest of the carcass will show signs of dehydration, namely dark red blood and sunken eyes. The pH of the rumen content will be below 5.

Mildly affected animals resume eating within three to four days, and their condition will be improved by administering antacids and supplying good-quality hay. They will need intravenous administering of bicarbonate fluid; and sometimes the removal of the rumen's content. Mortality is high in severe cases and emergency slaughter should be considered, as animals will need intensive veterinary treat-

ment to save them.

Prevent the condition by ensuring animals don't accidentally overeat on grain. Feedlot animals should be allowed three weeks to adapt to a gradual increase of carbohydrate in the ration.

Alkalosis (urea poisoning)

Alkalosis is the opposite of acidosis, a systemic excess of alkali insead of acid. In small stock, this is caused mainly by urea poisoning. Urea is a non-protein source of nitrogen which is a valuable form of protein supplementation. Because it's toxic, it must be fed gradually so that the rumen flora can adapt. Sudden large intakes in urea are often caused by urea blocks dissolving in water and this causes deaths in stock when they drink the water (see Poisoning, page 126 - 127, for more details).

Blue tongue

This viral disease occurs in summer, and causes mouth ulcers and swelling of the head and tongue. There are other symptoms too, including lameness. The disease is discussed in more detail in the section on lameness (page 57).

Bloat

Bloat is the massive distention of the abdomen resulting from the accumulation of

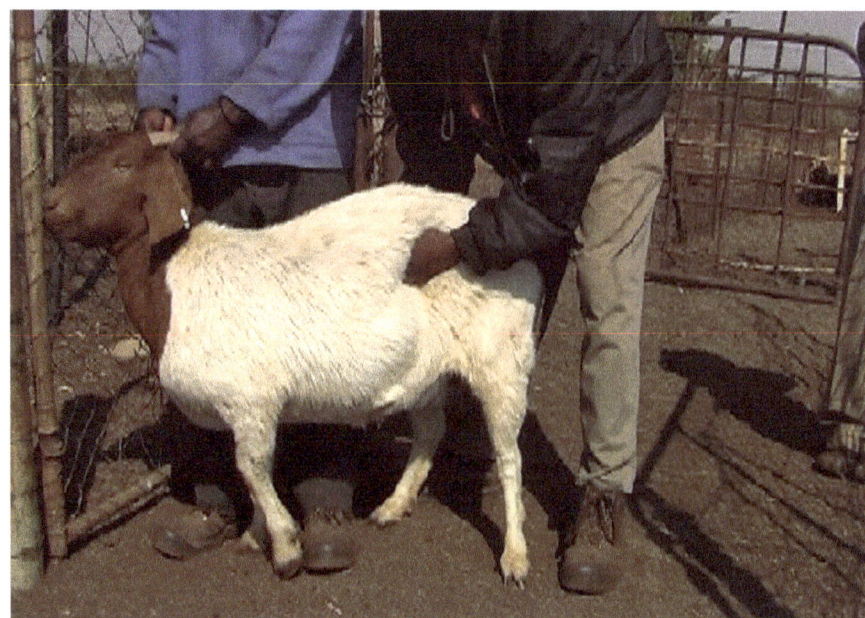

The rumen can be felt and injected through the para-lumbar fossa

gases fermentating in the rumen and reticulum. Under normal circumstances, the gas produced in the rumen is eructated (burped) out through the oesophagus, but in cases of bloat, this cannot happen for a number of possible reasons. There are two different kinds of bloat.

The most common type seen in small stock is frothy bloat, which occurs as outbreaks when animals graze on leguminous pastures such as lucerne and clover. The high level of protein in these pastures causes carbon dioxide to form frothy gas bubbles, which accumulate in the rumen causing severe pressure on the abdomen and later on in the lungs.

Free gas bloat can be caused by paralysis of the rumen as the result of plant poisoning or blockage of the oesophagus (choke). Prussic acid poisoning and krimpsiekte are two of the most common causes of paralysis in the rumen (see Plant poisoning, page ??). Obstruction of the oesophagus occurs in sheep and goats most often by blockage – with potatoes, fruit or vegetables, or pelleted rations. Greedy feeders or hungry animals tend to develop this type of bloat. Another type is seen in sheep/goats that have worn teeth, and feed on poor-quality grazing. The animals are unable to ruminate effectively, resulting in a blockage of the rumen with poor-quality roughage.

The symptoms are the massive distention of the abdomen, difficulty in breathing, regurgitation of rumen contents, froth exuding from the nose and, finally, collapse and death. Life-threatening cases of free gas bloat is relieved by inserting a trocar into the rumen. The cause must then be determined. Choke can be diagnosed by a veterinarian's trying to pass a stomach tube down the animal's throat. An obstruction will prevent the tube's passing into the stomach.

Bloat caused by paralysis of the rumen from plant poisoning is often irreversible, especially in the case of opblaaskrimpsiekte. See Prussic acid poisoning (page 126) and krimpsiekte (page 122 - 123).

Frothy bloat is treated by administering anti-foaming agents directly into the rumen through the para-lumbar fossa, a triangle on the animal's left side formed between the ribs, vertebrae and the hind leg (see Fig 50). If the condition is very serious, the rumen will have to be opened and emptied by a veterinarian. Prevent frothy bloat by dosing animals with anti-foaming agents before placing them on grazing, feeding hay before allowing them on pastures, or limiting the time spent grazing on leguminous pastures.

Braxy
(See Acute (sudden) death, page 73)

Coccidiosis
Coccidiosis occurs mainly in animals under one year of age. (See Lambs and kids, page 32 - 33, for more details.)

Dental attrition
In ruminants, as in other animals, the teeth begin to show wear as the animals age. Animals on the veld in sandy and semi-arid areas show greater wear to the teeth than animals on pastures. Animals whose teeth are worn or missing cannot eat or ruminate properly and will show a progressive weight loss. It is important to inspect the teeth when purchasing animals, to determine the age and check on overall condition. Overgrown incisors may be seen in stall-fed animals, as a direct result of lack of wear. Such animals will show signs of teeth-grinding and loss of condition.

Diarrhoea
Diarrhoea – the production of liquid faeces – arises from the rapid passage of the contents of the gastrointestinal tract (GIT). Irritation of the gut mucosa caused by parasites or plant poisons may also cause diarrhoea. Osmotic factors, e g high levels of magnesium ions in salt fed as a lick, can cause diarrhoea because it draws water into the cavity of the gut.

Certain bacteria cause diarrhoea because they contain toxins that interfere with the water-flow dynamics of the intestine, e g *E coli* (see Lambs and kids, page 34, 35). Other agents such as coccidia cause diarohhea due to damage of the intestine (see Lambs and kids, page 34, 35). Young animals in crowded, intensive systems may occasionally show outbreaks of diarrhoea, due to rota and corona viruses. In older animals, common causes of diarrhoea are intestinal parasites such as roundworms, brown stomach worms, bankrupt worms, whips and bowel worms. Other parasites that can cause diarrhoea are liver fluke, conical fluke or (rarely) bilharzia. A number of poisonous plants also cause diarrhoea in sheep and goats.

E. coli
(See Lambs and kids, page 34 - 35)

Endoparasites
Most endoparasites in livestock occur in the gastrointestinal tract and cause various syndromes, ranging from anaemia and weight loss to diarrhoea, even death. (See Endoparasites, page 76 - 81, for the worms that affect the various species.)

Enterotoxaemia
See Acute (sudden) death, page ??.

Gall bladder enlargement (grootgal)
Many farmers believe an animal showing an enlarged gall bladder at post-mortem has died from a specific disease, which they refer to as grootgal or gal-lamsiekte. An enlarged gall bladder is not an indicator of a specific disease. It is seen when animals haven't eaten for some time, usually because of a chronic disease, such as botulism (lamsiekte) or because of impaction of the rumen with poor-quality grass (droë galsiekte). Bile – a greenish black fluid produced by the liver – is shed into the intestine to help the digestive process.

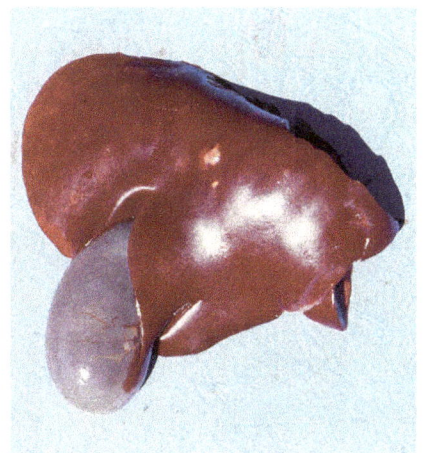

An enlarged gall bladder

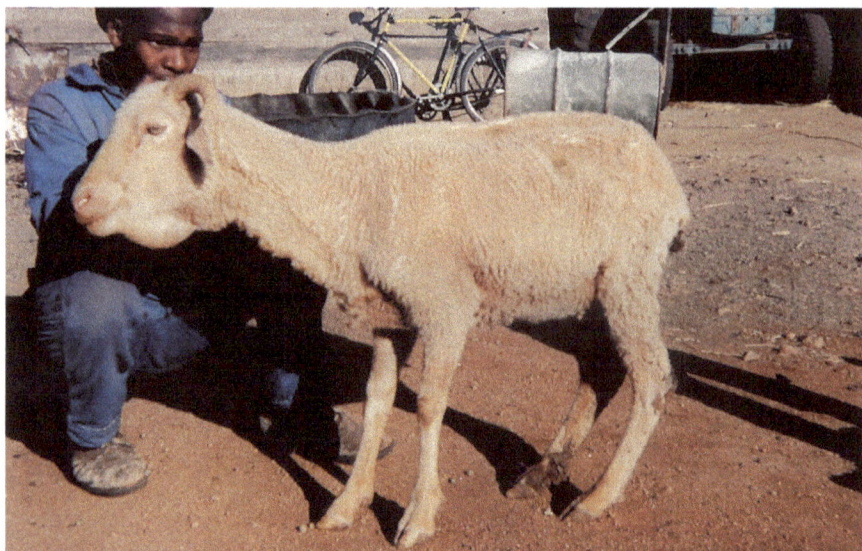

A sheep suffering from Johne's disease, showing bottlejaw and emaciation

When the animal doesn't eat for a protracted period, the bile builds up in the gall bladder, causing noticeable enlargement.

Johne's disease (paratuberculosis)

This is a bacterial infection of sheep and goats caused by *Mycobacterium avium* subspecies paratuberculosis. It is now a notifiable disease in South Africa, which means that all cases have to be reported to the veterinary authorities. The disease is becoming more prevalent because it's difficult to identify initially; it has a long incubation period and diagnosis is complicated. In South Africa, the disease is prevalent in the Eastern and Western Cape, especially in farms around Ceres, Caledon and Mossel Bay, where the acid soil is thought to promote the survival of the organism. The bacterium is highly resistant, surviving in soil and water for up to a year in these areas.

Farms become infected when animals shedding the bacterium through the faeces and milk are introduced. Because the incubation period of the disease is roughly two years, by the time the signs of infection appear on the farm the bacteria have established themselves on the property. Young animals are the most vulnerable to infection. The bacteria invade the intestine, causing a chronic granular infection of the small intestine which inhibits the

Corrugations of the colon caused by Johne's disease

absorption of nutrients. As a result, there is a progressive loss of condition over a number of years. Sheep and goats show gradual wasting and develop bottlejaw. The faeces may appear soft, but small stock don't develop the chronic diarrhoea seen in cattle. Sheep may shed their wool.

The diagnosis of Johne's disease is most often made when infected animals are slaughtered or die, and the typical corrugations of the small intestine are seen on post-mortem. The diagnosis can be confirmed by a number of laboratory tests, some of which can be used to identify infected animals in the flock.

There is no economically viable treatment for the condition. Control on infected farms must has to be focused on reducing the level of infection in the animals' environment; this includes identifying and re-

moving infected animals, regular removal of faeces, and feeding young animals on pasteurised colostrum and milk. A vaccine is available for sheep and goats, on prescription from a State veterinarian, to be used in conjunction with eliminating infected animals. All vaccinated animals have to be clearly marked. The vaccine will reduce the number of clinical cases by reducing the number of organisms shed.

In areas where the incidence of Johne's disease is high, prevent the introduction of the infection by buying from clean farms. Local veterinarians will be able to advise on whether or not serological tests such as ELISA should be performed on the animals to be bought.

Mouth ulcers

In sheep, the main cause of ulcers in the mouth is the viral disease blue tongue but we should always be aware of the possibility of foot and mouth disease. Other causes are trauma resulting from hard or spiny feed, or dosing injuries.

Oesophageal paralysis

This is a plant poisoning which occurs in sheep (vermeersiekte), and can cause paralysis of the oesophagus. (See Plant poisoning, page 125)

Obstruction of the bowel

Sheep are less inclined to eat foreign objects than goats, but in semi-arid areas they do suffer from bowel obstructions because of plant fibre balls. These are formed when the animals eat bushes

Certain karoo bushes cause the formation of plant balls which may lodge in the abomasum and cause an obstruction

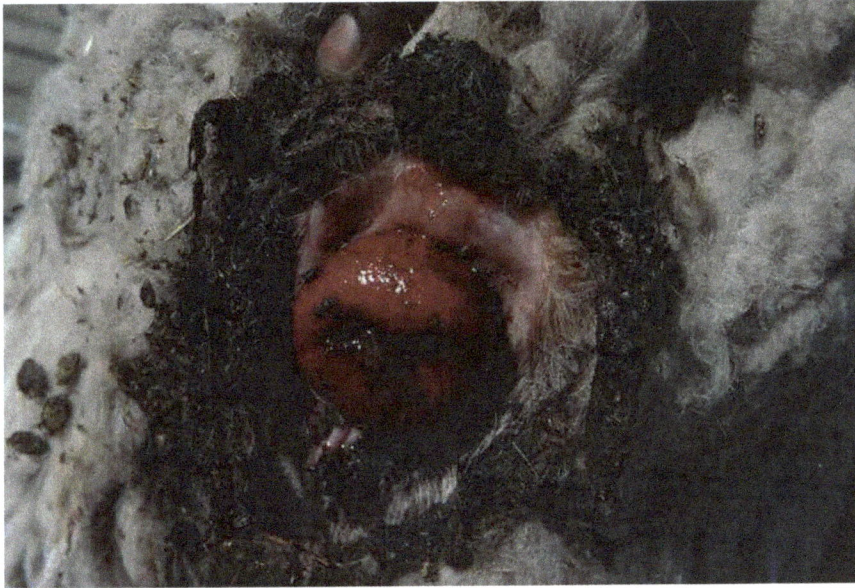

Rectal prolapse in a sheep

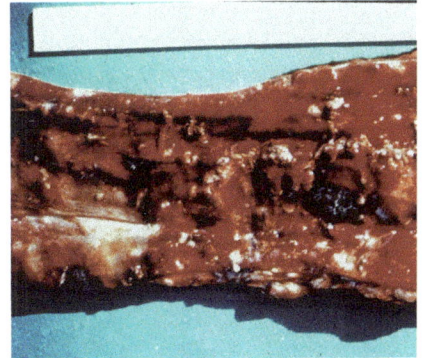

Salmonella infection causes a severe bloody enteritis

and grass that have woolly flowers: *Stipagrostis obtusa* (boesmansgras), *Eriocephalus* (kapokbos), *Chrysocoma* (bitterbos) and *Gnidia* (januariebos). Goats are particularly fond of eating these flowers and often suffer from plant ball impaction. If the balls are large, animals will show signs of emaciation and bloating. The fibrous plant balls are easily seen at post-mortem, when the abomasum is opened up.

To prevent the condition, the problem plants have to be avoided when they're in flower.

Plant poisoning

Most plant poisons that affect the GIT cause diarrhoea (chinkerinchee, castor oil plants, Sesbania, for instance), but these are accompanied by other symptoms. Exceptions are vermeersiekte in sheep, which causes damage to the muscles of the oesophagus and results in the muscular walls thinning and dilating. The affected animals are unable to swallow, and regurgitate feed (see Plant poisoning, page 125, for more details).

Rectal prolapse

This condition occurs in certain sheep flocks which seem to have a genetic predisposition to developing it. The condition is breed-related and is seen in mutton sheep, particularly Dorpers. It's speculated that docking tails too short may contribute to damage which predisposes to this condition. Rectal prolapse occurs particularly in animals on high-energy rations, that don't have exercise. It can also occur in ewes that have had a prolonged dystocia, or lambs that have developed severe coccidial diarrhoea.

The symptom is the protrusion of a fold of the rectum. Initially, it can be replaced in the body, but the protruding fold gradually becomes swollen, damaged and infected and then can no longer be replaced. At this stage, the animal shows signs of pain, straining and may develop a fever. Ewes may develop a uterine prolapse simultaneously.

Veterinary help is essential, as resolving the condition requires surgery. In the early stages, the protruding rectal fold can be replaced and contained by loosely stitching the rectum to close it. Damaged rectal folds have to be amputated by a veterinarian.

Avoid breeding animals that have a tendency to rectal prolapse, and cut tails longer. Animals prone to rectal prolapse should not be used in feedlots.

Salmonellosis

Salmonella infection in sheep and goats occurs in extensive and intensive systems in sheep of all ages, but usually two- to four-tooth animals. The precipitating factor appears to be stress, since clinical disease occurs in animals transported over long distances, or those introduced into feedlots, or animals crowded together for shearing or dipping.

The most common salmonella strain in South Africa is *Salmonella Typhimurium*, which infects all species of animals, including humans, and isn't specific to small stock. The source of infection is usually difficult to determine but it's thought that pens, paddocks, trucks or water points can be sources. Certain feeds, such as carcass meals, may be infected with salmonella bacteria.

The symptoms appear a week to a month after a stressful experience, and affect 2 – 50% of animals. Sick animals develop a fever of 40°C , lose their appetite, are listless, weak, reluctant to move, and experience blood-tinged or watery diarrhoea. They often die within seven days. Survivors show severe dehydration and loss of weight. Abortions may occur in pregnant sheep.

Suspect salmonellosis when sheep or goats develop severe diarrhoea after being transported or introduced into feedlots. On post-mortem, there's typically a severe inflammation of the gut. Isolating salmonella bacteria from the gut and organs will confirm the diagnosis. Sick animals may be salvaged by a veterinarian treating the animal with scheduled antibiotics and administering fluid. Survivors usually recover sufficiently to regain condition.

When salmonellosis is diagnosed on a

property, recurring outbreaks should be prevented by minimising stress, improving hygiene and avoiding overcrowding. In feedlots, animals should get sufficient roughage and be introduced gradually to concentrates. Using a live vaccine containing *S Typhimurium* may be recommended by veterinarians but their usefulness has not been established.

Wooden tongue

This is caused by the bacterium *Actinobacillus lignieresi*, a normal inhabitant of the mouth.

Cases of wooden tongue arise in small stock as a result of feeding on coarse grass or exposure to feed, such as prickly pears, from which the spines haven't been removed.

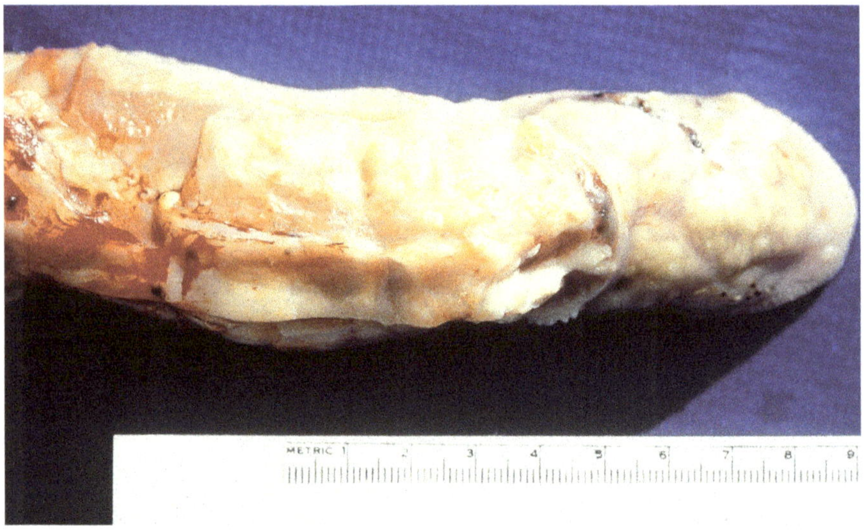

The tiny *A lignieresi* abscesses that develop in the tongue as a result cause it to enlarge, harden and develop a lumpy surface. As a result, the tongue becomes less mobile and the affected animal has trouble chewing and swallowing. It shows signs of salivation and weight loss which gradually proceeds to death from starvation.

By the time the symptoms have developed, the condition cannot be treated effectively and animals have to be slaughtered. Abscesses on the face are caused by the same bacterium, which infects wounds caused during feeding by coarse grass, sharp grass lawns, spiny plants like vyebos, prickly pears; and also, sometimes, by tick bites (see Skin conditions and wounds, page 63).

Sheep and goats use their lips and graze close to the ground, so the condition often involves the lips and corners of the mouth. The small abscesses that arise spread via the lymphatic system to form extensive lesions all over the face.

In the case of face abscesses, small external wounds can be treated by regularly applying an iodine solution, but extensive cases are usually not worth treating. Both conditions can be prevented by avoiding sharp, spiny or hard feed.

A case of wooden tongue in a sheep

NOTES

_____
_____
_____
_____
_____
_____
_____
_____
_____
_____
_____
_____
_____
_____
_____
_____

RESPIRATORY DISEASES

Caseous lympadenitis (*Corynebacterium ovis*)

Corynebacterium ovis is a bacterium that causes abscesses in the lungs and lymph nodes in sheep and goats, although the lungs are less often affected in goats. Sheep contract the infection during shearing or dipping, when bacteria from infected sheep are able to contaminate wounds. Once the bacteria have penetrated the skin they're spread through the lymphatic system and lodge in the lymph nodes, and sometimes also in the lungs. The most commonly affected lymph nodes in sheep are the ones at the point of the shoulder and the groin; in goats, the lymph nodes of the head and neck are usually affected.

In sheep, fresh abscesses are very yellow with a greenish tinge, but later the pus dries out and develops a layered effect, like the cross-section of an onion. In goats, the pus is very dry and doesn't show the typical layered pattern seen in sheep.

In live animals, lymph node abscesses are often not noticed unless the abcess ruptures, often during handling of the animal.

Sheep in which lung abscesses develop show gradual loss of weight and eventually have difficulty breathing, because of the extensive invasion of the lung tissue. At this stage, the condition can be confused with bacterial or viral pneumonia. These animals die soon after showing respiratory signs.

Apart from the deaths due to lung abscesses, *C ovis* infection causes an estimated loss of 5% in wool production. In mutton sheep, losses are caused by trimming and carcass downgrading.

Antibiotic therapy is not effective in affected animals because the drugs cannot penetrate the thick capsule layers of the abscess. *C ovis* abscessation can be controlled by using a vaccine that helps to limit the spread and protect young, uninfected animals.

Killed vaccines for the control of CLA have to be repeated four to six weeks after an initial injection, and then repeated annually. Vaccination has to be combined with good hygiene; when dipping sheep, young animals have to be dipped first to prevent their becoming contaminated. When shearing, castrating, docking and tagging, use wound disinfectants such as iodine solutions. If an abscess ruptures during handling, wipe this up with paper and use disinfectant to decontaminate this material and the surroundings, to prevent other animals becoming infected.

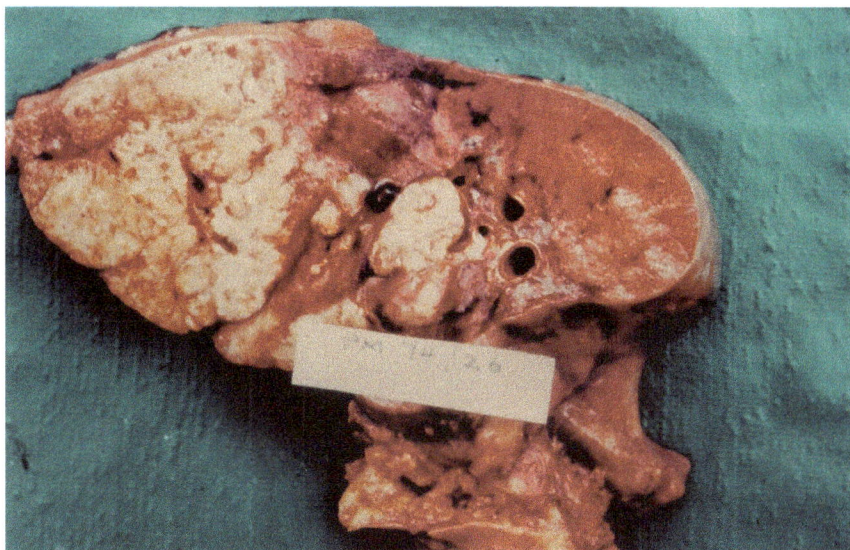

***Corynebacterium ovis* abscess in the lung**

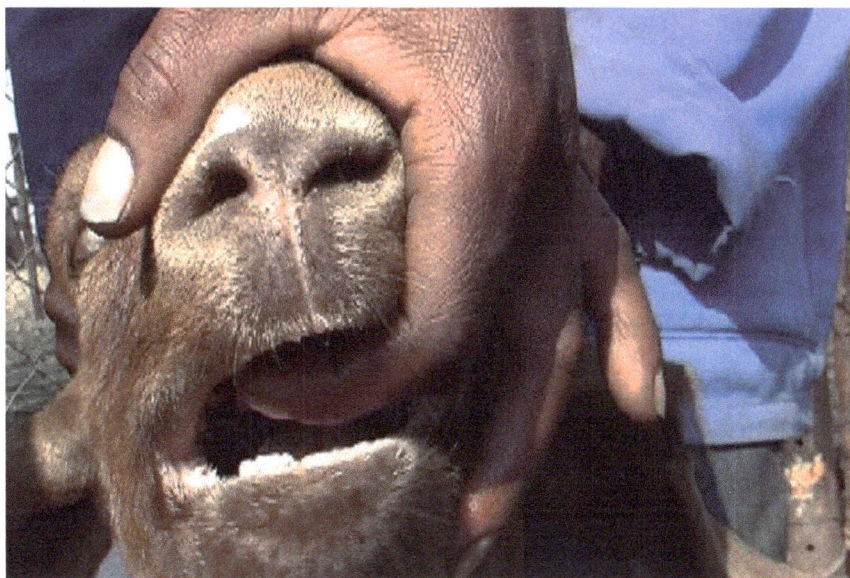

The correct way to dose small stock

Dosing (gangrenous) pneumonia

This condition can occur as a result of poor dosing techniques when administering stock remedies, or when ruminants lying on their sides regurgitate rumen content. For dosing pneumonia, the remedies are delivered directly into the lungs instead of down the oesophagus.

The symptoms of gangrenous pneumonia are fever and difficulty breathing one to three days after the dosing or inhalation incident. The mortality rate is usually high because of the extensive damage caused to the lung tissue. If dosing pneumonia is suspected, prompt treatment with a broad-spectrum antibiotic, such as

A sheep suffering from jaagsiekte, showing the copious watery discharge from the nose

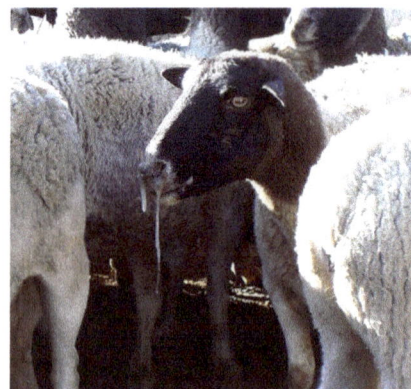

A sheep infested with nasal worms, showing severe mucous nasal discharge

oxytetracycline, is indicated and supportive treatment by a veterinarian may be useful for valuable animals. Guidelines for the correct dosing of small stock are:

- Don't dose faster than the animal can swallow
- Don't lift the animal's head up as this prevents swallowing
- Don't pull the tongue out, because it's needed in the process of swallowing.

Pulmonary adenomatosi (Jaagsiekte)

This is a cancer of the lungs, induced by a retrovirus, in sheep and (rarely) in goats. The infection is introduced into a clean flock by an infected animal, which spreads the virus by coughing. Lambs less than six months old are the most susceptible and usually contract infection from infected mothers.

The disease has a long incubation period, and signs of infection can take as long as eight to 24 months after initial infection to appear. The most prominent symptom is shortness of breath, especially when the sheep are driven. Severely affected animals will lag behind the flock and have a severe cough. They may have a copious watery discharge from the nose. Infected animals deteriorate gradually and they die two to four months after the initial symptoms appear, usually as a result of secondary bacterial infections which cause fatal pneumonia.

On post-mortem, the lungs are clearly abnormal: they have a grey colouration and are solid instead of having the usual spongy texture. When placed in water, the lung tissue sinks instead of floating, as normal lung tissue does. There's usually an increase in volume of the affected lung lobes. The lung lesions seen with jaagsiekte are characteristic, and histopathological examination by a veterinary pathologist will confirm the diagnosis.

There's no treatment. Infected sheep have to be identified by serological testing and eradicated from the flock as soon as possible.

Lungworm infestation

Lungworm infestation occurs in focal areas of the country which experience cool, misty conditions, such as the coastal areas of Natal and the Eastern Cape, and in mountainous regions such as Lesotho. Animals become infested when they ingest larvae on infested grazing. The worms migrate to the lungs and cause respiratory symptoms such as coughing and nasal discharge. Most roundworm remedies are effective against lungworm infestations. (For more details about treating and controlling the condition, see Roundworms, page 80.)

Nasal worms

This condition, which occurs in sheep and goats, is an infestation of the sinus cavities with the larval stages of the sheep nasal fly *Oestrus ovis*.

The fly is active during summer, when it seeks out small stock and lays its larvae around the nostrils. The larvae enter the nasal cavity and climb up into the sinus cavity where they feed on the secretions. Here they moult a number of times to become fairly large, before they are sneezed out. The larvae then pupate in the ground. Nasal fly larvae cause severe irritation of the sinuses, resulting in a sometimes copious nasal discharge which can become thick and yellow. Infested animals sneeze and shake their heads and progressively lose weight because of the discomfort caused by the larvae. Heavily infested rams may refuse to mate and ewes may refuse to suckle their lambs.

Nasal worm infestations are treated by dosing with remedies containing rafoxanide or closantel, or injections having macrocyclic lactones (ivermectin, moxidectin, etc). For more details about control, see Ectoparasites (page 105-106).

Pasteurellosis (bontlong) (*Mannheimia haemolytica*)

This is a pneumonia caused by, among other organisms, *Mannheimia* (formerly *Pasteurella*) *haemolytica* serotypes. It occurs in small stock of all ages but causes a very severe septicaemic form in young lambs.

The precipitating factor for outbreaks of disease are thought to be management or environmental stressors, as deaths occur in association with dipping, castration, dosing, and herding.

In lambs younger than three months old, acute death is the most common sign; older animals tend to show signs of pneumonia such as fever, lack of appetite, difficulty breathing, coughing and nasal discharge. Milder cases may show a discharge from the nose and eyes and occasional coughing. The condition can be confused with nasal worm infection, blue tongue, jaagsiekte and photosensitivity. Death follows if the animals are not treated promptly with broad-spectrum antibiotics, such as oxytetracyclines.

At post-mortem, the lungs show areas of thickening and darkening, so that they resemble liver tissue. The diagnosis can be confirmed by isolating a *Mannheimia haemolytica* serotype from the lung and other tissues.

Vaccination with a good-quality multivalent product such as the IRP vaccine (Multivax P) has been shown to give good protection against *Mannheimia haemolytica* as well as the bacterium *Pasteurella trehalosi* which causes septicaemia in sheep

Pneumonia caused by *Mannheimia haemolytica* (pasteurellosis)

(see Acute (sudden) death, page 74). The Multivax P vaccine also contains all the important clostridia.

To protect flocks against pasteurella pneumonia, sheep of all ages – including week-old lambs – should be vaccinated and given a booster four to six weeks later. Annual vaccination will maintain immunity. Lambs of vaccinated ewes will have colostral immunity so vaccination should be delayed.

Plant poisoning
Certain plant poisons are occasionally a cause of respiratory conditions in sheep; diseases such as *Crotalaria* spp (jaagsiektebossie), *Gnidia* (harpuisbos) and *Hertia pallens* (springbokbos).

NOTES

REPRODUCTIVE DISEASES

A number of infectious diseases of ewes and does cause abortions or the birth of weak lambs. These are discussed in detail below. The most important infectious cause of infertility in sheep rams is *Brucella ovis* which results in a low lambing percentage. Other causes of reproductive failure in small stock are non-infectious factors, such as congential problems of the genitalia, injuries, inappropriate breeding season, inadequate nutrition, and incorrect ram to ewe ratio. These factors can all affect the lambing percentage. Investigating reproductive problems in small stock requires taking a full history of the symptoms, the number of animals involved, the stage of abortions, the history of introduction of new animals, vaccination programmes, etc.

Aborted foetuses, weak or malformed newborns can be valuable material on which to do post-mortems and microbiological isolations. This material should be submitted as soon as possible to veterinarians or veterinary laboratories. Never freeze this material and use gloves or plastic bags when handling it. The foetus must be double-bagged in strong, non-leak plastic bags and must not be frozen but kept cool on cool packs. It can sometimes be difficult to ascertain the cause of reproductive problems, but in the long term a successful diagnosis will justify the trouble taken.

Abortions

There are various causes of abortions in sheep and goats, including genetic factors and some infectious agents, such as *Chlamydiophila* and, less often, *Brucella melitensis* and *Coxiella burnetti*. Other causes are Rift Valley fever and various plant poisonings.

Abortion in Angora goats

Although the infections that affect other species can affect Angora goats, the breed is known to suffer from "habitual abortion". This is a heritable metabolic problem of certain individuals in the breed and its high prevalence is due to inbreeding, as it occurs particularly in ewes that show fine hair quality. These ewes abort most commonly at four months, without showing any signs of illness or abnormalities such as retained placentas. The only control measure is the elimination of habitual aborters from the flock. Adverse weather conditions or stress of any other kind, especially poor nutrition which causes ketosis, can precipitate such abortions.

Testicular abscessation

Abscesses of the testes of rams, usually caused by *Arcanobacterium* (*Corynebacterium*) *pyogenes*, may occur as a result of tick bites or as a sequel to other infections. The feasibility of veterinary treatment for such abscesses depends on whether they're localised under the skin or whether there is testicular involvement, in which case the prognosis for drainage and treatment is poor. (See Skin conditions and wounds, page 63 for the treatment of abscesses.)

Big lamb disease

This is caused by a plant intoxication that triggers a failure of the birth process. The causative plant is a Karoo bush *Salsola tuberculatiformis* (the cauliflower saltwort) found in the arid areas of the country; the problem is therefore limited geographically. The condition occurs primarily during periods of drought, when sheep are forced to eat this shrub.

The toxic components are thought to interfere with the hormonal trigger for the birth process, resulting in the pregnancy being extended, and resulting in abnormally large lambs. Pregnancy can be prolonged to 213 days. Typical signs are ewes with enormously distended abdomens but no sign of udder development. Affected sheep have to have the birth induced with injections of oxytocin or, if the lambs are too large, they should be removed by caesarean section. These lambs can weigh up to 12kg and have erupted teeth and long hooves. The plant only affects ewes in the last 50 days of pregnancy, so pastures containing this plant have to be avoided during this period.

Blue udder/mastitis

A number of bacteria can cause mastitis (or the so-called "blue udder") at different stages in sheep and goats. Some conditions occur shortly after lambing (*Staph aureus*); others result from the trauma large lambs cause to the udder (*Mannheimia* (*Pasteurella*) *haemolytica*) later in lactation. Wounding to the udder and unhygienic conditions are the main causative factors.

In the early stages of infection, the ewe separates from the flock and refuses to allow the lamb to suckle. Examination of the udder will show either one or both quarters to be hard, red and swollen and when milk is expressed, it is blood-stained and contains clots. If the ewe isn't treated with injectable antibiotics at this stage, the condition may become gangrenous, and the affected quarter turns blue. Mannheimia mastitis can be effectively treated with injectable tetracyclines. Taking a sterile milk sample before administering antibiotic therapy will allow for identification of the organism involved.

Big lamb disease, or prolonged pregnancy, can be caused by plant poisoning or deformation of the foetus

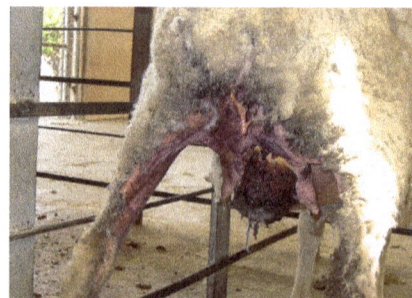

A severe case of blue udder or mastitis in a sheep

Some types of mastitis can be prevented by allowing the ewes to lamb on the veld instead of in camps. Injuries caused by shearing, and missing or scarred teats are a severe liability as the ewe won't be able to raise lambs, even if she has one intact teat. Affected ewes should be culled before the breeding season.

Brucella melitensis

Brucella melitensis is a sporadic cause of abortion in sheep and goats, which has been seen in flocks in Mpumalanga, Limpopo and KwaZulu-Natal. Although not widespread, the importance of these outbreaks is that, apart from the losses suffered by stock owners, *B melitensis* is a cause of Malta fever in humans.

In small stock, the disease initially causes abortion storms in late pregnancy and retained placentas may be seen. Reduced fertility may be seen in rams. As the disease progresses, the incidence of abortion declines but infection persists and may become invisible. Definitive diagnosis of this infection is made by isolating the organism from foetal or placental material, or even from milk samples of lactating does or ewes. Serology can also be used to detect the presence of infection in a herd. Control of the disease can be achieved by vaccination of ewes/does, but this must be done before the breeding season as the Rev 1 vaccine causes abortion in pregnant animals.

Coxiella burnetti (Q fever)

This organism is widespread in livestock in South Africa and is transmitted primarily by ticks. It is an occasional cause of abortion in sheep (3% of abortions investigated by Onderstepoort). Sporadic outbreaks of abortion and the birth of weak lambs occur in association with this organism. It's usually diagnosed on examination of the foetus in veterinary laboratories, in conjunction with serology. Abortions are sporadic and there is no treatment or prevention that can be applied economically.

Dystocia

The term "dystocia" means a difficult birth, and the cause may either be maternal or foetal. Maternal factors include weakness

A foetus aborted due to *Coxiella burnetti* infection

of the mother because of malnutrition, malformation of the pelvic cavity or the presence of tumours or large quantities of intra-abdominal fat. Foetal factors include oversized foetuses, deformation of the foetus due to infectious agents (see Foetal malformation, page 33-34), or faulty position of the foetus.

The normal presentation of the foetus is anterior; in other words, with the forelegs facing forward. Less common is a posterior presentation with hind legs first. Under normal circumstances, both of these usually have a trouble-free delivery, unless one of the limbs is bent. Breech presentations (tail first) are usually problematic unless the foetus is very small. Minor presentation problems can be corrected by straightening the limbs, but more complicated ones must be left for a veterinarian, who will do a caesarean section.

The farmer needs to know when to intervene in lambing; this should be done in the the following instances:
- when after an hour of straining, the lamb doesn't appear
- when the tail is seen protruding from the vulva (breech presentation)
- when the waterbag protrudes but the lamb doesn't appear
- when the ewe has blood-stained or wet hindquarters and no lamb or placental membrane appears.

Before the ewe is examined, she should preferably be placed on newspaper or clean feed sacks on a table or the back of a bakkie. The working surface should slope gently downwards in the direction of the ewe's head; before placing the hand in the vagina the hands and arm should be thoroughly washed with soap and water and liberally smeared with lubricant such as liquid paraffin or KY jelly. Failure to use enough lubricant will cause tearing of the tissues and the ewe may bleed to death. Insert the arm and assess the number of lambs, condition and presentation of the lambs, as this will determine what action should be taken:
- **Live normal lamb with correct presentation:** The lamb is probably too big. In this case, use plenty of lubricant and, using very gentle downward traction, try to ease the shoulders and hips through the birth canal, one at a time. If the lamb is so large that the ewe's abdomen is distended (as in grootlamsiekte) the lamb will have to be removed by caesarean section.
- **Live normal lamb with head or limb retained:** The head or limb must be straightened by gently pushing the lamb back down the birth canal and correcting the flexion. Protect the birth canal from damage by placing the hand over the hoof.

- Twins or triplets: Deliver each lamb separately; gently push the others back into the uterus.
- Breech presentation: The hind limbs must be straightened one at a time so that the lamb can be delivered by posterior presentation.
- Dead lambs: If the lamb has died in the uterus and is swollen, the foetus will have to be delivered by caesarean section; in some cases, the ewe may have to be destroyed.
- Deformed lambs: They usually have to be removed by caesarean section as the deformity causes the obstruction.

Enzootic abortion (*Chlamyophilia abortus*)

Enzootic abortion is a contagious condition caused by the rickettsial organism *Chlamydophilia abortus*. The organism invades the placenta and causes abortions and the birth of weak offspring in sheep and goats. A small percentage of animals are carriers of the bacterium which is shed onto the pastures through the faeces.

When infected ewes/does are introduced onto a farm they infect a flock by contaminating pastures during lambing, giving rise to an abortion storm. Very often, this occurs during the last month of pregnancy, usually two to three weeks before term.

Other manifestations can also be seen, however; the birth of weak premature lambs, or low lambing percentages due to early abortions. The lambs/kids that survive may be stunted and have joint infections or diarrhoea. Although the incidence of abortion drops as the ewes in the flock become immune, weak lambs will still be seen.

Enzootic abortion is suspected when there is a history of abortion storms and weak offspring. The foetuses are well-developed and fresh. Ewes that abort may show a vaginal discharge but are otherwise normal. A definitive diagnosis of enzootic abortion can be made on veterinary examination of the foetus, by making impression smears of the placenta and taking blood samples. The treatment of pregnant ewes with tetracyclines during abortion storms may limit the extent of infection

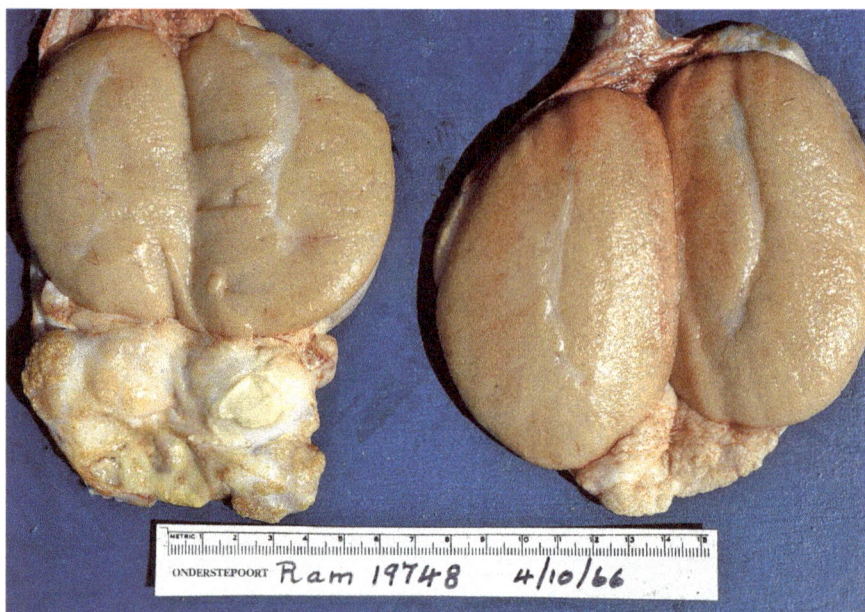

Epididymitis caused by *B ovis*; note that the fibrotic epididymis on the left has caused shrinkage of the testis. The testis and epididymis on the right are normal

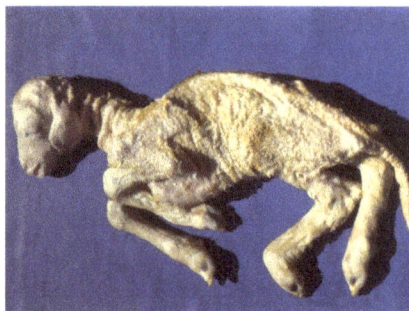

A foetus aborted due to enzootic abortion

but the best control method is vaccination of the ewes before the breeding season. The killed EA vaccine must be given annually four weeks before mating. The live EA vaccine should be given to young ewes at five months of age and repeated four weeks before mating. If it is given later, it may adversely affect the pregnancy.

Epididymitis

The epididymis is the duct which carries sperm from the ram's testicles. If this duct becomes infected by bacteria it causes the swelling and blockage of the tubules, resulting in infertility.

There are two causes of epididymitis in sheep rams, of which *Brucella ovis* is the most important.

Brucella ovis (ovine brucellosis)

This is a contagious cause of epididymitis in ovine rams which causes infertility and therefore results in a low lambing percentage. Goats are not susceptible to this disease.

B ovis bacteria are transmitted from adult carrier rams to young susceptible rams by direct contact, during mating or homosexual activity, by fly transmission, or by licking of the genitalia. The bacteria enter through the mucosal surfaces of the body (eyes, mouth, genitalia, rectum) and can migrate to the genital tract where they lodge in the epididymis – the system of tubules that transport semen from the testes. The epididymis lies on the outer surface of the testis and forms a tail at the lowest point of the testis. *B ovis* bacteria cause inflammation of the epididymis, which becomes red and swollen in the acute stages but later hardens into a large, fibrous lump. This can cause partial – and eventually total – blockage of the tubules. As a result, affected rams cannot inseminate ewes effectively because their fertility is reduced. Rams having affected testicles may nevertheless be dominant, monopolising ewes but not inseminating them efficiently.

The farmer doesn't usually notice the

condition until the lambing percentage is considerably reduced. On examination, infected rams show a hardening of the epididymis of one or both testes, which can become atrophied (shrink). The diagnosis is made by a veterinarian taking a semen sample which is examined in the laboratory. Confirmation of the presence of *B ovis* by culture or by staining is important to differentiate it from *A seminis* epididymitis. Serology can also be used to confirm the cause of epididymitis in rams.

To control the disease, all affected rams should be culled because they are a constant source of infection; and even if only one testicle is affected, the ram's fertility is reduced. Young rams in infected flocks should be given a single inoculation at weaning with the Rev 1 vaccine, since vaccination of adult rams can cause epididymitis. The vaccine will be less effective if infected rams aren't removed from the flock because they are a constant source of infection. Using the vaccine reduces the prevalence of the disease. Continue to examine the ram flock regularly until the flock is clean. It is unnecessary and undesirable to vaccinate ewes, as the vaccine can cause abortion. Examine all new rams carefully before introducing them into clean flocks.

Actinobacillus seminis in rams

A group of bacteria, including *Actinobacillus seminis*, can be a sporadic cause of epididymitis in sheep rams. It's thought that many rams may carry the bacteria but don't necessarily develop the condition. Ewes may also carry the bacteria, but don't suffer any disease symptoms. Factors which could promote the development of the condition are high nutrition levels and crowding in small camps. The cause and method of transmission are as yet unknown.

A small percentage of rams develop swollen, inflamed testicles for a number of days, which then subsides. Most rams recover but a few develop hardening of the epididymis of the testicle which indicates that they've been permanently damaged, and this causes blockage of the tubules transporting the sperm. The affected testicle later becomes flabby and atrophied.

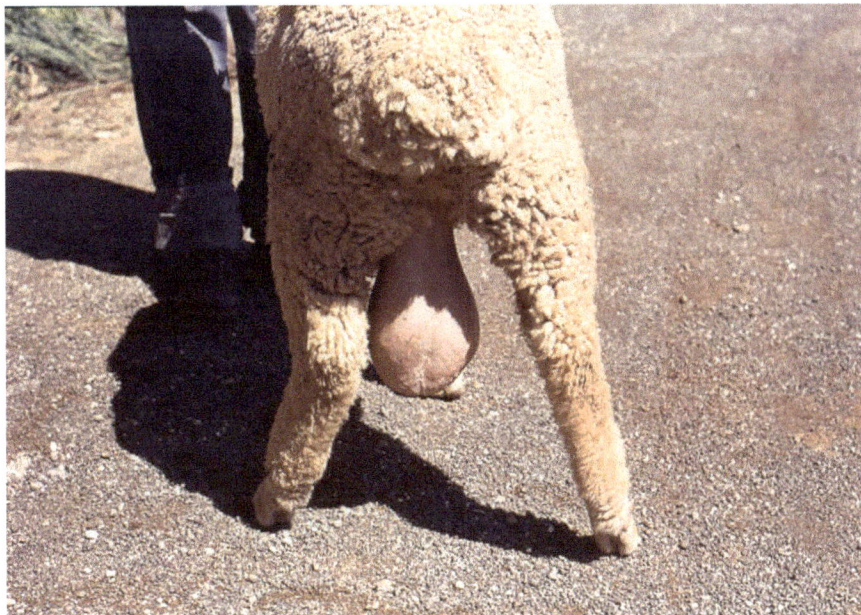

Swollen, inflamed testicles caused by *A seminis* infection in the initial stages

It's important to differentiate the condition from *Brucella ovis*, which is contagious and causes a high percentage of epididymitis in rams. This can be done by taking semen samples for bacterial culture. Ovine brucellosis can be eliminated from the flock with vaccination and culling (see *Brucella ovis*).

There's no cost-effective treatment for epididymitis caused by *A seminis*. Affected rams should be removed from the flock because they will be infertile. Culling or treating rams with antibiotics doesn't necessarily remove the organism from the flock or prevent damage to the epididymis. There is some evidence that rams kept in camps on high levels of nutrition are most affected and that turning young rams out into the veld may reduce the incidence of the condition.

Foetal malformation

A small percentage of foetal malformation is caused by genetic factors but when the prevalence increases, the involvement of infectious agents should be suspected. The culprits are generally a group of insect-borne viruses predominant in summer. The *Akabane* virus group causes sporadic abortion and foetal malformation in ruminants, chiefly joint and brain deformities. The degree of prevalence of problems

caused by this virus does not, however, justify importating or producing a vaccine.

Certain live vaccines can cause a low percentage of foetal abnormalities if administered early in pregnancy – for example, blue tongue, some live RVF vaccines and Wesselsbron vaccine (no longer available). History and post-mortem examination can usually establish the cause of these foetal malformations.

Infertility

In rams, non-infectious causes of infertility include underdevelopment or malformation of the genital tract and conformational features which make mating difficult. Structural defects such as hernias and any kind of lameness can affect the ability of rams to mate. Rams can acquire injuries to the penis from grass seed penetrating it, which causes permanent scarring, preventing the movement of the penis during erection. Other external factors such as overwork, high environmental temperatures and age can affect the work rate of rams. Brucella ovis is one of the most common causes of infertility in sheep rams causing low lambing percentages (see epididymitis).

Non-infectious causes of ewe infertility are various hereditary factors, nutritional factors such as vitamin A deficiency, the

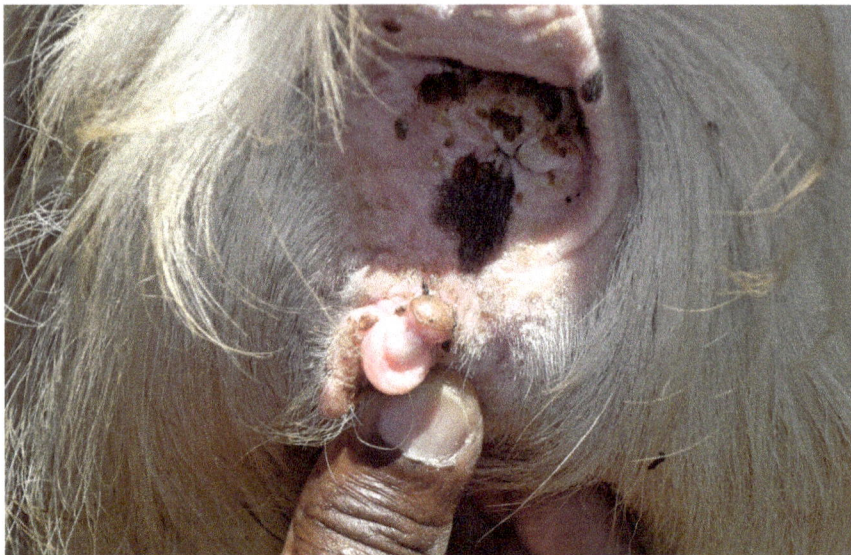

Anatomical abnormalities such as hermaphroditism, seen here, can be responsible for failure of animals to breed

high oestrogen content of clover pastures and selenium deficiency. Physiological infertility results when the oestrus cycle is irregular due to poor management, nutrition or genetic factors.

Ketosis (domsiekte)

Ketosis is a disease of pregnant ewes and of goat does, usually those carrying more than one foetus, so the condition is also referred to as twin lamb disease. It occurs when the ewe/doe has insufficient energy intake during the last six weeks of pregnancy. This is especially crucial in ewes carrying more than one foetus, because it doubles the amount of energy required at this stage. Any factor that prevents the ewe/doe from ingesting sufficient energy – for example, being too fat, poor grazing, long periods of handling of heavily pregnant animals, bad weather, heavy parasite infestations, and anatomical factors like worn teeth and lameness - can trigger ketosis. When the animal has insufficient energy, the body starts to break down fat, resulting in the production of ketones. These ketones cause acidosis, liver damage and brain damage and leads to a change in behaviour.

In the early stages of ketosis, ewes or does separate from the herd, are listless, refuse to eat and seem to be unusually tame or "stupid" when approached. They may appear to be blind. Some stand, pushing their heads against objects. Later, the ewe lies down and refuses to rise. If she isn't treated she will progress into a coma. The whole process can take about 10 days before the animal finally dies.

Ketosis is diagnosed based on the symptoms and the history of multiple births in the flock. Injecting calcium borogluconate under the skin (about 50ml) will eliminate milk fever as an alternative diagnosis. Veterinary intervention will be needed to treat affected sheep, because merely administering glucose is usually insufficient to reverse the condition, except in early cases. Caesarean section may be required to save the ewes' lives, but if liver damage is too severe this may not be successful.

At post-mortem, a typical sign is fatty degeneration of the liver which manifests as a yellowish colour and a friable texture. The uterus will be very large since it contains more than one lamb foetus. Ketones will be detected in the urine.

To prevent ketosis, don't allow ewes to become fat during pregnancy – not more than a body condition score of 4; those carrying twins should have a score of 3 (see page 29 for a discussion of body condition). The nutritional level should be improved during the last six weeks of pregnancy. Avoid unnecessary handling of ewes during late pregnancy.

Goat does develop ketosis under the same circumstances as ewes; the main difference is that they may abort, resulting in a reversal of the condition. Those that don't abort will lose their appetite, wander around listlessly and eventually go down, fall into a coma and die. The treatment is the same as for ewes.

Listeriosis

Listeria monocytogenes is an occasional cause of abortion in sheep and goats. *Listeria* bacteria are widespread in the environment, in the soil and pasture, and in the

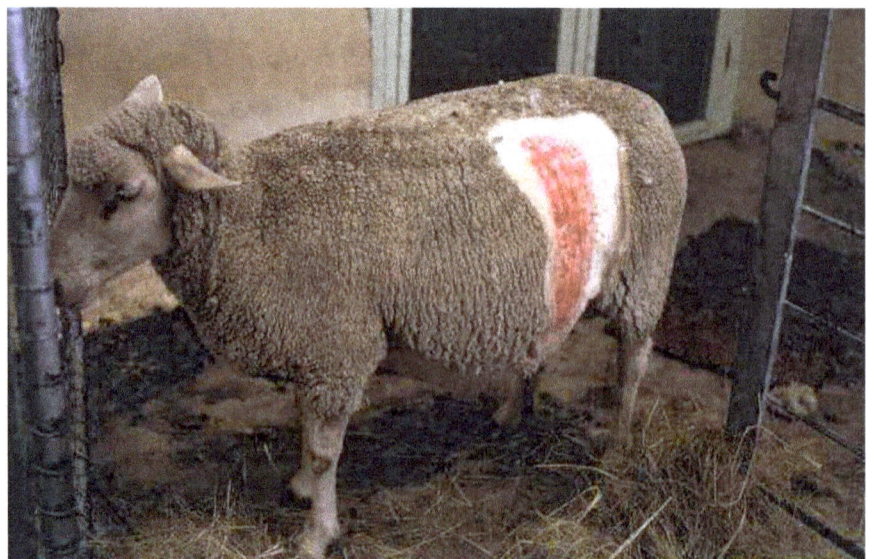

A ewe suffering from ketosis, showing head-pressing behaviour

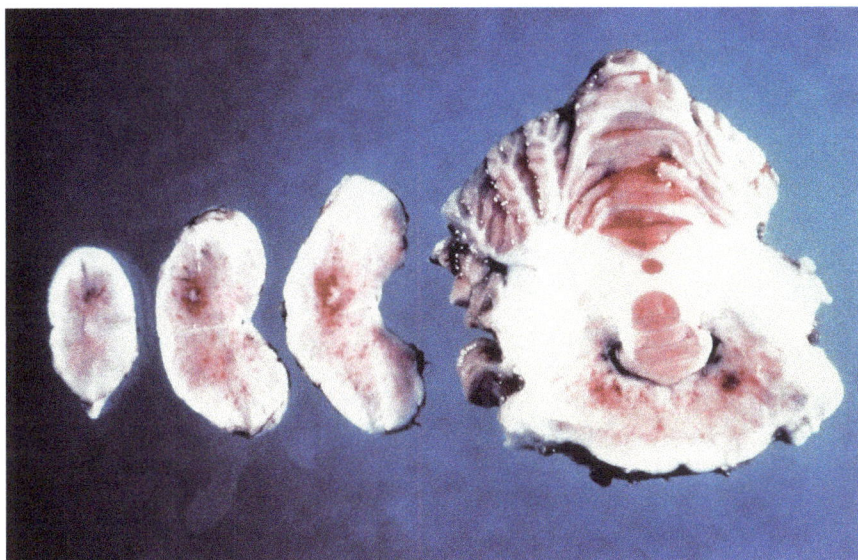

Brain damage caused by the bacterium *Listeria monocytogenes*

intestines of animals. They have a particular affinity for plant material flourishing on wet or flooded pastures, where they can survive for long periods. The organism grows particularly well on poor-quality silage which has become alkaline, and this is often a source of infection.

Under stressful conditions, *Listeria* organisms cause infections, either encephalitis or abortions. Abortions occurs in up to 15% of a flock, usually a month before lambing. The abortions will be accompanied by retained placentas, clinical illness in the ewes, and fever. Ewes can also give birth to weak lambs which may die later.

Encephalitis is seen in small stock of all ages. The symptoms are dullness, loss of appetite and separating from the flock. They show lack of co-ordination, head tilting or circling, after which they become recumbent and die within a week of showing signs.

The diagnosis is based on the history of symptoms of abortions or encephalitis, often in conjunction with feeding silage. Examination of aborted foetuses on post-mortem may reveal typical signs, such as the focal areas of damage in the liver.

There is no treatment for the condition. Silage use should be discontinued if this is the source of infection.

Mycotoxins

The presence of mycotoxins in feed can cause abortion. For more information, see Plant poisoning, page 116.

Post-lambing gangrene

Post-lambing gangrene is a clostridial infection common in goats, although it also occurs in sheep producing multiple lambs. The condition occurs after birth, usually if the ewe has had a difficult or multiple birth or is confined to stables during the birth-giving process. The bruising caused to the uterus during the birth process allows *C septicum* (or other clostridia) to invade, and this causes a gangrenous infection of the muscle of the uterus. Affected ewes develop a fever, show straining and have a reddish discharge and a purple discoloration of the vulva.

Prompt treatment with a broad-spectrum antibiotic like tetracycline may save the ewe's life. At post-mortem, the red-purple discoloration of the uterine muscle will be clearly seen. The condition can be prevented by annual vaccination with a multi-component clostridial vaccine during pregnancy. For more discussion of this condition, see acute death, page 73.

Prolapsed vagina

Prolapse of the vagina occurs in mature ewes in the later stages of pregnancy, usually if they are too fat. Occurrence has also been linked to high oestrogen levels in certain feeds, particularly clover pastures. Other typical signs of clover poisoning are infertility, difficult births, or prolapses, even in non-breeding ewes. When this occurs, the animals should be withdrawn from the pastures.

It's important to treat a prolapsed vagina early, before it dries out and becomes damaged, in which case the ewe will have to be slaughtered. To replace the vagina, wash it very well using clean lukewarm water, and then lubricate it well with antiseptic cream. Gently replace the vagina and hold it in place for five minutes. If necessary, a veterinarian could put stitches in

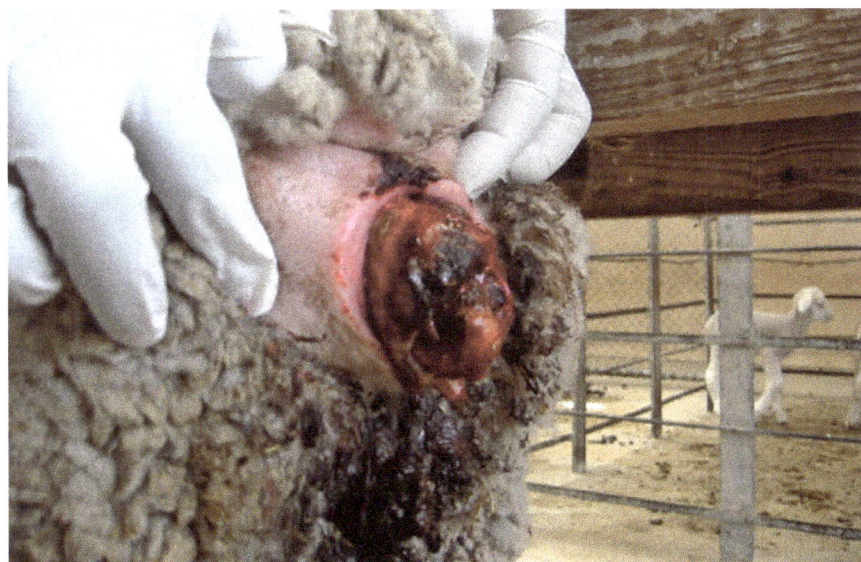

A prolapsed vagina being treated and replaced

Ulcerative lesions on the penis in a case
of balanopostitis

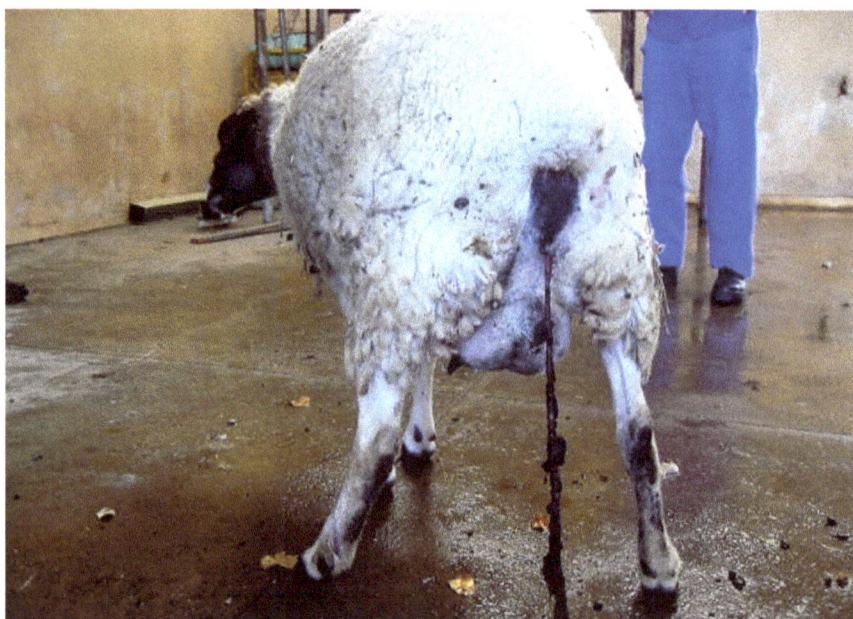

A ewe with a retained afterbirth

the vulva to retain the vagina until the ewe lambs.

Retained afterbirth

The foetal membranes (afterbirth) are usually expelled soon after the lamb has been born, but in some cases they may remain attached for longer periods. Infection, damage to the uterus, or exhaustion of the ewe may cause the afterbirth to be retained longer than 72 hours after birth. A retained afterbirth that remains untreated will rot and cause toxaemia in the ewe. In such cases, use a gloved hand to gently pull on the protruding afterbirth. If this is unsuccessful, administer a long-acting tetracycline to prevent the ewe becoming ill.

Rift Valley fever (RVF)

Rift Valley fever is a viral disease primarily of cattle, sheep and goats which occurs as an epidemic in SA under certain conditions. The virus is transmitted by a mosquito species that feeds on livestock rather than humans. In years when there is heavy rainfall early in summer, enormous numbers of these mosquitoes are bred. Such conditions allow massive numbers of these mosquitoes to breed, usually in shallow surface water or pans. Livestock become infected as a result of mosquito bites and abortion storms occur, as well as

death among newborn and young animals. It is estimated that millions of animals died during the outbreaks of the 1950s, before vaccines were available. The last major outbreaks occurred in SA in the 1970s during which there was a huge demand for vaccine but in many cases the application was too late for protection. During RVF outbreaks, pregnant sheep and goats show an abortion rate of between 40 – 100%, and stock younger than two weeks old show 90% mortality.

Young animals under two weeks of age die acutely with a mortality rate of 90%. Those over two weeks old may show fever, weakness, diarrhoea and they refuse to eat. In adult animals the only sign of infection may be abortions.

The RVF virus is transmissible to man when infected animals are handled in the course of farm work, veterinary investigations and when samples are handled in the laboratory. The infection in humans is serious, occasionally life-threatening, and may cause blindness in some individuals.

RVF outbreaks should be suspected when abortions and deaths in newborns occur in late summer, especially during high rainfall years. Cases of influenza-like disease in humans handling these animals are extra evidence of possible RVF outbreaks. A presumptive diagnosis can be

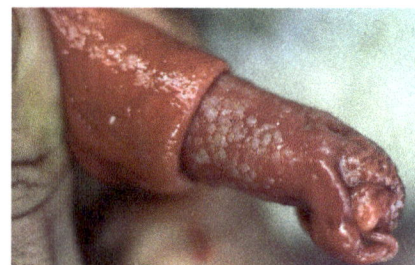

made by veterinary examination of aborted foetuses or young animals which show massive liver damage. The disease can be confirmed on the isolation of RVF virus from the tissues of foetuses or young animals that have died.

There is no treatment for RVF. Annual vaccination of stock with the live Smithburn RVF vaccine is recommended because it gives the best immunity. Avoid vaccinating early in pregnancy since the Smithburn strain can cause a low percentage of foetal malformations in sheep. The killed vaccine gives poor immunity and is of little use during outbreaks as two to three vaccinations are required before significant immunity is achieved. During outbreaks it should be borne in mind that vaccination will take up to three weeks to be protective, so emergency treatment with the pyrethoid deltamethrin will be needed to repel mosquitoes.

Wooled sheep should be belly-bathed with deltamethrin dip and treated along the spine with a water-based pour-on. Non-wooled sheep and goats may be dipped in deltamethrin or treated with an oil-based deltamethrin pour-on. Lambs and kids must be hand-dipped with a deltamethrin dip.

Ulcerative balanoposthitis and vulvitis (peestersiekte)

This venereally transmitted infectious condition of the genitalia of ewes and rams is thought to be caused primarily by a *Mycoplasma* sp. It occurs in an estimated 2 – 4% of flocks in South Africa and is seen predominantly in Dorpers, Karakul and indigenous sheep, although it is also seen in Merinos. A similar condition is seen in Angora goats.

The condition has been described in the North West, Limpopo, and Eastern Cape provinces and the southern part of the Free State.

The condition appears at the beginning of the mating season; the first signs are that the rams refuse to mate and show signs of severe pain of the penis. When examined, they show ulcerative lesions on the penis and sometimes the sheath. These can be so extensive that the penis adheres to the inside of the sheath or is too swollen to be retracted into the sheath. Ewes show ulcerations of the vulva but can lamb without incident, but they do experience discomfort which they show by constant tail-stump wagging.

It's essential to withdraw affected rams from the breeding herd, and to treat their lesions with the local application of acriflavine-glycerine, obtained from a veterinarian. Injecting infected animals with oxytetracyclines will help recovery. These treatments do not, however, eliminate the infection and the symptoms will reappear in the rams when they engage in sexual activity again. The condition seems to disappear in a flock after two to three years, but experts advise the culling of infected rams.

Before buying and introducing new animals into the flock, examine ewes and rams for ulcers of the genitalia, and repeat this examination while they are in quarantine.

Vitamin A deficiency

Vitamin A deficiency causes low conception rates, an increased incidence of retained placentas, eye problems and dry hair/coat.

Although the vitamin is plentiful in fresh green pastures, as soon as the pastures are made into hay, the level declines. Winter pastures and pelleted rations are also low in vitamin A.

The vitamin is light-sensitive, which means its inclusion in rations isn't very efficient as it breaks down rapidly. Supplementation with injectable or oral vitamin A preparations will improve breeding performance and general health of livestock on dry rations.

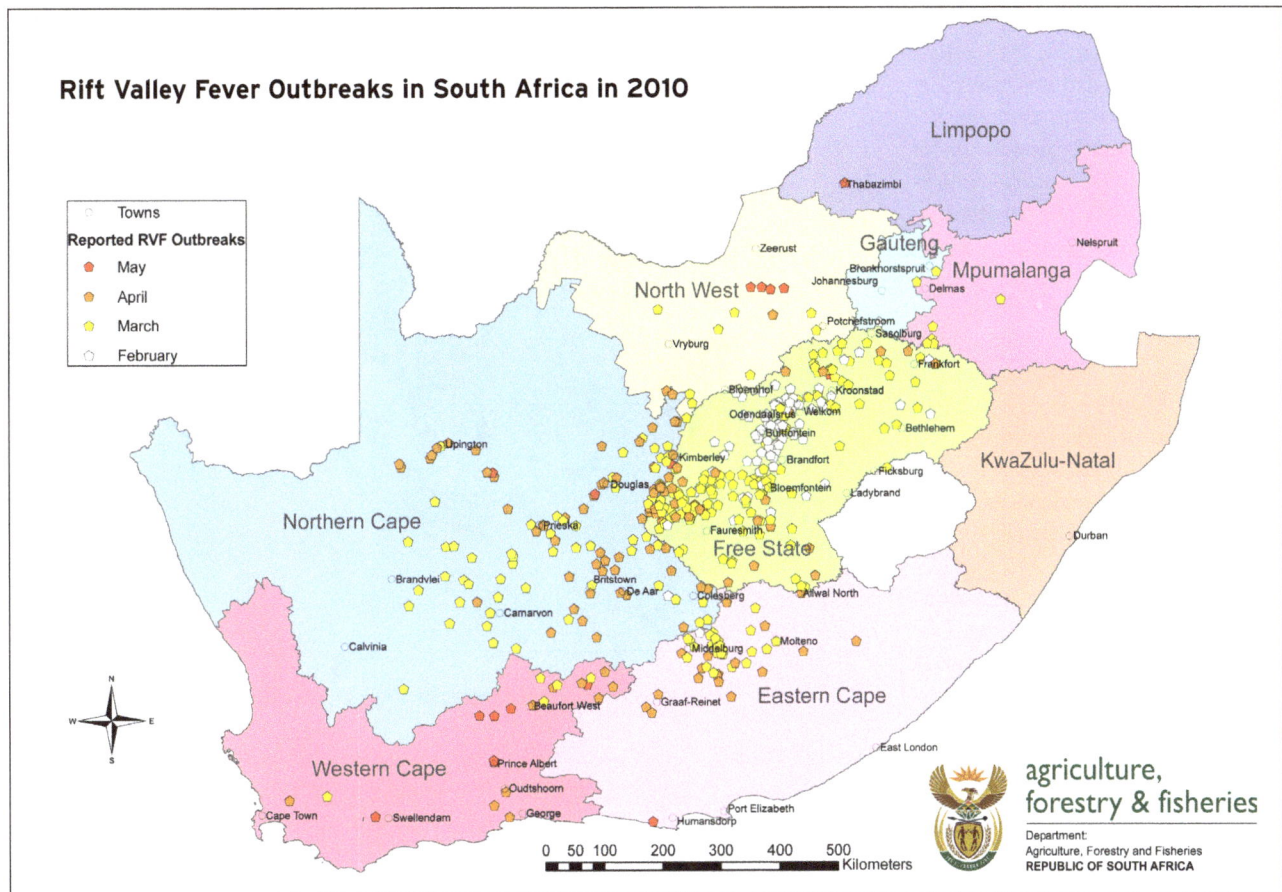

Rift Valley Fever Outbreaks in South Africa in 2010

Towns
Reported RVF Outbreaks
- May
- April
- March
- February

Limpopo
Thabazimbi
Zeerust
Gauteng
Bronkhorstspruit
Johannesburg
Nelspruit
Mpumalanga
North West
Delmas
Potchefstroom
Sasolburg
Vryburg
Frankfort
Bloemhof
Kroonstad
Odendaalsrus
Welkom
Upington
Bethlehem
Kimberley
Buttontein
Brandfort
Ficksburg
Douglas
Bloemfontein
Ladybrand
KwaZulu-Natal
Northern Cape
Prieska
Fauresmith
Durban
Brandvlei
Britstown
Free State
Camarvon
De Aar
Colesberg
Aliwal North
Calvinia
Molteno
Middelburg
Graaf-Reinet
Eastern Cape
Beaufort West
East London
Prince Albert
Western Cape
Oudtshoorn
Port Elizabeth
Cape Town
Swellendam
George
Humansdorp

0 50 100 200 300 400 500 Kilometers

agriculture, forestry & fisheries
Department:
Agriculture, Forestry and Fisheries
REPUBLIC OF SOUTH AFRICA

NOTES

_____

_____

_____

_____

NERVOUS CONDITIONS

The nervous system is composed of the brain, spinal cord and nerves. Nervous conditions can show a range of symptoms including blindness, lameness, and partial or total paralysis. Some of these conditions are, therefore, discussed in other chapters. The most common causes of nervous conditions in small stock are gid (draaisiekte), heartwater, botulism, tetanus, ketosis, milk fever and various plant poisonings. Some less important conditions are also discussed.

A clinical case of gid in a sheep

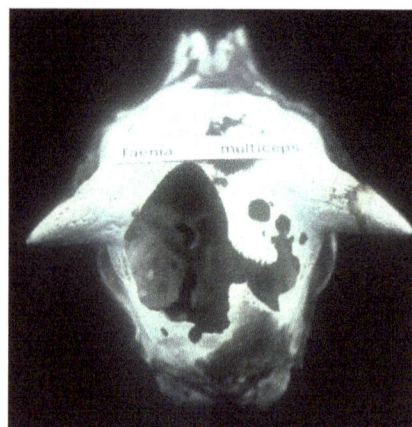

Erosion of the skull caused by a large *T multiceps* tapeworm cyst in the brain

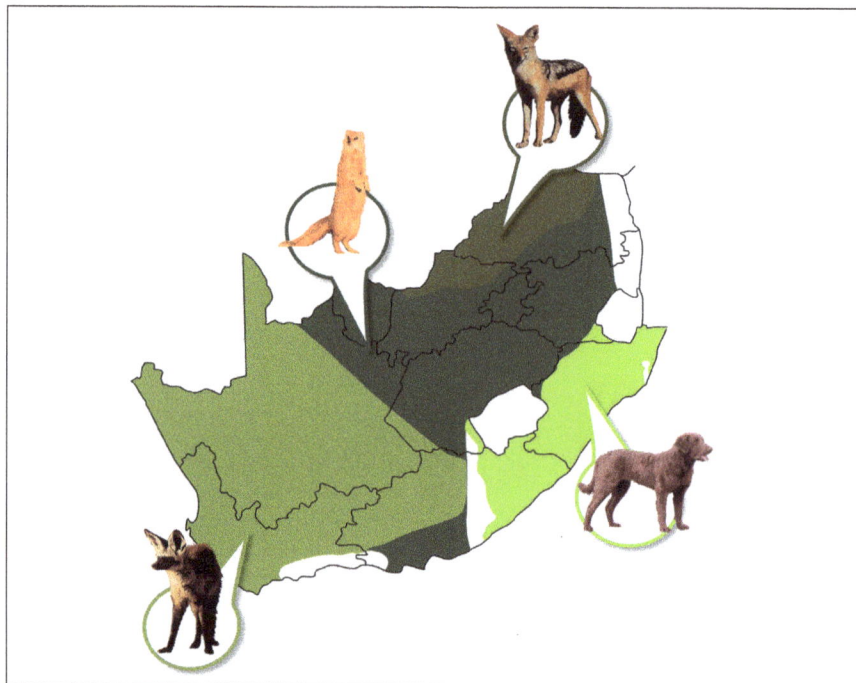

Cerebrocortical necrosis (*Polioencephalomalacia*)

This condition is occasionally seen in grazing sheep. It results from a deficiency of vitamin B$_1$ (thiamine) which is usually produced by rumen micro-organisms. Under certain circumstances, not yet understood, a shortage of this vitamin occurs.

The first signs are listlessness, loss of appetite and separation from the flock. Affected sheep wander aimlessly, or appear blind. Typical symptoms are "star gazing" (staring upwards) or staring downwards at the ground. These sheep eventually lie down and appear to go into spasms. They gradually weaken, fall into a coma and die. Some sheep die having shown few signs; others may be mildly affected and recover after a while.

The thiamine deficiency causes brain damage which can be demonstrated on microscopic examination of the tissues. If the condition is diagnosed timeously, thiamine injections will reverse the condition, sometimes within a few hours. The nutrition of affected flocks should be changed or supplemented to prevent recurrences.

Gid (draaisiekte)

Gid is the name given to a condition seen in sheep and goats, caused when the intermediate or larval stages of the tapeworm of dogs, *Taenia multiceps*, lodge in the brain. The eggs of this tapeworm are picked up from the faeces of carnivores (domestic or wild dogs) by grazing sheep. On reaching the intestine, the eggs hatch

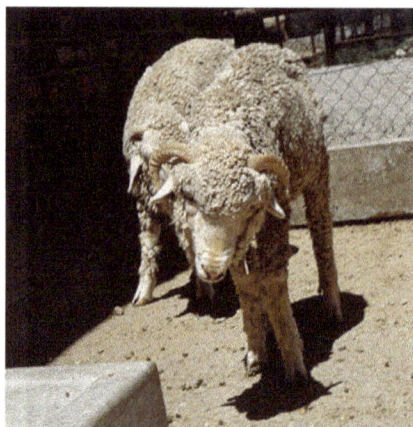

The vectors of rabies in the different geographic regions of South Africa

and give rise to a cyst which eventually finds its way to the brain of the sheep. The life cycle is completed when a dog (wild or domestic species) eats the brain of an infected sheep and the cyst then develops into a tapeworm in the intestine of the dog. Humans are incidental hosts and can become infected with the cysts if they pick up the eggs from the faeces of infected dogs.

The presence of the cyst in the brain causes varying symptoms, depending on the size and location. Affected sheep are seen walking around in circles or stand-

ing with their heads pressed against an object. The animal may behave as if it is blind, bumping into things, and the head may be held to one side. Sometimes sheep may show a high-stepping gait, a symptom also seen in heartwater. The animals may be completely paralysed if the brain is extensively affected and the cysts can be so large that they cause the bones of the skull to be worn away.

There is no treatment for the condition. The cyst can be seen when the skull is sawn open at post-mortem. It is a fluid-filled

bladder which, if large, causes shrinkage of the brain to a fraction of its usual size. Gid is prevented by dosing domestic dogs on the farm with tapeworm remedies containing the active ingredient praziquantal every three months. Don't reinfect dogs by feeding them infected sheep offal.

Rabies

Rabies is a fatal viral disease which can affect a wide range of mammalian species, including livestock, wildlife, domestic cats and dogs, and humans. It occasionally affects sheep and goats. The main vectors or transmitters of infection vary in different areas of South Africa (see map). These include bat-eared foxes, jackals, yellow mongoose or domestic dogs.

Sheep and goats probably become infected when investigating the strange behaviour of rabies-infected wild animals, which lose their fear and display either docility or aggression. They may enter farmyards, even buildings. The most common method of transmitting the disease is through a bite from a rabid animal, but contact with infected saliva can also transmit the infection. After being bitten by a rabid animal, the incubation period for the disease can be long, as the virus moves along the nerve tracts until it finally reaches the brain tissue. Once it reaches the brain it begins to affect the tissue and the animal starts to show symptoms, particularly changes in behaviour. Sheep rams infected with rabies show heightened sexual excitability, while goats bleat excessively and are even more aggressive than cattle. It should be borne in mind, however, that the symptoms can vary considerably.

Rabies is a notifiable disease and, if suspected, the local state vet or a private veterinarian must be contacted. The diagnosis is based on the history, namely incidence of the disease, in the area and the presence of wild animals acting strangely, as well as the symptoms of the domestic animal infected. There is no economically viable treatment for rabid animals, and since they pose a threat to other animals and to humans, they should be destroyed. The diagnosis of rabies has to be confirmed by a veterinarian taking a brain sample for laboratory examination.

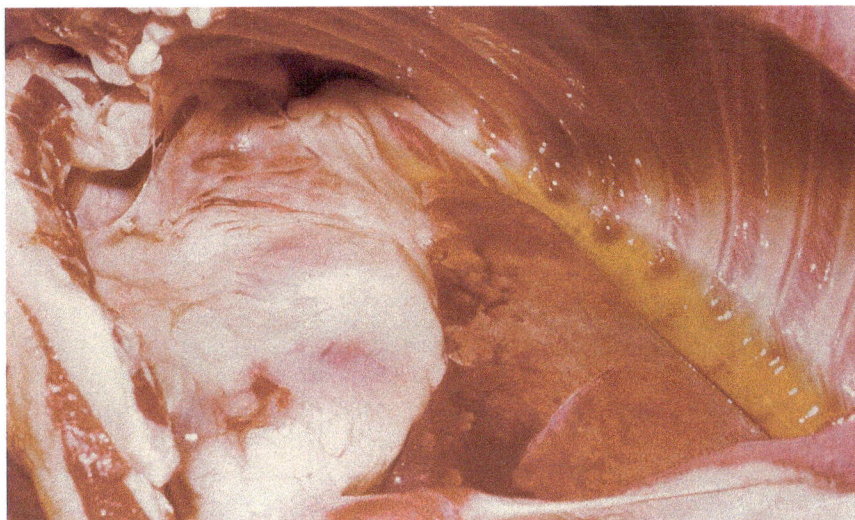

A heartwater case showing fluid accumulation in the thorax (chest cavity)

Vaccination is done in areas where rabies is prevalent in a particular species, most commonly cattle, dogs and cats. If it is deemed necessary to vaccinate sheep and goats, they should be vaccinated at 12 weeks of age and then repeat vaccination every two years. Wild animals such as meerkat or jackals may not be vaccinated, in gterms of animal health laws.

A sheep that died of heartwater, showing the fluid accumulation (lung oedema) issuing from the lungs

Important notes
- **Never handle animals suspected of being rabid.**
- **If human contact has occurred, report it immediately to the district surgeon who will arrange for treatment.**

Plant poisoning

There are currently 20 plants and fungi that can potentially cause nervous symptoms in livestock. Many do not cause any specific pathological lesions, and the diagnosis often has to be made based on circumstantial evidence or the presence of recognisable plant parts in the gastro-intestinal tract, or on the presence of fungal growth on grazing or feed. (See Plant poisoning, page 121-123, for a discussion of the main plants involved.)

Heartwater

The heartwater organism, *Erlichia* (formerly *Cowdria*) *ruminantium*, is transmitted by the bont tick, which occurs in warm, moist regions of the country, namely the bushveld and the eastern coastal areas. The immature bont tick feeds on small mammals and ground birds, and this makes it impossible to eradicate the species. The transmission of heartwater occurs throughout the year but is less prevalent in winter. Losses resulting from the disease occur in animals introduced into heartwater areas, or when animals in heartwater areas aren't exposed frequently enough to tick immunisation, usually during drought years.

Infected sheep and goats begin to show symptoms seven to 35 days after being bitten by an infected tick. Initially they show a fever, listlessness, high-stepping gait, difficult breathing, and later they show prominent nervous symptoms such

as chewing and head pressing. They lie down, frantically paddling, and death follows soon after.

Typical post-mortem signs are the accumulation of fluid around the heart, in the chest cavity, and in the lungs where it is seen as foam.

To confirm the diagnosis a veterinarian will take a brain smear for laboratory examination, in which the heartwater organisms can be seen when the smear is coloured with a specific stain.

Treatment of sick animals is most effective when done early in the course of the disease.

Once nervous signs have developed, the chances for successful treatment deteriorate dramatically. An oxytetracycline injection should be given immediately, preferably intravenously, at a dose rate of 10mg/kg, and this should be repeated at least twice at 24-hour intervals.

Slow administration of intravenous preparations is essential to prevent shock reactions. Long-acting formulations can also be used in less severe cases. These are given at 20mg/kg via the intramuscular route and may need to be repeated after 72 hours.

Supportive treatment can be given by a veterinarian to reverse lung oedema and nervous symptoms. Once the animal's temperature has returned to normal, the stock owner should provide the animal with good-quality feed to encourage the animal to eat.

Vaccination against heartwater in small stock as an aid to creating a stable or endemic disease situation has been mainly unsuccessful. Experts in heartwater areas where small stock are kept report that sustained intensive tick control will prevent outbreaks.

Susceptible animals newly introduced into the area should be dipped by belly bathing with tick remedies weekly for the first three weeks. For sustained control, dipping can be done every two to four weeks in summer. The dipping intervals can be extended in winter if tick challenge is low (Dr R J Taylor). It should be noted that this intensive tick control renders the flock totally susceptible to heartwater and dipping must be sustained to prevent outbreaks.

Hypophyseal abscess

This condition is most common in goats and results from tick infestation or wounding around the horns.

The wounds made by the ticks allow for the penetration of bacteria such as *A pyogenes* which invade the bloodstream in a specific part of the brain, the hypophysis, or pituitary gland, where infection lodges causing nervous symptoms similar to those seen with heartwater, although a fever is seldom seen.

High doses of tetracycline can be administered for seven days to treat the abscess but the prognosis is usually poor, resulting in death of the animal.

Prevent the condition by practising localised tick control on the head, using tick grease or a pour-on preparation registered for tick control.

Milk fever

Milk fever is a deficiency of calcium which occurs in ewes in late pregnancy, or in other animals that have a disrupted calcium/phosphorus or magnesium deficiency.

In pregnant ewes, this condition is usually due to a low dietary intake of calcium. It generally affects animals grazing on lush pastures such as lucerne or oats, or on grain diets low in calcium. Outbreaks of milk fever in flocks can be precipitated by stress such as transport, shearing or cold weather.

Because calcium is essential for muscle activity, the animals show muscle tremors and stagger around. Eventually they are too weak to stand. They lie down with the head held against the flanks. Unlike ewes suffering from ketosis (domsiekte), the animals are alert and will try to struggle when handled, but cannot get up. Animals suffering from milk fever will die within 24 hours if not treated.

The diagnosis of milk fever is based on the history of late pregnancy and the typical symptoms. There is no typical post-mortem sign. Treat milk fever cases as early as possible by subcutaneous injection with a calcium solution, using the dose recommended on the packaging. The response to treatment is rapid, but animals may suffer relapses and need additional treatment. To prevent milk fever in pregnant ewes/does, don't graze them on lush pastures in late pregnancy, and give a calcium supplement if they're on grain rations, for example, in drought feeding (15g limestone per ton of feed).

NOTES

_____
_____
_____
_____
_____
_____
_____
_____
_____
_____

LAMENESS

The term refers to any difficulty in walking, and the condition has a wide range of causes, ranging from physical injury to various infectious diseases that affect the limbs or the brain. The primary causes include hoof problems, conditions affecting the muscles, or spinal lesions which may cause paralysis. It is therefore important to diagnose the cause correctly. It must be stressed that there are many causes of lameness; only the most common ones are discussed here.

Botulism (lamsiekte)

Clostridium botulinum bacteria occur widely in the environment and grow in rotting material like carcases, in which they produce a powerful toxin. Livestock contract botulism when they chew on bones or tortoise shells on the veld, and when kraaled and fed hay or silage.

The veld form involves *C botulinum* type D, found on the carcases of dead animals or old tortoise shells. When the phosphate levels of veld grass begin to drop, animals develop a phosphate hunger or "pica" which causes them to eat old bones, carcases or tortoise shells, and these often contain botulism toxin.

Under kraal conditions the source of contamination is the carcases of small animals such as rats, birds and cats. This type of botulism usually involves *C botulinum* type C. Broiler manure is commonly contaminated with *C botulinum* because it almost always contains chicken carcases.

If animals have ingested botulism toxin, the symptoms are seen two to three days later.

In sheep the early signs are separating from the flock, standing with the neck bent to one side. The animals may show spasm of the tail stump. As the disease progresses, the animal begins to walk stiffly and then becomes recumbent. In some cases, the tongue may protrude from the mouth, due to paralysis. The animal will later be unable to rise and will die from suffocation resulting from paralysis of the respiratory muscles. A post-mortem of an animal that died of botulism will reveal nothing specific, but bones or tortoise shells are

A Dorper ewe suffering from botulism shows the typical bending of the neck

occasionally found in the digestive tract. Confirmation of botulism cases can only be done by taking intestinal content for isolation of the toxin from the gut – and this is usually very difficult to do.

Treating animals with botulism antiserum can be tried, but it's usually unsuccessful except in cases detected very early. The most economical control measure is vaccination administered before or at weaning; a booster vaccination is needed three to four weeks later. Vaccinate annually to maintain immunity. Supplementating with phosphate licks in winter will reduce the eating of bones and improve the condition of animals. The symptoms of botulism can be confused with *Stenocarpella* (Diplodea) poisoning (a fungus that grows on mealies), krimpsiekte plant poisoning and rabies.

Blue tongue

Blue tongue is a viral disease of sheep, transmitted by Culicoides midges. It occurs virtually all over South Africa except in certain mountainous areas. To date, 21 types of blue tongue virus that can cause disease have been identified. Because there is no cross-immunity between them, all these types have to be included in the vaccine. The disease is seen in summer and autumn, when Culicoides midges are numerous. Because the midges need moist areas to breed, they occur especially in vleis and around dams, and are active in the evenings, after sundown, until sunrise. Indigenous and Asian sheep breeds are less susceptible than imported breeds, and usually develop mild symptoms. Goats

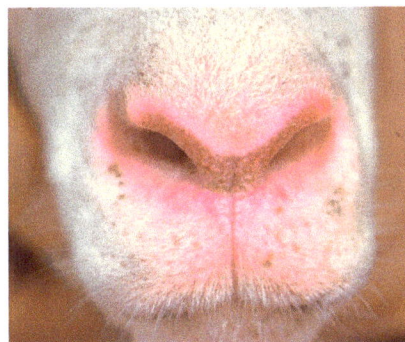

A blue tongue case showing inflammation of the nose

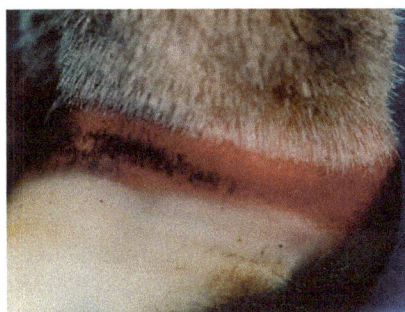

Inflammation of the coronet of the hoof resulting from blue tongue infection

Sheep with severe cases of blue tongue may show a break, or shedding of the wool

do not get the disease.

In the early stages of infection with the blue tongue virus, sheep have a fever and lose their appetite. They develop reddening of the nose and mouth, and a while later they show erosions on the nose and inside the mouth. Occasionally, severe swelling of the tongue (blue tongue) and the head may occur. Affected animals may become lame because of inflammation of the coronet of the hoof. This may be so severe that sheep walk on their knees.

Blue tongue infections cause severe economic losses as there is a break in the wool (due to the fever reaction), weight loss because the sheep isn't eating and there may be permanent damage to the muscles of the neck causing a bent neck (torticollis). The hooves grow out unevenly and have to be trimmed to allow for normal locomotion. Young lambs, if affected, may die of starvation and secondary infections. There is no specific treatment for blue tongue because it is a viral disease, but severely affected animals can be treated with a broad-spectrum antibiotic, such as an oxytetracycline, to prevent secondary infections.

The only effective prevention for blue tongue is vaccination. The vaccine, which comprises three separate inoculations (A, B and C) that have to be administered three weeks apart. Vaccination must be repeated annually, preferably in spring before the height of the blue tongue season. The schedule can be adapted to accommodate the lambing season. Lambs of vaccinated ewes should be vaccinated at weaning age, when colostral immunity is waning (see Vaccination programme, page 14-16).

Other control measures are to limit exposure to the midges by avoiding of low-lying vlei areas from sundown to sunrise, and to graze cattle with sheep as the midges prefer to feed on bovines.

Although goats may also become infected with the blue tongue virus, they don't get ill, so vaccination is unnecessary.

Copper deficiency

In small stock, a copper deficiency may arise due to low levels of the mineral in the grazing or to a high intake of sulphur, molybdenum zinc, iron, cadmium or calcium in the diet which reduce absorption in the intestine. In general, copper-deficient grazing is usually found on sandy soils, or pastures that have been top-dressed with molybdenum.

Copper is needed for various bodily functions, so a shortage causes a variety of symptoms depending on the age of the animal and the severity of the deficiency. In young animals, moderate deficiencies may show bone fragility, being predisposed to bone fractures but they not showing any deformities. Pregnant animals having a copper deficiency give birth to lambs or kids with swayback, a nervous condition that causes the animals to stagger and be unco-ordinated. This may be seen at birth, or it may only become noticeable within two weeks after birth. These lambs/kids deteriorate and eventually die. The wool of older animals loses its sheen and strength, showing more crimping (steely wool). Black and coloured wool loses its colour, showing white banding when the wool is parted.

It's important to investigate suspected deficiencies tnoroughly, as the availability of copper in grazing can fluctuate, causing temporary shortages, and unnecessary copper supplementation can cause toxicity. Submitting liver samples to a suitable laboratory for analysis will allow scientists to determine whether animals are copper deficient.

The decision to supplement animals with copper should, therefore, be taken in conjunction with experts. Copper injections can be given to treat deficient animals. Long-term strategies, such as copper top-dressing, may be employed if the losses caused by deficiency are extensive.

Foot abscess

Foot abscess in small stock should be differentiated from footrot, which has a different cause and epidemiology. Foot abscesses develop as a result of wounding of the skin around the claw. The primary cause is wounding by tick bites, or (particularly in goats) by thorny bushes. The wounds become infected with the bacterium *Arcanobacterium* (*Corynebacterium*) pyogenes, causing the formation of an abscess which eventually affects the joint.

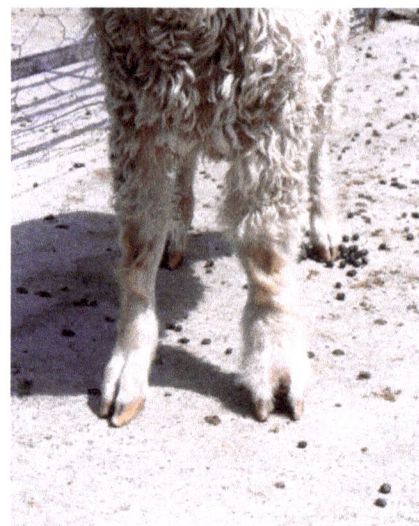

An Angora goat suffering from foot-abscess (right), showing the reddening of the skin between the toes

Affected animals become lame − usually only in one leg, but sometimes in more than one.

The affected foot becomes red, swollen and painful, swells above the claws and may burst open, oozing pus, but unlike footrot there is never separation of the sole. Animals having foot abscess lose condition rapidly and could die from septicaemia. Because antibiotics penetrate abscesses poorly, treatment is not very successful but if combined with proper care, valuable animals may be saved if treated with oxytetracycline injections for two to three weeks.

Because of the poor recovery rate with treatment, prevention should be implemented by removing the cause of the condition (avoiding thorny or stony pastures) or, if this isn't possible, using foot-baths containing 5% formalin. This will reduce the level of bacterial contamination. If ticks are the primary cause, use a foot-bath containing a tick remedy or apply a pour-on tick remedy to the feet.

Although using the *A. pyogenes* vaccine has been advocated to control this condition, there is no scientific proof of its efficacy.

Footrot

Footrot in small stock is caused by a specific bacterium (*Dichelobacter necropho-*

Footrot in sheep undermines the sole and causes deforming of the hoof material

Foot-and-mouth lesions in a sheep

rum) which is carried in the hooves of infected sheep and goats. The infection only becomes evident under certain conditions, when the animals develop symptoms, and these carrier animals can spread the infection to others. Some breeds, such as Merinos, are more susceptible than mutton breeds. The bacterium causes problems when the hoof is softened by wet, muddy conditions after heavy rainfall and in places where there is poor drainage. In SA it is seen in areas such as KwaZulu-Natal or on irrigated pastures, but it may become more important in other areas as rainfall patterns change. Severe forms of footrot may cause serious economic losses, resulting in weight loss and reduced wool production. Mild strains cause inflammation of the skin between the toes; severe forms progress to involve the tissues of the hoof.

Mild footrot outbreaks begin with a few animals becoming lame. One, but usually more, feet are involved. Early examination will show reddening, and swelling of the skin between the claws; later, a grey-yellow scum develops. This differentiates the disease from foot abscess. In virulent or severe forms of footrot, the interdigital inflammation progresses, undermining the sole of the foot and causing separation of the hoof material and the skin. Severe lameness develops and animals whose front feet are affected may be seen walking on their knees.

During footrot outbreaks, affected animals have to be isolated, and placed in dry camps or sheds to limit the spread. A daily walk through footbaths containing 10% zinc sulphate helps to heal the affected claws and is inexpensive. If the hoof is involved, the sheep's claws must be trimmed and treated with antibiotics or disinfectants. Injectable antibiotics such as oxytetracycline and sulphas will help clear up the infections. Infected animals should be removed from the flock, if possible, as they act as a source of infection.

Prevent outbreaks at the beginning of the season in which problems occur by using formalin (5%) or zinc sulphate (10%) footbaths. Poorly drained, muddy camps should be improved by laying gravel. Footrot vaccines are available, but the usage is too small in SA to warrant their import by distributors.

When buying sheep, examine the flock for signs of foot problems; malformed hooves, inflammation of the interdigital spaces and underunning of the hoof material, for instance. Repeat the examination during the quarantine period.

Foot-and-mouth disease (FMD)

In South Africa, FMD is confined to a focus of infection in the Kruger National Park, where buffalo serve as carriers of the virus. To prevent the spread of the disease from the park, authorities use fences, and maintain a buffer zone in which livestock

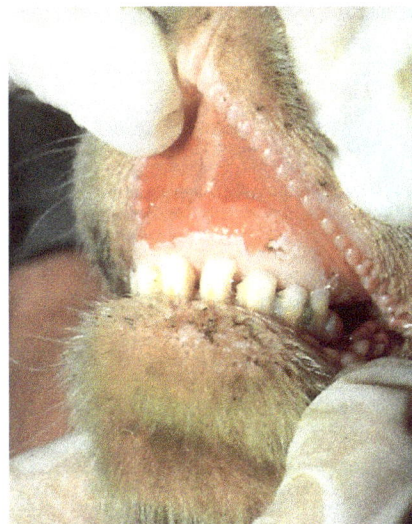

are vaccinated and examined regularly. The country has a strict importation policy to prevent the re-introduction of the disease, especially across SA borders, as some neighbouring countries are infected.

In spite of the strict controls, however, FMD outbreaks have occurred as a result of the importation of infected animals and feed, and it is essential for the authorities and all involved in the animal health industry to be vigilant in preventing outbreaks.

The disease, in itself, doesn't cause high mortalities, but it is catastrophic for commercial farming because it erodes production and prevents the exporting of any agricultural product to developed countries. Eradication requires a massive logistical exercise involving the slaughter, burial or burning of large numbers of animals and the imposing of disruptive quarantine measures.

Small stock, cattle, pigs and wild antelope can develop clinical FMD. Early in the disease, blisters form in the mouth and between the claws. The blisters rupture, leaving raw and painful erosions. The animals salivate and show signs of lameness. Indigenous sheep and goats tend to show less dramatic symptoms. In small stock, the lesions of FMD can be confused with other conditions such as blue tongue, laminitis, footrot or other hoof conditions. Any stock owner suspecting the presence of FMD on his property must immediately contact the local state veterinarian. All FMD vaccination

is done by animal health authorities and may not be done by private stock owners.

Ill-thrift (wasting disease)
This is a poorly defined condition of young sheep which occurs in certain areas of the Eastern Cape, specifically the high rainfall areas of the coastal region of Port Elizabeth and Humansdorp.

It has been suggested that the blood parasite *Eperythrozoon ovis* is the cause, but sheep in other parts of the country are also infected with this organism without showing the syndrome; therefore, multifactorial (as yet unknown) causes may be involved. Mixed infections of *E ovis* with blood parasites such as *Anaplasma ovis* have been proposed as possible causes.

The ill-thrift syndrome is characterised by a mild to moderate suppression of growth which affects a large proportion of animals, but few mortalities occur. In affected flocks, lambs grow well up to two to three months of age, after which their growth slows down. They're listless, pot-bellied, eat poorly, have a stiff staggering gait and may collapse and die when stressed. On post-mortem, there are signs of anaemia and sometimes jaundice. In severely affected flocks, there may be a high mortality rate, as well as stunting of bone growth and late sexual maturation.

The condition is diagnosed based on the symptoms, presence of *E ovis* and the demonstration of mild to moderate anaemia.

Ill-thrift is only marginally improved by treatment with injectable tetracyclines, which supports the theory that the cause is multifactorial, and not merely a blood parasite infection. Good nutrition and protection from the elements are essential for vulnerable animals such as pregnant and lactating ewes, and lambs. Other factors such as trace element deficiencies and parasite should be eliminated.

Another cause of an ill-thrift type of syndrome is a vitamin E-selenium deficiency, which also results in poor growth and poor wool production. This condition usually occurs from grazing on dry pasture. It causes typical "white muscle" lesions which are seen on post-mortem. The condition can be treated with supplements or by giving green feed.

Laminitis
See Acidosis, page 38.

Osteoporosis (rickets/bowie)
This is caused by poor bone mineralisation, caused by any deficiency or disruption of the minerals needed for strong bone formation. The condition affects lambs, weaners and young goats under various grazing conditions. Grazing weaners on lush pastures such as lucerne or oats which contain low levels of calcium may cause osteoporosis. Pastures having marginal or low copper levels and high levels of molybdenum are a cause of osteoporosis in some areas (see Copper deficiency, page 58).

Osteoporosis causes bones to fracture easily after relatively minor injuries. The limb bones may be distorted, especially the front legs; a clinical syndrome known as bowie. The bones of the skull may also be affected. Affected animals also show poor growth and an increased susceptibility to worm infestation.

Young animals affected by osteoporosis will recover if grazed on mature pastures; administering a vitamin D supplement also helps. If the cause is copper deficiency, it should be addressed.

Post-dipping lameness
The bacterium *Erysipelothix rhusiopathiae*, which occurs in the faeces of sheep, is able to survive and grow in dipwash used over more than one day. These bacteria penetrate the wounds caused by shearing, wounding caused by other management practices, or the abrasions that arise around the skin on the hooves. *E rhusiopathiae* enters these small wounds, causing local inflammation of the skin. The skin infection spreads to the joints, causing lameness and eventually chronic arthritis, which leads to a rapid loss of condition.

Post-dipping lameness is usually seen two to seven days after dipping and usually affects large numbers of sheep - sometimes causing up to 80% to show signs of lameness. The feet become hot and swollen, and later become hairless. The joints may be permanently affected, causing mild but chronic lameness.

Animals suspected of having post-dip-

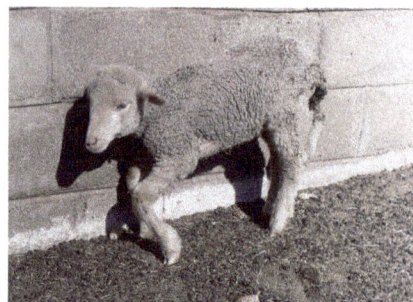

A lamb suffering from post-dipping lameness

A lamb suffering from spinal abscessation (sitsiekte), showing hindlimb paralysis

ping lameness have to be treated with antibiotics such as oxytetracycline before the condition becomes chronic. Prevention is simple and efficient: A dip used for more than a day should have 10% Zn SO$_4$ added to suppress bacterial growth.

Spinal abscessation (sitsiekte)
This condition often occurs in lambs as a result of poor hygiene during tail docking or when ticks with long mouthparts attach around the rectum. The wounds become infected with abscess-forming bacteria such as *Corynebacterium ovis* or *Arcanobacterium pyogenes*, which are then spread through the bloodstream to the spinal cord. Here the abscess grows and eventually becomes so large that it puts pressure on the spinal nerves, causing the so-called sitsiekte. These lambs cannot move their hindlegs and drag their hindquarters along the ground. They lose weight rapidly because they cannot feed and usually die. Although treatment with high doses of antibiotics such as oxytetracycline can be tried in order to salvage such animals, but it's usually just as un-

successful as for other kinds of abscesses, and animals may have to be slaughtered.

The abscess can be demonstrated on post-mortem by opening up the spinal cord. Prevention involves disinfecting docking wounds with iodine spray or other suitable preparations, and thoroughly cleaning knives used for docking or castration. If the problem is caused by tick infestation, measures have to be implemented to control ticks. Applying dressing by hand, in addition to dipping or spraying, may be required to reach areas under the tail. (For more information, see Tick control, page 108-113, in the chapter on External parasites.)

Tetanus (klem-in-die-kaak)

Tetanus is caused by the toxin of the bacterium *Clostridum tetani*. These bacteria occur widely in soil in the form of resistant spores. When the spores contaminate deep wounds, the germinating bacteria secrete a powerful toxin. Castration and docking using elastrators (rekkies), create the ideal conditions for the growth of the tetanus bacteria. The powerful tetanus toxin causes a spastic paralysis which is almost always irreversible. Lambs die soon after showing symptoms, because the respiratory muscles are paralysed (see lambs and kids, page 36). Vaccinating ewes with clostridial vaccines containing tetanus will give lambs optimal colostral immunity at three weeks of age, when it will be safe to castrate and dock them.

Treating affected animals with antibiotics usually comes too late, as the toxin has already been produced when the symp-toms appear. Using tetanus antiserum is generally not very effective unless given early in the course of the disease.

Tick paralysis

A number of tick species produce a toxin in their saliva which affects nerve transmission and causes paralysis.

The Karoo paralysis tick (*Ixodes rubicundus*) causes paralysis, especially in sheep and goats. This tick is found in hilly areas of the northern Cape, the Free State and patchily in Mpumalanga – especially on the cooler southern slopes, where overgrazing has resulted in the encroachment of unpalatable scrubs (such as besembos, taaibos and renosterbos) and sour grasses (suurpol).

This vegetation provides an ideal habitat for the intermediate hosts of *I rubicundus*, a three-host tick that has a long life cycle. The intermediate hosts are elephant shrews, the red rock rabbit, caracal and mountain reedbuck which frequent these habitats.

The adult ticks feed on stock from February to November, with peak incidences of paralysis occurring after the first frosts in March, April and May. To reverse the paralysis, the ticks must be removed immediately in the early stages. If this is done, the animals recover within one to two days.

Control of the Karoo paralysis tick can be achieved by avoiding affected camps on the southern slopes of the hills during the peak season (March to May). If this is unavoidable, using belly-bath dips or pourons can be extremely effective if applied properly, at the correct time. Amitraz and pyrethroids are suitable chemicals to use (see External parasites, page 97).

Spring lamb paralysis is caused by the red-legged tick (*Rhipicephalus evertsi evertsi*). Unlike Karoo paralysis, this condition occurs only when large numbers of ticks infest the host. The larger the host, the more ticks are needed to cause paralysis, which is why the condition is seen in small lambs. As the name indicates, the tick is most active in spring. The ticks have to be removed to reverse the condition and tick control must be implemented to prevent the condition in spring.

Angora goat kid paralysis although similar to spring lamb paralysis in its symptoms, this is caused by *Rhipicephalus warburtoni* and is confined to the Free State and Northern Cape. The adult ticks cluster on the head and in the ears of young Angora kids and cause heavy losses. Prevention is essential, as kids may die even if the ticks are removed. Amitraz is the ideal remedy for use as it causes rapid detachment. It can be applied in the form of a pour-on to the head and ears during the danger periods September to February.

Sand tampan toxicosis occurs when large numbers of sand tampans, *Ornithodoros savygni*, which occur in dry areas such as the Kalahari, suppress the immunity of young animals. Cases of severe allergic reaction to tampan bites also occur. Regular dipping with a pyrethroid helps reduce the numbers, but as they take only 20 minutes to feed, tampans are difficult to control. Ground-feeding birds (guineafowl, francolin etc) should be protected in these areas as they feed on tampans.

NOTES

URINARY PROBLEMS

Bladder stones (urinary calculi)

Bladder stones are mainly a problem in wethers (castrated rams) because the urethra in these animals is narrower than in rams and ewes. There are two main types of bladder stones, and they develop under different conditions:

Phosphate stones are the most important and problematic. They occur in castrated animals in feedlots, that are on high phosphate/low calcium diets. The stones are chalky, white and irregular in shape. Because they're fine and crumbly, the stones may block the urinary tract, usually in the urethra or the penis.

Silica stones occur mainly in sheep on grazing in areas of the Karoo where the plants have a high silica content. These stones are round with a pearly appearance, and tend to be confined to the bladder. They're usually found as an incidental finding at post-mortem.

When phosphate bladder stones block the urethra, the animal is in severe pain and will have difficulty urinating. If the urethra is totally blocked it may rupture and urine will collect under the skin around the penis (waterbelly); the bladder could also rupture as a result of the pressure that builds up. In both cases, the animal will die of ureamia.

The symptoms of urethral blockage are restlessness, and attempts to urinate producing only a few drops at a time over a long period. The animal shows signs of abdominal pain and an increase in tail wagging. The sheath is usually swollen and red in the early stages, and often turns blue as necrosis sets in.

As the condition progresses, there are

A urolith (stone) trapped in the urethral process of the penis

Bladder stone material removed from the penile urethra

signs of abdominal swelling, loss of appetite and the animal may lie down. It could suddenly die, or death may be preceded by neurological signs.

In the early stages, if the stones are lodged in the urethral section at the tip of the penis, this can be snipped off, but blockage further up the urethra can only be resolved by veterinary intervention. At this stage, most animals can be salvaged by emergency slaughter. At post-mortem, the stones may be found in the kidney, the ureter, the bladder or the urethra. It is helpful to have bladder stones analysed so

that the correct control measures can be implemented.

To prevent phosphate stones forming, the calcium:phosphate ratio has to be corrected to 2:1 in feedlot animals, by adding 15g limestone per ton of feed. Including 0,5 − 1% ammonium chloride or 0,5% − 0.8% ammonium sulphate in the ration to acidify the urine will reduce the formation of stones.

In the case of silica stones occurring on pastures, male animals should be moved off the problem pastures and fed an alternative diet. Good-quality, potable water must always be available as dehydration increases the risk of bladder stones forming.

Copper poisoning

Poisoning known as geelsiekte occurs in sheep in certain areas of the Karoo, because of the high copper level in the soil. Copper poisoning can also occur if chicken or pig manure is used as fertiliser on pastures, or from copper sulphate dosing, or sheep drinking copper sulphate added to dips or used as footbaths. The epidemiology, symptoms, treatment and prevention are discussed in the chapter on poisoning (page 125-126).

Oxalate poisoning

A wide variety of plants in SA contain oxalates. Depending on how heavily these plants are grazed, poisoning may occur as a result of primary damage of the kidney. Sheep and goats are both susceptible to this problem (for details, see Plant poisoning, page 125).

Pulpy kidney

See Acute (sudden) death (page 71-72).

NOTES

_____

_____

_____

_____

_____

_____

_____

SKIN CONDITIONS AND WOUNDS

Skin conditions in small stock have many causes. They may specifically involve the skin or can be part of other disease complexes. As many skin conditions look similar, it's essential to obtain a diagnosis by careful examination and the taking of samples for laboratory testing. This will make it possible to treat the condition correctly.

Abscesses

The most common causes of skin abscesses in sheep and goats are *Corynebacterium ovis* and *Arcanobacterium pyogenes*. These bacteria are spread by infected animals and are picked up by susceptible animals during management procedures such as ear-tagging, castration, and docking, but also through wounding by ticks, thorny plants, stony ground, ticks and grass seed awns and weeds. In sheep, grass seeds penetrate soft skin around the throat causing abscesses around the tongue and pharynx. When abscesses develop, the animals refuse to feed because of the discomfort, and lose weight. These abscesses are seldom detected in live animals but will be seen if a careful post-mortem is performed.

C ovis causes abscessation and massive enlargement of the lymph nodes around the head and neck, sometimes rupturing to the outside. Infection can spread to the lungs causing abcess formation. *C ovis* infections, also known as caseous lymphadenitis, are usually associated with wounds caused by shearing. Effective vaccines are available for preventing the infection of young animals and limiting infections in adult animals (see Respiratory problems, page 43, for more information).

Good hygiene practices, such as disinfecting shearing equipment, are essential to prevent the spread of infection.

Face abscesses are seen in sheep forced to graze on thorny forage such as prickly pears, thorny bushes such as vyebos or grass with sharp seeds. These wounds become infected with Actinobacillus lignieresi organisms which occur in faeces

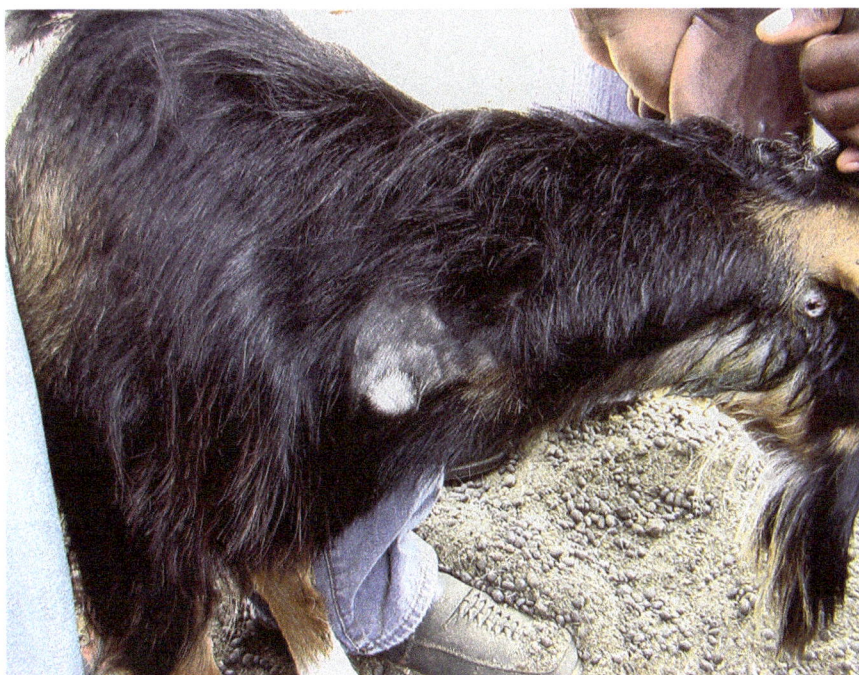

Corynebacterium ovis abscess in the prescapular lymph node of a goat

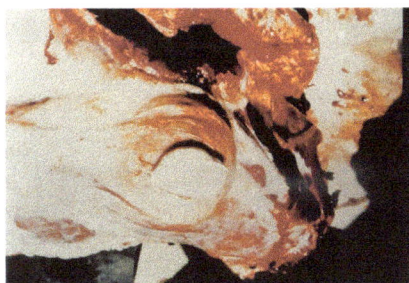

A C. ovis abscess cut open

Facial abscess caused by A. lignieresi

and soil. Abscesses formed this way can spread extensively all along the skin of the head and to various other parts of the body (see GIT, page 42, for more about wooden tongue and facial abscesses).

To ensure effective control of abscesses, it is essential to identify the causative organism as this will determine the control measures to be taken. Samples of pus can be submitted to veterinary laboratories for bacterial culture. The treatment of abscesses with antibiotics is usually ineffective. General abscess problems should be tackled by culling heavily infected animals, destroying infected material by burning or treating with strong disinfectants, applying stringent hygiene and disinfecting practices during surgical procedures and eliminating predisposing causes such as

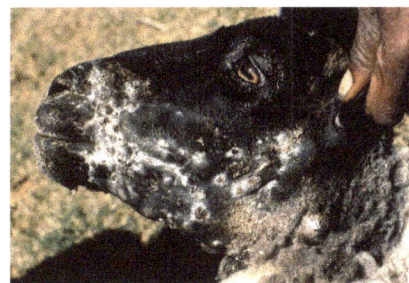

thorny grazing. Tick control may be necessary if foot abscesses (sitsiekte) are encountered (see chapter on Lameness, page 58).

Bolo disease

Bolo disease is a condition of the fleece of Merino-type sheep. It occurs mainly in the Eastern Cape areas of Stutterheim and Cathcart, although it has also been described elsewhere. The cause is thought to be an unidentified *Corynebacterium* species which invades the skin, causing a dermatitis. This is seen as dark patches of wool which, when shorn off, show chalky white patches. The skin of affected animals is inflamed and scabby, and tears easily at shearing. Bolo disease develops in sheep of roughly two years of age and

A sheep showing the typical signs of Bolo disease

becomes progressively worse with increasing age. Severely affected animals lose body condition.

Bolo disease doesn't respond to antibiotic treatment, but mild cases can benefit from dipping in a solution of 3% flowers of sulphur. Severe cases do not respond and these animals should be culled. Segregating age groups during shearing may help prevent the spread of the condition and stringent disinfecting of shears with formalin is recommended.

Burns

Sheep and goats often get caught in veld fires and suffer burn wounds. Burnt animals should be assessed as soon as possible to decide whether they need to be destroyed on humane grounds. Wooled sheep are generally protected by their fleece and suffer minor skin burns, but shorn or hairy sheep and goats may suffer extensive injuries. Australian vets recommend grouping animals in three categories:

1. Poor survival prospects:
- animals with burns to the legs, as the hooves usually fall off
- animals with breathing difficulties, as they will have irreversible lung damage
- milk goats with burnt udders, as they

will be in severe pain and have a poor prognosis for recovery
- **These animals should be euthanased for humane reasons.**

2. Salvageable:
- Animals with burns to the face, groin, anus, sheath, scrotum and vulva may survive with good nursing, but can also be sent for emergency slaughter. These animals will survive if they're given proper nursing and protected from fly strike.

3. Good survival prospects:
- sheep with a good fleece cover are often insulated from fire damage and they have a good chance of surviving without intervention.

Blowfly strike

Blowflies are a group of flies that, in nature, are adapted to laying their eggs on carrion. Some of these species have adapted to attack live sheep, and occasionally goats, under certain conditions. The problem is seen particularly in fine-woolled Merinos when the fleece becomes soiled with faeces, or becomes wet. Animals having heavy folds are strongly predisposed to fly strike because the fleece inside the folds retains moisture and results in local areas of fleece rot (the breakdown of fine fleece and softening of skin; see Lumpy wool,

below). These areas emit a smell that attracts blowflies which settle and lay their eggs on these patches.

The larvae feed on the softened skin, causing large open sores. Affected sheep are restless and anxious, and bite and kick at their lesions. Heavily infested animals may die if not treated. For the treatment and prevention of blowfly strike see Ectoparasites, page 104-105.

Fleece rot
See Lumpy wool (below).

Lumpy wool (dermatophilosis)
This condition results from the infection of the skin hair by the bacterium *Dermatophilus congolensis*. It can be a serious problem in wooled Merinos, although it also affects non-wooled sheep such as Dorpers. It can also affect Angora goats. The bacterium is carried by infected sheep and transmitted to others, usually by infected dipwash to which no bacteriostats have been added. The organism invades the skin during shearing, or with the constant wetting of the fleece resulting from rain or dipping. Young animals are more susceptible because they have less wool fat, which makes the hair more susceptible to wetting.

The bacteria invade the skin, causing inflammation which results in the wool forming hard scabby lumps; removing these lumps exposes bleeding skin lesions. In a more generalised form the wool becomes matted into hard pyramid like lumps of wool. A scabby localised form shows crust formation along the topline of animal, but also the head and face; the so-called hardelam syndrome. This is seen especially in young Merinos, during the rainy season. The skin above the hooves may also be affected causing raw red areas to develop, a condition referred to as strawberry footrot. In Angora goats, the hair shows clumping and then falls out. Apart from the damage to fleece or hair, severely affected animals may die of exposure to cold or loss of weight resulting from discomfort.

Diagnosis of this condition is based on a history of wetting and the appearance of the skin lesions. The diagnosis can be

Lumpy wool in a Dorper

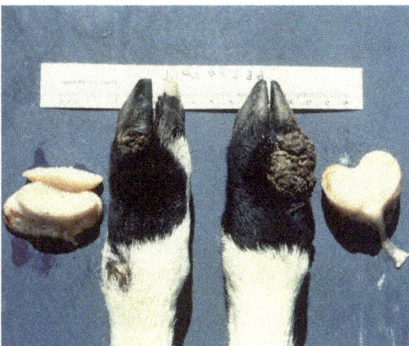

Strawberry foot rot – *Dermatophilus congolensis* infection of the feet

confirmed by laboratory isolation of the causative organism or microscopic examination of impression smears made from the scabs. This is important, as lumpy wool can be confused with other conditions of the skin and fleece. The most commonly confused condition is that of fleece rot, which is a result of the bacterium *Pseudomonas aeruginosa* growing on wool that remains wet for consecutive days. In fleece rot, the wool may sometimes (but not always) have a green discoloration, but there are no hard scab formations. Fleece rot occurs on long wool, with a growth of six months or more, in sheep of all ages. There's often secondary blow fly strike (see Blow fly strike, page 104-106).

Animals suffering severely from lumpy wool can be treated with a course of long-acting oxytetracycline. Affected flocks can be treated by applying quaternary ammo-nium disinfectants, diluted to 1:200, by dipping or hand spraying. Treatments should be repeated at three-week intervals. The application of zinc sulphate powder along the topline during wet seasons is said to be effective in preventing hardelammers.

Prevent lumpy wool by adding 5% zinc sulphate to dip solutions to inhibit bacterial growth.

Orf (vuilbek)

Orf is a contagious viral infection of sheep and goats seen on many farms in South Africa.

It occurs particularly in young animals, as older animals gradually develop immunity with exposure. The virus is very resistant in the environment and can survive in kraals and camps for long periods.

Outbreaks occur in lambs grazing on thorny shrubs such as vyebos or thorn trees, which cause wounding of the mouth. The lesions seen are wartlike outgrowths which develop around the lips, nose and (occasionally) on the rest of the face and head, or on the feet in wet areas. Internal lesions may also arise. Lambs and kids transmit the infection to ewes who then develop lesions on the udder, sometimes leading to cases of mastitis. Although orf lesions are usually small and localised, they can become extensive, may bleed and become secondarily infected. Goats usual-ly develop the lesions around the corners of the mouth, but generalised cases can also be seen.

A diagnosis of orf is usually made on the appearance of the lesions, but samples can be sent to a laboratory for confirmation. The lesions resolve within a few weeks, but can be treated locally with wound oil or antibiotic spray to prevent secondary bacterial infection. Severely affected animals may need veterinary assistance if they cannot feed or walk.

Vaccination can be used on farms experiencing severe, recurrent cases of orf, where wounding by thorns cannot be avoided. Lambs can be vaccinated from as early as two days old and vaccination can be repeated six to eight weeks later. Ewes should be vaccinated eight weeks before lambing; they have to be vaccinated in the axilla (armpit) so that the udder doesn't get infected. Orf vaccines are not as effective as other live viral vaccines, so the correct application is most important. The skin is scarified (scratched) with a sterile needle and a drop of vaccine is placed on the scratches. Successful vaccination is indicated by the development of a scab

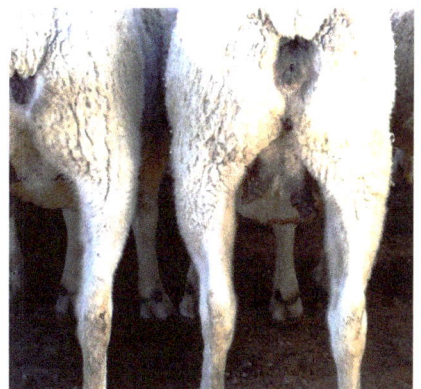

Orf lesions on an ewe's udder

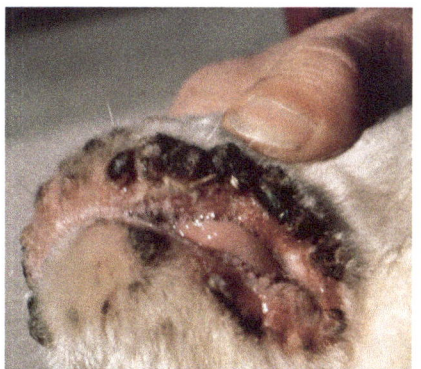

A severe case of orf in a lamb

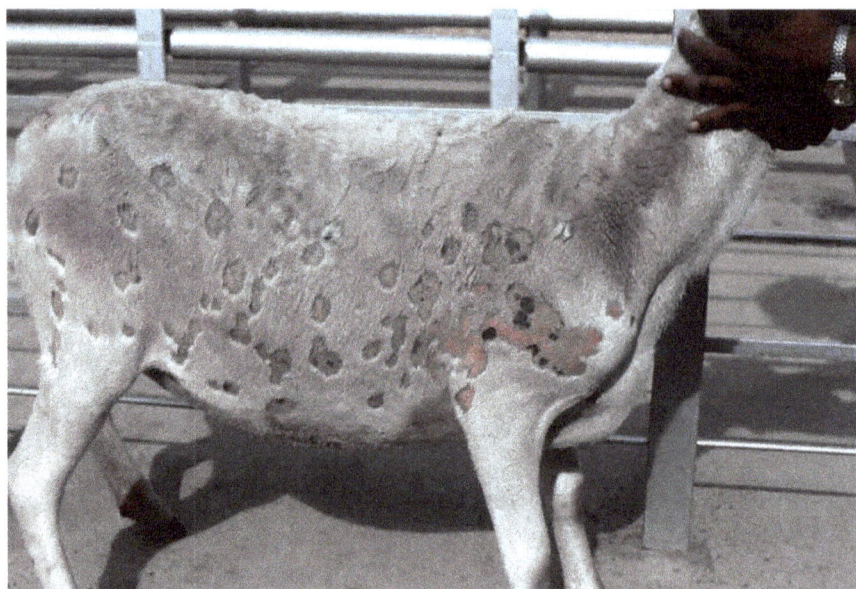

The typical focal lesions seen with ringworm cases in sheep

at the site of scarification. Disinfectants should not be used at the injection site because this will kill the vaccine virus.

NOTE: Humans can also be infected by the orf virus, so wear gloves when handling cases or administering the vaccine.

Parasites

A number of parasites are able to infest the wool of sheep and cause them to show signs of fleece disturbance. The most common problems are sheep scab, caused by the mite *Psoroptes ovis*, and biting and sucking mites which affect both sheep and goats. Australian itch mite and ked flies are less common causes of skin irritation. Descriptions, treatment and prevention of all these conditions are discussed in External parasites (page 94-113).

Photosensitivity (light sensitivity)

The most common cause of photosensitivity in sheep and goats is the ingestion of certain plants or fungi containing toxins. There are a number of these plants and it's useful to familiarise oneself with local plants which can cause this condition.

Common causes are dubbeltjies (*Tribulus terrestris*) which causes geeldikkop, buffalo grass (*Panicum*), *Lantana camara* and various Karoo bushes such as *Athanasia* and *Assemia*. The distribution and description of these plants are dealt with in Plant poisoning (page 118-120).

Photosensitivity is caused when the plant toxin damages the liver, resulting in a breakdown product being able to reach the bloodstream. When the skin is exposed to sunlight this breakdown product causes a severe inflammation of the skin, reddening and severe swelling, usually on the head, and sometimes causes the skin to burst. The skin then oozes serum and a crust forms. The eyelids are often red and swollen.

Jaundice is also seen, because of the liver damage. The diagnosis of the condition is based on the symptoms and history of eating specific plants. Treatment is the withdrawal of animals from the grazing and the providing of complete shade and water, but animals can be so badly affected that they need specific veterinary treatments such as fluid and cortisone administration.

Ringworm

Ringworm is a fungal infection of the skin (dermatophyte) seen in many animal species, including man. Among small stock, non-wooled sheep in areas such as the Northern Cape and the Free State are most commonly affected by ringworm. There are a number of species of dermatophytes, but the most common is *Trichophyton* spp. The infection is introduced into a flock by an infected animal and the infection then spreads if animals are kept in close contact. The lesions are usually circular, scabby or crusty areas of hairlessness, usually found on the head; but it can spread to the rest of the body, to sites such as the legs, the groin and around the tail. The condition is slow and progressive, but if severe, the animal will lose condition. The diagnosis is usually based on the typical appearance of the lesion. Culture of the affected hair by a veterinary laboratory will confirm the cause.

Treatment of the affected areas with an iodine wash will kill the fungus. Severely affected animals may need to be plunge-dipped in 2% lime sulphur solutions, once or twice a week for a month.

Skin cancers

The most common cancer found in sheep is squamous cell carcinoma, which affects the bare skin of the face, the anus and the vulva of ewes. All unpigmented sheep breeds and goats, especially Angoras, are susceptible. Melanomas − typically dark pigmented growths − are also seen in Angoras and sheep in South Africa.

Skin cancers develop in response to physical injury and/or UV radiation (sun-

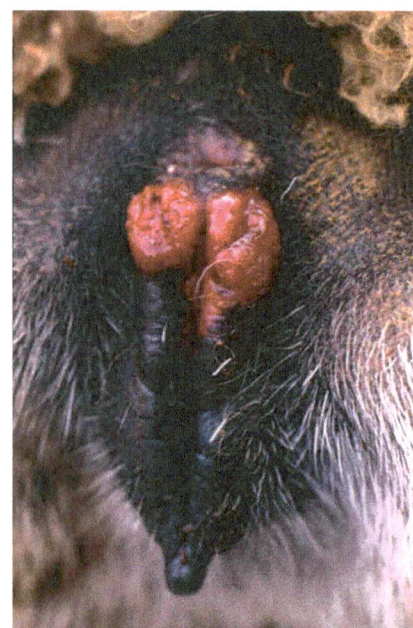

Squamous cell carcinoma of the vulva on a sheep

A melanoma on the ear of an Angora goat

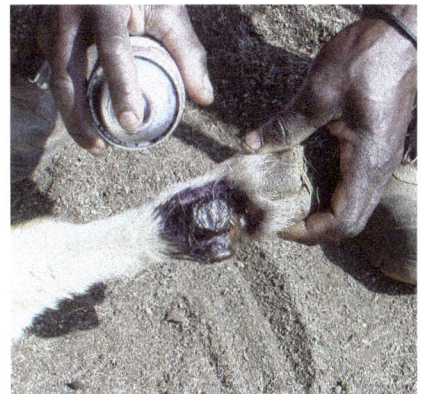

Prompt wound management will prevent further complications

light). It is therefore most common in un-pigmented sheep, which have had some type of wounding, such as ear tagging. When tails are cut too short it exposes the vulva and anus to solar radiation.

The most common age group affected are animals between four and six years of age.

The initial sign of the disease is a thickening of the skin, which expands, sometimes becoming very large. These cancers bleed when injured, show crusting and cracking and may be attacked by screwworm flies. Affected animals may die when the cancers bleed or become secondarily infected.

The diagnosis of skin cancer is based on the symptoms, but it can be confirmed by a veterinarian taking a biopsy from a live animal or submitting post-mortem samples for examination. There is no economically viable method of treating this condition, so affected sheep have to be slaughtered.

Prevent the condition by limiting injury such as ear tagging, and by reducing exposure to sunlight by docking tails so that they cover the anus in rams and the vulva in ewes. Provide shade in camps where small stock are held.

Wound management

The most serious wounds are those in which large blood vessels have been severed, resulting in massive bleeding. In such cases, it's essential to apply pressure to the blood vessel and stop the bleeding. This can be done by applying pressure with a finger and then clamping the blood vessel closed with a forceps. Less serious bleeding can be stopped with a pressure bandage made of cotton wool and a bandage. The cotton wool absorbs the blood and applies pressure to the wound, when wrapped tightly with a bandage.

Large gaping wounds should preferably be sewn, as they won't close properly if left unattended, but this must be done within 24 hours of the injury's happening. Smaller wounds can be managed with basic wound management; rinsing the wound with clean water and applying wound oil, ointment or spray is usually sufficient. The use of irritant substances such as hydrogen peroxide or disinfectants, should be avoided. In areas where screw worm occurs, wound oil containing insecticide should be applied to prevent maggot infestation. Injectable antibiotics will only be needed in cases of large, deep wounds or those which have become severely infected because of neglect.

NOTES

_____

_____

_____

_____

_____

_____

_____

_____

EYE AND EAR PROBLEMS

Genetic conditions

Genetic problems of eyes can be seen at birth; these include cataracts, squinting and conformational problems regarding the structure of the eye or eyelids. Entropion – the inversion or turning in of the eyelids – is sometimes seen in lambs; the farmer usually doesn't notice this, but as the affected lamb gets older it will show watery eyes, and later the surface of the eye becomes cloudy. Severe cases of entropion could, eventually, lead to blindness. It's not economically feasible to correct this defect surgically. These animals shouldn't be used for breeding, and should perhaps be culled.

Cancer of the ears

See Skin cancers (page 66-67)

Deafness

The spinose ear tick *Otobius megnini* occurs in the arid areas of the country and inhabits kraals and stables. The ticks infest the ear canal of a variety of animals, including sheep and goats. They cause severe irritation and can lead to the rupture of the ear drum, resulting in deafness.

Ear loss

Animals may lose ears as a sequel to the secondary infestation of tick wounds by the cattle screw worm *Chrysomyia bezziana*. (For control measures, see Ticks, page 111-113, and Flies, page 104-106.)

Gedoelstia (popeye or uitpeuloog)

The invasion of the eyes of sheep and goats by the larval stages of Gedoelstia flies causes popeye, the protrusion of the eye because of severe tissue inflammation and damage. For more details see the section on flies, page 104-105.

Infectious keratoconjunctivitis (pink eye)

The primary cause of keratoconjunctivitis (eye infection) in sheep and goats is believed to be the infectious agent *Mycoplasma conjunctivae*. The organism is car-

ried by animals that have recovered from the disease. They transmit the infection to other animals by direct contact when animals are kraaled together.

Certain factors, such as dust and sunlight, may predispose animals to infection, and the spread is then promoted by flies. Weaners are the most commonly affected age group.

The first signs of the condition are watering eyes, sensitivity to light, reddening and swelling of the eyelids. The watery discharge later becomes yellow and thick. The surface (cornea) of the eye becomes blue and later white (the so-called pearl formation) and may, in some cases, ulcerate and cause deep infection of the eyeball. Two to three weeks after the initial infection, the eye begins to heal and blood vessels may grow onto the surface causing a pink colour to develop, which later disappears.

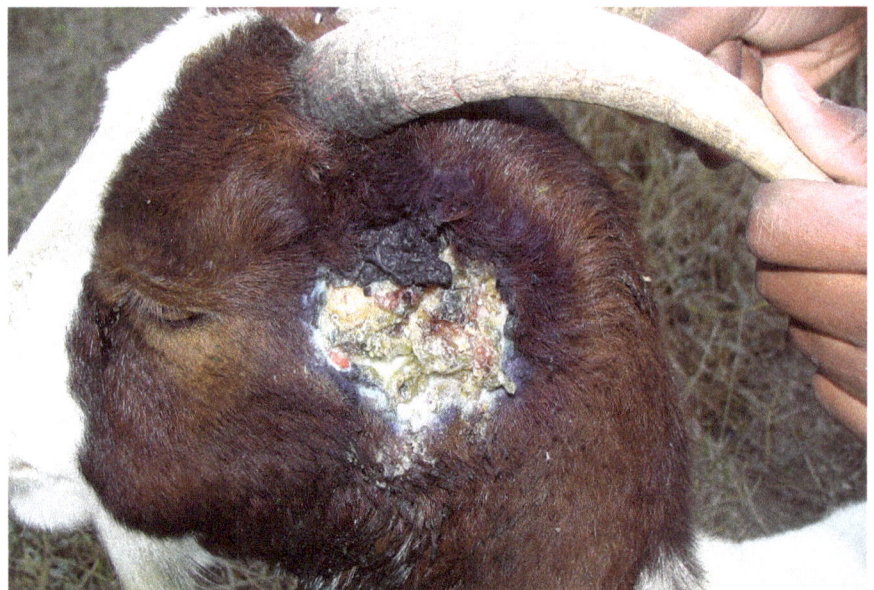

Clustering of certain species of ticks in the ear causes primary damage

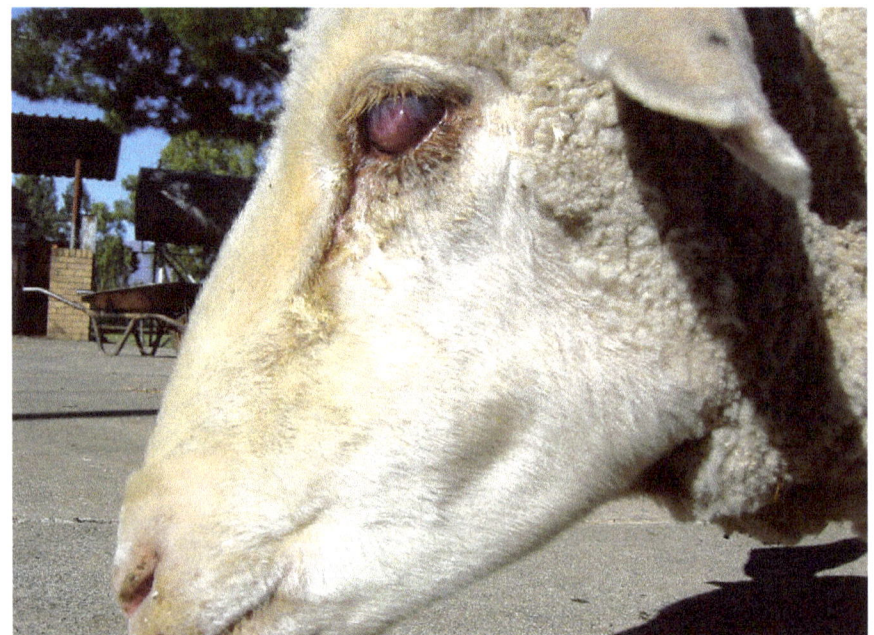

Keratoconjunctivitis in sheep

Secondary attacks on tick damage by cattle screw worm larvae could lead to ear loss

The scarring of the surface of the eye may resolve or may remain permanently causing partial blindness in that eye. Animals in which both eyes are affected can be temporarily blinded, unable to eat or move around effectively.

The diagnosis of pink eye is based on the clinical symptoms. Affected animals must be separated from the herd and placed in shady, dust-free conditions. Intramuscular injection with long-acting tet-racyclines is the most effective treatment and is preferable to using eye ointments, as this is painful for the animal and needs regular application to be effective. Blind animals will need special care. It may be necessary to control flies and so prevent transmission to uninfected animals. Vitamin A injections may enhance resistance to eye conditions.

Ketosis (domsiekte)

Ketosis is a metabolic disease of ewes, which occurs shortly before lambing. Because of a glucose deficiency in the diet, fat is broken down for energy and ketones are produced as a by-product. Ketones are toxic, affecting the brain and causing symptoms of docile behaviour and blindness. If the condition is left untreated, the animal will die (for more information, see Reproductive problems, page 50).

Poisoning

Certain remedies can cause blindness in stock if the recommended dose is exceeded. Examples of such remedies are rafoxanide and closantel. Poisonous plants such as chinkerinchee (*Ornithogalum* spp.) are a known cause of blindness in sheep. (See Plant poisoning, page 116, for more details.) Acidosis can cause brain damage and subsequent blindness.

Trauma

If small and superficial, lacerations of the cornea (the tough outer layer of the eye) may heal uneventfully – or become infected, with resultant blindness or loss of the eye.

Irritation of the eyes from plants having sharp seeds, such as *Hibiscus cannabinus* (wild stock rose), found on old lands, may cause infections and resultant blindness. Since eye surgery is a delicate and expensive procedure, it is seldom done on livestock. Animals blind in one eye cope well, but totally blind animals have to be euthanased.

NOTES

ACUTE (SUDDEN) DEATH

The term acute or sudden death refers to diseases in which few, if any, symptoms are seen before death, especially in extensive farming areas where animals are not monitored every day. The most common causes of acute deaths in sheep are anthrax, the clostridial diseases – including pulpy kidney and various forms of gas gangrene infections (sponssiekte), septicaemic pasteurellosis (*Mannheimia*) and plant poisoning.

Anthrax

Anthrax is caused by the bacterium *Bacillus anthracis* which, because it forms resistant spores, persists for very long periods in the soil. The spores are exposed when infected soil is grazed during dry seasons or when soil is disturbed by river courses or agricultural activities. Many livestock

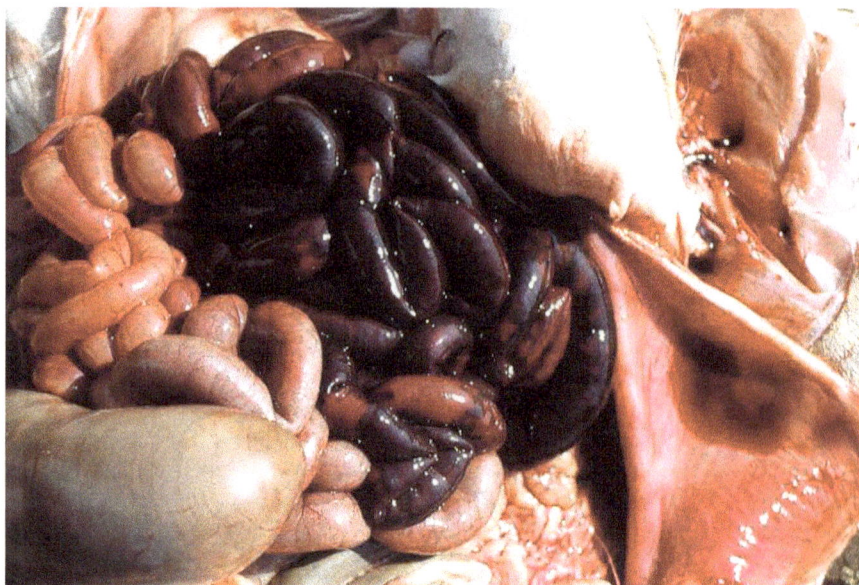

Anthrax organisms in a bloodsmear

The typical black-red congestive lesions of the organs seen in an animal that died of anthrax

A case of redgut showing the blood-filled intestine

species are susceptible, including cattle, sheep, goats, pigs and horses. Game animals are also susceptible and outbreaks occur from time to time in the Kruger National Park and Etosha Game Reserve.

Once anthrax spores have been ingested or inhaled by the grazing animals, the bacteria multiply, invade the bloodstream and cause rapid death from the production of potent toxins. During the incubation period, animals have a fever but no typical symptoms are noticed by the stock owner. Occasionally, animals may show convulsions in the terminal stages. Blood seeping from the nose or the anus is typical of anthrax carcases, but is seen with other diseases as well.

If anthrax is suspected, a bloodsmear should be taken and examined by a veterinarian, as the organism can be seen clearly under the microscope. Anthrax carcases should not be opened, as this spreads the infection and can cause human infections when the carcass is cut up. Anthrax is a notifiable disease, which means all confirmed cases must be reported to the state veterinarian. Infected farms are quarantined until the outbreak is deemed to be over. Anthrax carcases should be disposed of to prevent contamination of the environment. The recommended method is to bury them at a depth of two metres, adding one part of lime chloride or quicklime

$(Ca(OCl_2)$ to three parts of soil. This helps the carcass to decompose more rapidly and prevents its being opened by scavengers.

Use the anthrax vaccine annually in small stock to prevent outbreaks. Note that goats sometimes develop severe swelling at the site of the injection, so avoid injecting in the neck area. Follow the manufacturer's instructions to prevent side effects or complications.

Clostridial diseases

The clostridia are a broad group of bacteria which cause a wide range of diseases by the toxins they produce. The clostridia can be divided into different groups based on the systems they affect: those that affect the muscles (gas gangrene group), those that affect the gastrointestinal system (enterotoxaemias), and those that affect the nervous system. The latter include botulism (page 57) and tetanus (page 36, 61). Clostridia are widespread in the environment and cannot be avoided or eradicated, which is why vaccination is the most effective control method.

C perfringens A (redgut and wound infection)

Whether this bacterium is the actual cause of the condition known as redgut is still a controversial issue. In South Africa, the

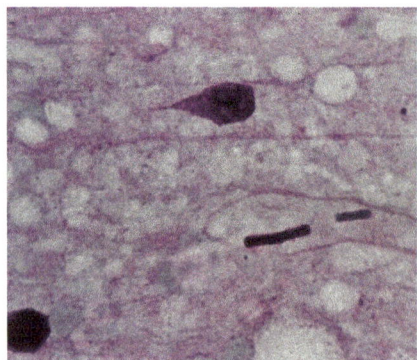

condition occurs in sheep grazed entirely on lucerne or clover pastures, without receiving any source of roughage. Sheep die suddenly and show blood-filled small intestines at post-mortem. The condition is thought to be caused by the production of a lot of gas, followed by displacement and strangulation of the intestines. Ensuring that animals on legume pastures receive some roughage every day has been shown to control the condition. *C perfringens* A is included in multicomponent clostridial vaccines because it sometimes causes fatalities. Manufacturers at present make no claim that the inclusion of Type A will prevent the redgut syndrome.

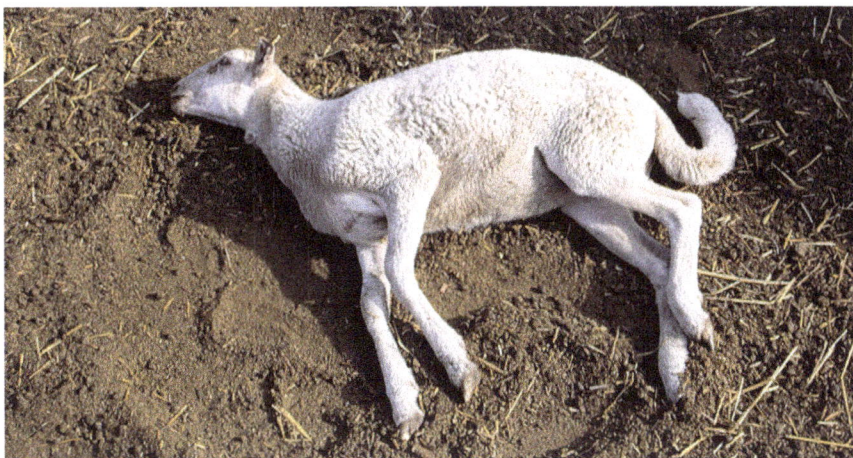

C perfringens B (lamb dysentery)

There are focal areas in South Africa where *C perfringens* B causes lamb dysentery. In the first week of life, infected lambs develop a gastrointestinal condition characterised by abdominal pain, bloody diarrhoea, and rapid death. At post-mortem examination the small intestine will show ulceration and haemorrhage. Treatment of affected lambs is seldom successful, so the only effective control measure is vaccination. To prevent the condition, the ewe must be vaccinated with a vaccine containing either type B or C organisms, since there is a cross-protection between the types. The ewes will then provide colostral immunity which will protect the lambs.

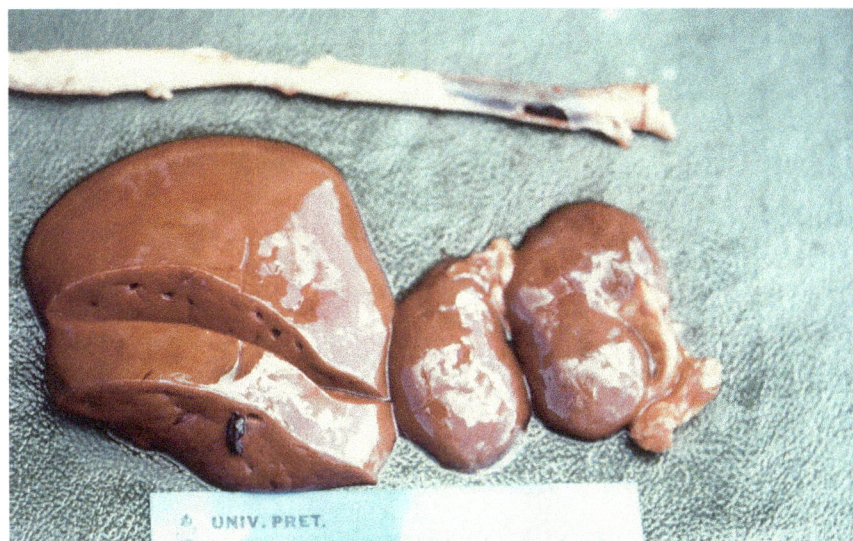

C perfringens C (necrotic enteritis)

It's not known whether this condition occurs in ruminants in South Africa, but the bacterium has been isolated from piglets here, so it does occur in the country. When this organism affects lambs, it causes a syndrome very similar to that of lamb dysentery. If diagnosed, the condition can be prevented by vaccinating ewes with clostridial vaccines containing type B or C organisms.

C perfringens D (pulpy kidney or enterotoxaemia)

Pulpy kidney is perhaps the single most important cause of deaths in small stock in SA.

It's sometimes called overeating disease

Pulpy kidney cases are usually found dead

The rapid breakdown of the organs in pulpy kidney cases can be confused with other conditions or the normal breakdown which occurs after death

because it is precipitated by the increase of the nutritional level of animals. The condition occurs when the organism *Clostridum perfringens* type D, which lives in the intestine of normal animals, suddenly multiplies rapidly, producing a powerful toxin which is absorbed into the system and causes severe damage to the blood vessels in body organs.

Pulpy kidney can occur in animals at any age, but most commonly in those on high levels of nutrition, such as weaners. It can also occur in other age groups when stock are given concentrated rations, placed on lush pastures or when heavily parasitised sheep are dewormed. The most common manifestations of pulpy kidney in a flock are sudden deaths, often in large numbers if flocks haven't been vaccinated. This occurs a few days after their nutritional level has been improved.

Lambs die acutely without showing symptoms; older sheep may show dullness, convulsions, frothing at the mouth before they die.

In goats, acute death is the most commonly reported sign but those with partial immunity may show signs of diarrhoea.

The diagnosis is usually made on the evidence of acute death of unvaccinated or inadequately vaccinated stock a few days after being given improved nutrition. Although there are some signs seen on postmortem, such as haemorrhages under

the skin, and rapid autolysis of the kidney (which gives the disease its name) these signs are not diagnostic. In particular, the "pulpiness" of the kidney can be seen in some other conditions such as prussic acid poisoning (geilsiekte) and pasteurellosis, and it must be borne in mind that after death internal organs begin to break down (autolysis) which will give the same picture as pulpy kidney. Goats that died of pulpy kidney may shows signs of enteritis.

There is no treatment for pulpy kidney; vaccination of small stock is the only method of control. Lambs/kids must be vaccinated from the age of three months, usually at weaning. As for all clostridial vaccines, pulpy kidney vaccination has to be repeated within three to four weeks and annually thereafter. Failure to give booster vaccinations at the recommended intervals will lead inadequate development of immunity.

Blackquarter (sponssiekte)

The syndrome known as blackquarter or quarter evil is a type of gas gangrene, or gangrenous infection of the muscles of the body. A number of clostridia can cause the syndrome, but *C. chauvoei* is the most common cause. Others are *C. septicum*, *C. novyi* and *C. sordelli*. *C. chauvoei* organisms occur as resistant spores in the soil and in the digestive tract and faeces of healthy stock. In small stock, the condition occurs when there's damage to muscles; for example, during shearing, marking, by dog bites or penetration by grass seeds. The wounding creates ideal conditions for this anaerobic (oxygen-avoiding) bacteria to germinate, multiply and produce a toxin that causes severe muscle damage. This toxin is then absorbed into the system and causes severe damage to the blood vessels of the body.

In sheep and goats, blackquarter usually develops after shearing or marking. Some days after the procedure, the animals develop a fever, refuse to eat, show depression and lameness, and die soon after the appearance of symptoms. If the wounds are examined they often show dark discoloration of the skin, and the skin may feel spongy because of the gas produced by the bacteria. Animals are usually found

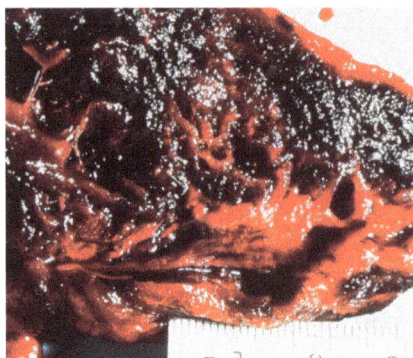

A case of quarter evil (sponssiekte)

dead on the pasture, without there being any prior indication of illness.

A post-mortem examination of the carcass shows rapid decomposition and the affected muscles will be swollen, blackened and show gas accumulation. Diagnosis of the condition can be confirmed by examining muscle smears in the laboratory, or performing bacterial isolations. This could be useful if the animals have been vaccinated because it may reveal the involvement of other gas gangrene-causing

Clostridial dikkop in a ram

clostridia, such as *C. novyi*, *C. septicum* and occasionally *C. sordelli* which can also cause blackquarter.

Acute deaths caused by clostridial gas gangrene could be confused with anthrax cases. If anthrax is suspected, a blood smear should be examined by a vet before the carcass can be opened up.

Gas gangrene infections in small stock must be prevented by vaccinating with a multiclostridial vaccine containing all the causative strains. The vaccine is generally

TABLE 4. Summary of the main clostridial diseases of small stock in South Africa

CLOSTRIDIUM SPECIES	DISEASE
C. chauvoei	Post-shearing quarter evil
C. septicum	Post-lambing gangrene, braxy
C. novyi	Big head
C. sordelli	Quarter evil
C. tetani	Tetanus
C. botulinum C	Botulism in water or feed
C. botulinum D	Botulism in veld animals
C. perfringens A	Redgut (this is not 100% certain)
C. perfringens B	Lamb dysentery
C. perfringens type C	Necrotic enteritis in lambs
C. perfringens type D	Pulpy kidney

given at weaning age, repeated after three to four weeks, then followed by annual re-vaccination.

C. novyi (big head) (dikkop)

This condition occurs when rams head butt each other and bruise the skin around the base of the horns. The *C. novyi* bacteria invade through small wounds in the skin and grow in the bruised tissue, causing massive swelling of the head. Affected rams may survive if treated with antibiotics, but most commonly they die of the toxins produced by the bacteria. Clostridial dikkop can be confused with bottlejaw (parasite infestation), blue tongue, dubbeltjies (geel-dikkop) poisoning and snakebite. Big head can be controlled by vaccinating with a clostridial vaccine containing *C. novyi* type B or D, as there is cross-immunity between the two types.

C. septicum (post-lambing gangrene) and braxy

Ewes that have difficult births – particularly when lambs are very big – or multiple births can develop gangrene of the uterus after lambing. *C. septicum* organisms invade the uterus through small wounds and multiply in the bruised tissue of the uterus. The ewes die very rapidly after lambing from the toxin produced by the bacteria. The carcass shows swelling and blue discoloration around the vulva and perineum. At post-mortem, the uterus shows typical signs of gas gangrene.

Another condition caused by this bacterium is braxy: This is the bacterial invasion of the abomasum or stomach with *C. septicum*, after the animal has consumed frozen grass or icy water. The low

A case of post-lambing gangrene showing the discoloration of the vulva

Small stock unable to shelter from cold weather develop hypothermia and die

temperature causes damage to the stomach muscle that provides suitable conditions for the invasion and multiplication by *C. septicum* organisms. Braxy causes acute death and is only diagnosed at post-mortem. It is unknown whether this condition occurs in South Africa. Both conditions can be prevented by using a clostridial vaccine that includes *C. septicum*.

Other Clostridia spp

Other, less common, clostridia, such as *C. sordelli*, are included in vaccines because they can occasionally cause gangrenous infections. *Clostridium haemolyticum* which causes a condition called redwater disease doesn't occur in South Africa. It secondarily infects the liver with primary liver fluke damage, producing a toxin that causes haemolysis (destruction of red blood cells, resulting in red discoloration of the urine, anaemia and death). The organism is included in some imported vaccines.

A note on clostridial vaccines and vaccination

Multi-component clostridial vaccines contain the clostridia that cause enterotoxaemias such as pulpy kidney, the most common causes of gas gangrene, and the tetanus organism. Because they provide broad coverage against the clostridial diseases, it eliminates losses and time-consuming investigations to identify specific clostrid-

ia. All clostridial vaccines must be given twice initially, with a three to four week interval and thereafter annually. Failure to give booster vaccinations within the specified period will not give adequate results.

Pregnant ewes should be vaccinated with multi-clostridial vaccines in the last four to six weeks of pregnancy to ensure protection against diseases of young stock, such as lamb dysentery and tetanus, as well as protection of the ewe against diseases such as post-lambing gangrene of the uterus and pulpy kidney. Ewes/does should be dewormed at the same time, because this is when they shed large numbers of worm eggs due to a phenomenon called PPRR (pre-parturient relaxation of resistance), which means increased susceptibility to worms during this time. Some clostridial vaccines contain deworming agents for the farmer's convenience.

Exposure (hypothermia)

Wooled sheep and Angora goats may die from chilling in cold conditions, usually after wetting the skin and subsequent exposure to the wind chill factor. Angora goats are very susceptible since they don't have much body fat as insulation. Even animals in good condition are victims of hypothermia because, although the body fat provides insulation, the animals are unable to change this fat into energy to raise the body temperature sufficiently, and in time. Stock confined to flat, open ground run a high risk of becoming hypothermic.

Chilled animals seek shelter downwind, are reluctant to move and they may collapse and fall into a coma and die within a few hours. Angora goats often abort after chilling because of the precipitous drop in blood sugar. Collapsed animals require urgent treatment; they should be placed in sheds, and insulated with dry sacks, wool or hay. When the animals' body temperature has been restored, they have to be provided through energy-rich feed and fresh water.

Prevent hypothermia by anticipating high-risk weather and providing protection for shorn animals ahead of these conditions. Provide downwind shelter for animals in all paddocks.

Prussic acid poisoning

Numerous plants contain prussic acid, which is poisonous to small stock. The details are discussed in Plant poisoning (page 126).

Pasteurella septicaemia (*Pasteurella trehalosi*)

The T biotypes of what was formerly known as *Pasteurella haemolytica*, are now referred to as *Pasteurella trehalosi*. They are present in the respiratory tract of small stock, but under certain conditions cause acute deaths in lambs six to nine months old due to systemic pasteurellosis or septicaemia. This usually occurs in feedlot lambs and yearlings during stress periods such as weaning, dietary stress and bad weather. The lambs affected are usually on a high level of nutrition. They die acutely without any noticeable symptoms, but close examination may reveal sheep in the incubation phase, typically looking depressed and separating themselves from the flock. The mortalities seldom exceed 10%.

The *P trehalosi* bacteria invade the lungs and liver where they multiply and then invade the bloodstream. Typically, the carcass shows signs of septicaemia; isolation of the organism from liver, lung and spleen will confirm the disease. It can be confused with other acute diseases such as pulpy kidney and pneumonia. If the condition is diagnosed early enough sick animals may be treated with a course of oxytetracycline injections.

P trehalosi serotypes included in the IRP vaccine Multivax P for protection against septicaemic pasteurellosis have been shown experimentally to protect against the condition. Multivax P also contains the pneumonia-inducing *Mannheimia* (*Pasteu-*

A case of acute septicaemia caused by *Pasteurella trehalosi*

rella) strains as well as the important clostridia (see Pasteurella pneumonia).

Plant poisoning

Various plant poisonings can cause acute death in small stock. The most important are plants containing cardiac glycoside such as tulp and slangkop (see the section on plant poisonings).

NOTES
_____
_____
_____
_____
_____
_____
_____
_____
_____
_____
_____
_____
_____
_____

Internal
PARASITES

Internal parasites and their control

The internal parasites of sheep and goats fall into three main groups: roundworms, tapeworms and flukes. The categories of parasite are discussed separately to illustrate the differences in life cycle and biology.

ROUNDWORMS

Young ruminants are born with no immunity to roundworms and are extremely susceptible to infestation. Although sheep and goats can develop resistance to roundworms on exposure, this occurs more slowly than in cattle and even adult animals can be severely affected when they're exposed to stress factors such as poor nutrition and cold weather.

Pregnant sheep and goats shed enormous numbers of roundworm eggs onto grazing because of the so-called peri-parturient relaxation of resistance (PPRR); a lowering of resistance during late pregnancy. This causes massive contamination of the pastures with worm eggs.

As a species, sheep are exposed to a high level of roundworm challenge because of various behavioral factors: They graze close to the ground so pick up more worm larvae than other species; they tend to graze more closely together; and they're less likely to avoid areas of high faecal contamination.

Most roundworms important in small stock are found in the gastrointestinal tract (GIT). There are many species, and because most are rather small, they're difficult to identify without a microscope.

The term "roundworm" refers to the fact that they have a round cross-section when compared with other parasites such as tapeworms and flukes.

Most roundworms have a direct life cycle, which means they have only one host during their lifetime.

After mating inside their host, female adult roundworms lay eggs which are passed out through the host's faeces onto pastures. A first-stage larva (L^1) develops

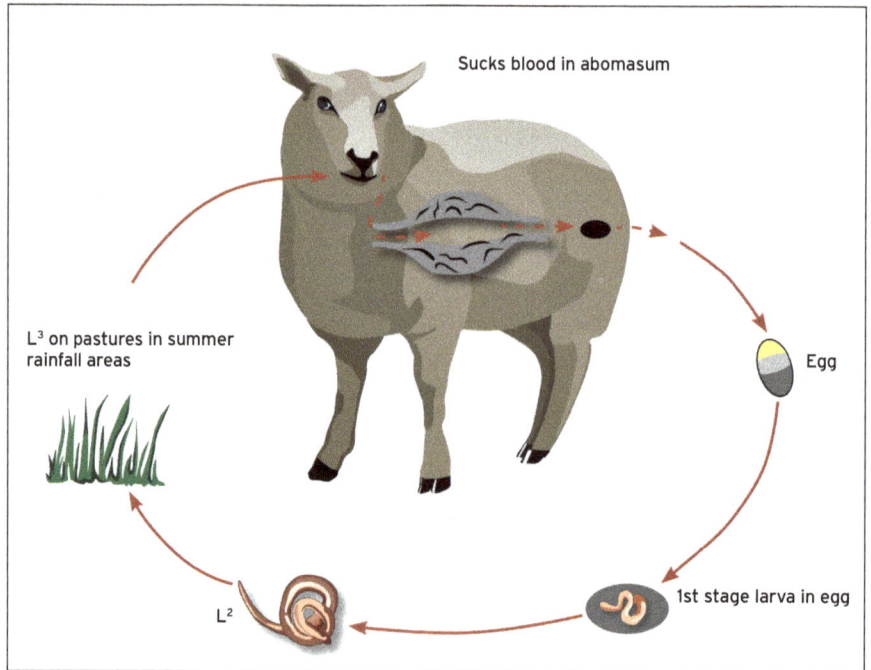

Life cycle of roundworm

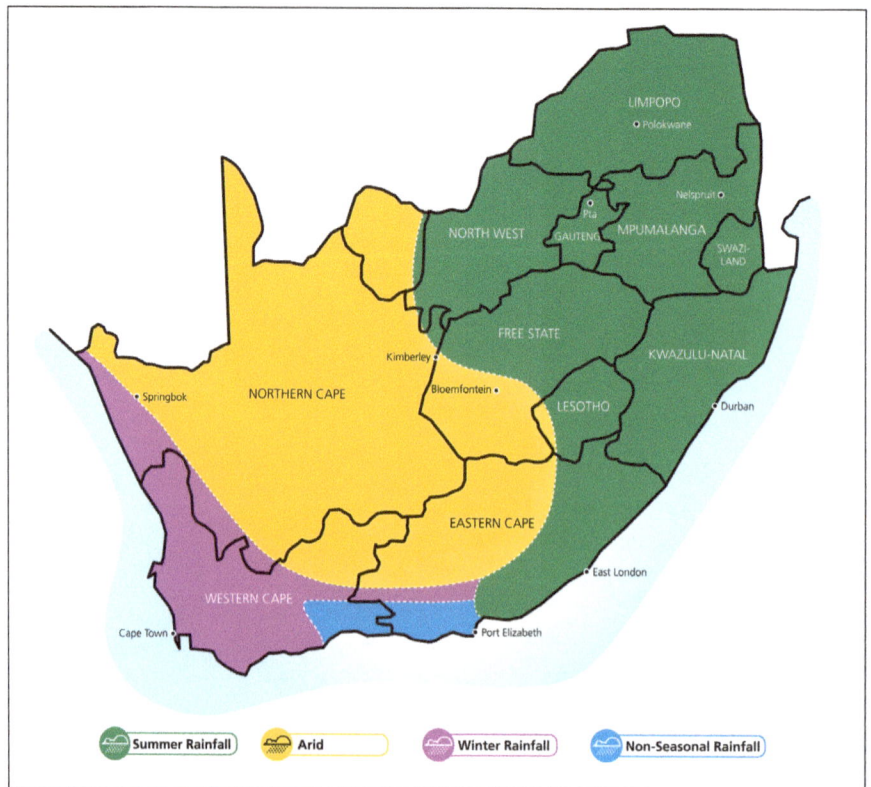

Rainfall areas of South Africa

in the egg, which hatches inside a dung pad and feeds on bacteria. The first-stage larva moults and becomes a second-stage larva (L^2). When the second-stage larva moults to become a third-stage larva (L^3), it moves out of the dung pad onto the grass stalks of the pasture. This is the infective stage, when the parasites wait for a suitable host to ingest them with the grazing.

The development of the larvae is influenced by temperature and moisture which, when optimal, can make it possible for them to complete their life cycle within one to two weeks; generally, it takes longer than this.

When the infective larvae are ingested by hosts they migrate to their preferred site in the gut; here they either feed on the surface of the gut, suck blood, or burrow into the gut tissues.

The migration and the method of feeding determine the symptoms that they cause. The worms mate and lay eggs which are shed in the faeces, completing the life cycle.

The roundworm species of small stock are summarised in Table 5. The most important worms are given in bold text. The distribution of these various species in South Africa occurs roughly according to the rainfall season, and they can be grouped in summer rainfall species, winter rainfall species and species which occur in arid or low-rainfall areas.

Areas in South Africa that get rain throughout the year (non-seasonal) are hosts for both winter and summer rainfall species (see map alongside).

Roundworms can have a variety of effects on their hosts, depending on the worm species.

One of the most important is the bloodsucking group, eg the very important wireworm *Haemonchus contortus* found in summer rainfall areas. Bloodsucking worms deplete the red blood cells, lowering the bloodstream's ability to supply oxygen, which results in less efficient functioning.

Blood may also be lost by leaking out into the gut and causing the appearence of black tarry faeces. In the early stages of anaemia, animals are weak and their growth and production are affected. More severe blood loss will result in animals becoming too weak to function normally; they could even die as a result of heavy infestations.

At the same time, bloodsucking worms remove serum proteins, causing a severe protein loss.

The combined effects of anaemia and protein loss caused by bloodsucking worms result in retarded growth in young animals, reduced production of meat and wool and sometimes deaths.

Other roundworms damage the gut, causing poor digestion and irritation and resulting in diarrhoea. Some species suppress the appetite, which leads to severe weight loss.

When roundworm infestations cause deaths the economic loss is easy to quantify, but researchers have shown that even roundworm infestations that show no visible external effects on the animal will start to erode production, as measured in sheep, by weight gain and wool production. So by the time clinical symptoms are seen the animals will already have suffered losses.

Ideally, then, the dosing programme to control roundworms should reduce the harmful effects on health and production without excessive application of dewormers, for reasons which will be discussed later.

Haemonchus contortus (Wire worm)

The worm This is a small worm, roughly 1-3cm long, found in the abomasum. The adult female is easy to identify because of their so-called "barber's pole" appearance as a result of the white spiral of uterus being wrapped around the red, blood-filled intestine. Male worms are small and reddish in colour.

Area The wire worm thrives in warm, moist conditions and is therefore mainly a problem in the summer rainfall areas. Irrigated pastures provide ideal conditions for this roundworm.

Biology The female wire worm lays 20 000 eggs per day, so there could be a phenomenal number of worms on pasture. Larvae hatch and mature rapidly on the pastures

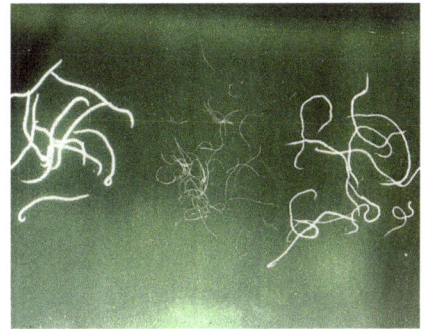

Various roundworms of stock. From left to right: Nodular, bankrupt, and wire worms

Wire worms (*H contortus*) in the abomasum

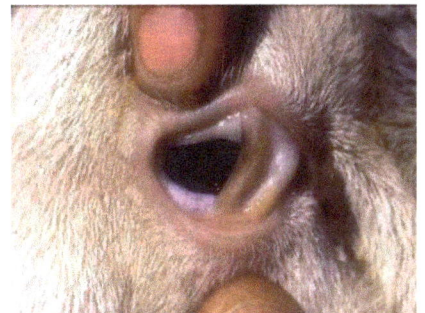

Anaemia caused by wire worm infestation

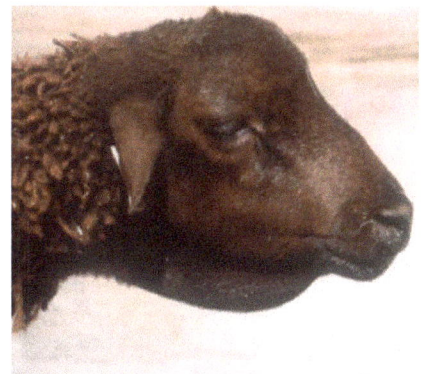

Bottlejaw caused by severe wire worm infestation

TABLE 5. Important roundworms of small stock in South Africa

SCIENTIFIC NAME	COMMON NAME	RAINFALL AREA	PART OF GIT
Haemonchus* contortus	wire worm	summer	abomasum
(Telodorsagia) Ostertagia Circumcincta	brown stomach worm	winter	abomasum
Trichostrongylus axei	stomach bankrupt worm	widespread	abomasum
Gaigeria pachyscelis	Sandveld hookworm	arid	small intestine
Trichostrongylus spp.	bankrupt worm	winter rainfall and pastures	small intestine
Bunostomum sp	Grassveld hookworm	summer and non seasonal	small intestine
Nematodirus spathiger	long necked bankrupt worm	Karoo and winter rainfall	small intestine
Strongyloides papilosus	white bankrupt worm	widespread	small intestine
Chabertia ovina	large-mouthed bowel worm	winter and non- seasonal	large intestine
Oesophagostomum sp	nodular worm	widespread	large intestine
Trichuris sp	whip worm	widespread	large intestine

*bold type indicates most important roundworms

after good summer rains and infest sheep in November. Conditions are optimal for the hatching and development of the worm from December to May.

This is a very important roundworm of sheep and goats; it has a large spike with which it pierces the abomasum of the host to suck blood, causing production losses and death.

Symptoms The presence of 100 – 1 000 adult wire worms is sufficient to cause a chronic, progressive anaemia, loss of appetite and death.

Higher burdens of 1 000 – 10 000 cause anaemia and weight loss and the typical bottlejaw syndrome which can terminate in death if untreated.

Heavy infestations of more than 10 000 wire worms will cause severe blood loss and rapid death. Signs of infestation are loss of weight, pale mucous membranes, tarry, black faeces, progressive weakness, loss of appetite and death.

Control On many farms *H contortus* is

resistant to almost all remedies – except the organophosphates. So in areas where the wire worm occurs, it's of cardinal importance to a) avoid introducing resistant worms by quarantine dosing (see under Preventing resistance, page 85); b) identify the remedies to which there is resistance c) in conjunction with a veterinarian, select a suitable remedy and implement a sustainable dosing programme, e g the FAMACHA© system (see page 83, 84, 85) which will limit stock losses, and at the same time prevent the development of resistance. See the discussion on preventing resistance (page 85).

Ostertagia (Telodorsagia) circumcinta (Brown stomach worm)

The worm This is a tiny, brown, thread-like worm (7 – 12mm long) found in the abomasum.

Area Ostertagia is particularly important in winter rainfall areas, because they prefer cool autumn and spring conditions.

Biology It occurs commonly in the Eastern and Western Cape, and the peak times for infection are April to September (autumn to spring). These worms are often a problem on planted pastures.

When environmental conditions are adverse for the larvae they are able to undergo a stage of arrested development (hypobiosis) in the animal, until conditions are favourable for the larvae to develop into adults and cause a sudden, massive increase in egg shedding.

Symptoms Brown stomach worms invade the gastric glands in the abomasum, destroying the acid-production function required for digestion.

The pH increases and digestion cannot take place efficiently, which gives rise to loss of appetite, weight loss, diarrhoea and death.

The overall protein deficiency results in severe wasting; in Angora goats the clinical syndrome is called waterpens because of the quantity of fluid that accumulates in

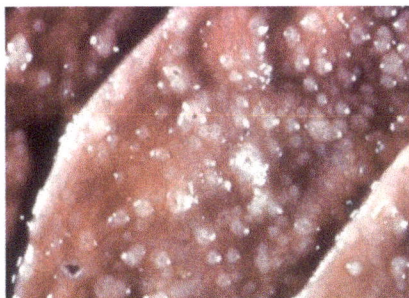

Lesions caused by brown stomach worm

the abdomen.

Control Some resistance to wormers has been seen. Refer to section on control of wireworm (page 80-81) for a discussion about how to the manage resistant roundworms, but note that the FAMACHA© system is not applicable to brown stomach worm control. When selecting remedies, bear in mind that thiabendazole doesn't remove hyperbiotic larvae, but levamisole and ivermectin will.

Trichostrongylus axei (Stomach bankrupt worm)

These are minute white worms, almost invisible to the naked eye. Infestations are often missed because of the difficulty of seeing the worms. Its presence inhibits the development of other abomasal worms. Dorpers are more susceptible than other breeds and large numbers of worms are required for significant infestations in sheep. The worms cause inflammation and thickening of the abomasum and an increase in pH. Symptoms are a foul-smelling diarrhoea, wasting, weakness and death. This worm has apparently become less common and is less likely to be a cause of problems nowadays.

Trichostrongylus spp. (Intestinal bankrupt worms)

The worm These tiny reddish brown worms (5 – 8mm) occur in the first few metres of the small intestine and are difficult to see.

Area Intestinal bankrupt worms thrive in areas having cold, wet winters and can be a problem on artificial pastures. The eggs and larvae resist drying and can survive for long periods until rain falls. These roundworms are therefore mostly of importance in winter rainfall and non-seasonal rainfall areas.

Symptoms Infestations cause insidious losses, especially in lambs and weaners. The worms suppress the appetite of the host, resulting in a protein deficiency and resultant muscle wasting.

Young growing animals are the most severely affected especially when the protein levels in feed are low. Very often the only clinical sign is weakness, although weight loss, constipation and diarrhoea are also seen. As the name of the worm indicates, the condition causes considerable losses because of the lack of dramatic symptoms. The diagnosis may also be easily missed because the parasite is difficult to see.

Control Some resistance to anthelminthics has been seen. Refer to section on the control of wire worm (page 78) for a discussion about the management of resistance, but note that the FAMACHA© system is not applicable to these roundworms.

Nematodirus spathiger (Long-necked bankrupt worm)

The worm These are fairly long, red worms (10 – 23mm) which show a narrowing at the tail end. They are found in the small intestine.

Area The eggs and larvae are resistant to drying and extreme temperatures. In the Karoo, infestations occur after rain when contaminated grass around camps greens up and attracts sheep. In winter rainfall areas, they're always present on pastures. The worm population peaks in late winter/ early spring.

Symptoms There is rapid deterioration in condition after infestation, especially in lambs which pick up massive infestations. The larvae cause severe damage to the intestinal lining, which results in loss of appetite, diarrhoea and weight loss.

Control Thus far, no problems with resistance have been seen in this worm.

Gaigeria pachyscelis (Sandveld hookworm)

The worm These worms of the small intestine are fairly long (20 – 30mm) and have a slightly hooked end.

Area Sandveld hookworm is found in arid areas of the North West Cape and Namibia. The worm larvae are found around leaking water troughs.

Biology They infect sheep through the skin and then migrate to the small intestine. Management practices which prevent water leakage or overflowing will control the problem.

Symptoms Even low numbers of worms can cause losses, because of their voracious bloodsucking. Five to six weeks after infestation, anaemia develops, and results in death. As few as 100 worms can result in fatal anaemia.

Control Thus far, this roundworm has shown no resistance to any of the dewormer groups.

Bunostomum spp (Grassveld hookworm)

The worm These small intestinal worms are thick and white with a hooked end (1 – 3cm).

Area They thrive in hot, moist conditions and are seen in summer and non-seasonal rainfall areas.

Biology The larvae are ingested either orally or through the skin. They finally lodge in the small intestine where they damage the intestinal epithelium with their large mouthparts. These areas bleed and cause anaemia in the animal. With heavy infestations, sheep show bottlejaw. Dermatitis can be seen at the site of skin penetration.

Control No resistance.

Stronglyloides papillosus (White bankrupt worm)

The worm This is a very small worm, found in the small intestine.

Area These roundworms are widespread throughout the country.

Biology Since young animals are most susceptible, these worms are most commonly seen as a problem in lambs and kids housed in kraals, during the summer months. Female larvae penetrate the skin, pass to the lungs and finally to the small intestine. Young animals can be infected through the milk of infected mothers.

Symptoms Massive infestations of young animals can cause severe diarrhoea, loss

of appetite and death. Goats show anorexia, diarrhoea, constipation and sunken eyes. Adult animals develop resistance and rarely show any clinical signs.

Control No resistance has been seen in this worm.

Chabertia ovina
(Large-mouthed bowel worm)

The worm These are large white worms (13 – 20mm long) which attach to the mucosa of the large intestine using their large mouth parts.

Area The eggs can survive low environmental temperatures but drying or exposure to sunlight will kill them. The parasites are therefore restricted to winter and non-seasonal rainfall areas.

Symptoms The worms browse on the intestinal mucosa, causing blood loss and leakage of plasma. This contributes to weight loss, especially if the animals are on poor feed. Diarrhoea may also be seen due to the damage caused by the worms feeding.

Control Benzimidazoles are effective and little resistance has been seen.

Oesophagostomum columbianum
(Nodular worm)

The worm These small, whitish-grey worms (12 – 18mm) have a hooked end, and are found in the large intestine .

Area They're found in summer rainfall areas because the young larvae need warm, wet weather and cannot survive drying. They are absent from arid, non-seasonal and winter rainfall areas. It is, however, seldom found on irrigated pastures.

Symptoms The infective larvae invade the wall of the gut where they moult and develop into the next stage.

From here the adult worms migrate into the large intestine. The larval invasion of the gut wall results in the formation of nodules which impair absorption of fluid. These nodules can be seen at post-mortem, which is a good indicator of the presence of the worm. Nodular worm infestation causes wasting and reduces production.

Control This worm responds well to benzimidazoles and no resistance has yet been detected.

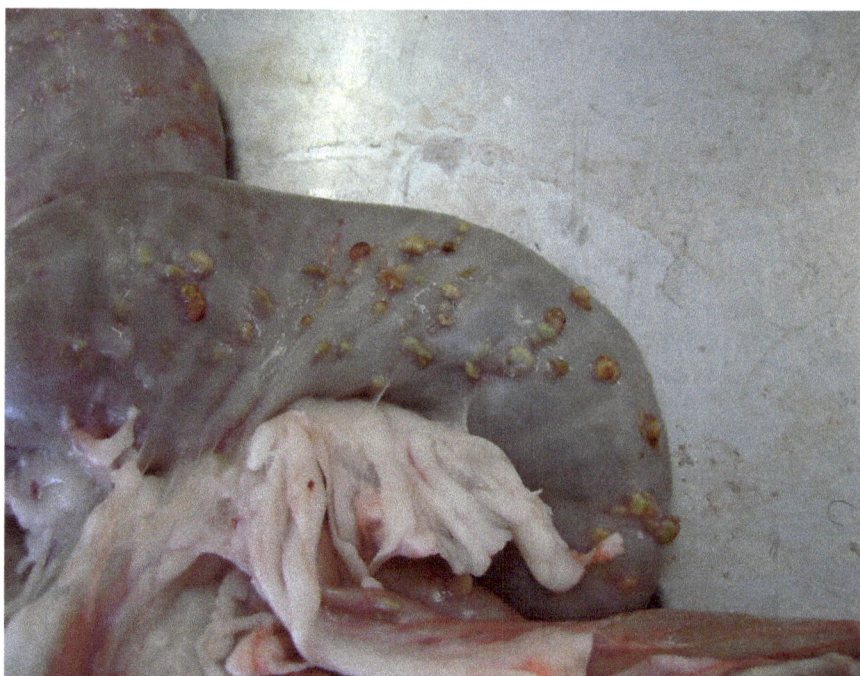

Intestinal lesions caused by nodular worms

Trichuris spp (Whip worm)

The worm The adult worm is very distinctive with a long, thin neck and thick posterior section. Found in the large intestine, its appearance has given it the name whip worm.

Area It is found in all areas and is quite resistant to temperature variation and resists dessication.

Symptoms Large numbers are required to produce the discomfort caused by the larvae when they burrow into the gut wall, mature and then migrate into the lumen of the colon. The main discomfort and damage are caused by the migration of the larvae through the intestinal wall but they can cause anaemia due to bleeding. The adults are not thought to cause problems unless they are very numerous, in which case they cause pain, diarrhoea and weight loss.

Control No resistance to dosing remedies.

OTHER ROUND-WORMS

Dictyocaulus filaria (lungworm)

This is a long, white (3 – 10cm) worm with a dark stripe down its length. It has a lim-

ited geographic range, being found on isolated farms in cool mountainous or coastal areas. The worms present in the lungs lay eggs, where they hatch and the larvae are coughed up, swallowed and excreted in the faeces. The larvae can survive until the infective stage develops, if conditions are moist and cool enough. The infective larvae are taken in with feed, penetrate the gut and migrate to the lungs. Within a few weeks of infestation the animals show difficulty breathing, coughing, nasal discharge and tiredness if chased. The worm is susceptible to most roundworm remedies.

ROUNDWORM DIAGNOSIS AND TREATMENT

Small stock can be infested with roundworms without showing symptoms, but if infestations are severe, they will show non-specific signs such as diarrhoea or weight loss. To detect the presence of roundworms, faecal samples can be taken from live animals for laboratory examination for their eggs.

Egg counts determine the severity of the

infestation, and the species of the round-worm eggs can usually also be identified (see Worm egg counts and FECRT for more information). Often the diagnosis of round worm infestation is made on a post mortem examination during which the worms themselves can be identified by a veterinarian or animal technician. Regular monitoring of roundworm burdens can be done by taking the intestinal tract of animals slaughtered for use for examination by a veterinarian or a vet laboratory. Animals infested with heavy worm burdens should be treated with dewormers (anthelmintics) registered for the type of worm infestation (see **Table 6**: dewormers, on page 83). However, because roundworms can cause huge losses in production it is preferable to deworm animals preventatively to control their effects rather than treat these when they are far advanced (see dosing programmes, page 85).

Post-mortem examination of the intestinal tract will give information on the roundworms infesting a flock

WORM EGG COUNTS AND FECRT

Intestinal roundworms shed their eggs in the faeces of the host animal. These eggs can be seen in faecal samples when examined under the microscope. Faecal egg counts are an extremely useful tool for identifying the worm species present and determining the severity of the infestation, and also for monitoring the effect of dosing programmes and roundworm resistance. Local veterinary laboratories and veterinarians are equipped to do faecal egg counts for roundworms and liver flukes. The samples taken from a flock for egg counts should represent the group of animals to be evaluated, eg five to 10 animals of a group showing signs of suspected infestation or, alternately, five to 10 animals treated 10 – 14 days earlier.

Send faecal samples, packed in small screw-top plastic containers, to suitable laboratories as soon as possible, since storage will result in decomposition and may affect the tests. At least 2g must be collected from each animal. Mark the samples clearly, recording the species of the animal, the identification number of the animal or group (e g weaners), and the

owner's details. It's important to specify if fluke egg analysis is needed, because that's a different test. Note that tapeworm infestations cannot be diagnosed using faecal egg counts.

The results of roundworm egg counts are expressed as eggs per gram (epg) and are usually reported as follows by laboratories/veterinarians:

O:	**No worm eggs present**
+:	**Slight infestation (1 – 500 eggs/gram)**
++:	**Moderate infestation (500 – 5 000 eggs/gram)**
+++:	**Heavy infestation (>5 000 eggs/gram)**

The results of these egg counts should be interpreted with care, as the number of eggs that occur in a sample is not necessarily proportional to the number of worms present; the animal may be infested with non-egg laying worms such as larvae or with a worm species which lays few eggs. Some species, such as wire worms (*Haemonchus*), produce massive numbers of eggs while others such as the brown stomach worm (*Telodorsagia*) produce low

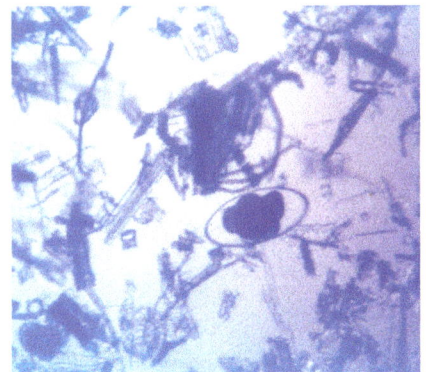

Microscopic examination of faecal samples allows for identification and counts of roundworm eggs

egg numbers.

The egg production of worms is cyclic so it will be low at certain times of the year, even at certain times of the day. Technical problems regarding egg counts may also give inaccurate results, so ensure they are being done by a professional.

Faecal egg counts should, therefore, be interpreted taking all these factors into account. They're most useful if done on a regular basis as a monitoring tool for building up a history and therefore developing and monitoring a dosing programme.

ROUNDWORM REMEDIES (DEWORMERS)

Anthelmintics, or dewormers, are chemicals that are poisonous to parasites but not to the host if given at the specified dose. The anthelmintics currently used act in one of two ways; either by affecting the parasite's neuromuscular system and causing paralysis, or by limiting energy by interfering with its respiration pathways.

Selecting a dewormer Choose a dewormer registered for the control of the roundworms present on the farm. Most roundworm remedies have a broad spectrum of activity, which means they control a variety of important species. On farms experiencing resistance problems (usually wire worms) a Faecal Egg Reduction Test should be performed to select a suitable remedy. A veterinarian may suggest the use of narrow-spectrum remedies to extend the range of available remedies for resistant worms.

Optimal use of dewormers Most anthelmintics are administered by mouth as drenches, although some are administered as injections or as pour-ons. The dose of anthelmintics given is based on the body weight of the animal to be treated. For control to be effective, the dose must be accurate as underdosing will lead to lowered efficacy. Underdosing occurs usually as a result of owners underestimating the weight of the various age groups of sheep. Weigh a few animals from each age group (weaners, ewes, rams) to obtain a mean weight. Another cause of underdosing is poorly calibrated dosing guns; calibration should be checked using a measuring cylinder. Goats are said to require higher doses of dewormers because they have a higher metabolic rate than sheep, but most dewormer manufacturers don't specify a goat dose. A veterinarian should be consulted before implementing this.

Overdosing with dewormers having a narrow safety margin (levamisole) can cause toxicity and must be avoided; weigh a few sheep from each age group as discussed previously. The FAMACHA© system allows farmers to identify only those animals that need to be dosed for wire worm and therefore reduces the risk of resistance developing (see overleaf).

TABLE 6. Chemical groups currently registered under Act 36/47

Code number*	GROUP	ACTIVES	SPECTRUM
1.	Macrocyclic lactones	Ivermectin Abamectin Moxidectin Doramectin	Roundworms (also nasalworm fly larvae)
2.	Benzimidazoles	Thibendazole Mebendazole Albendazole Triclabendazole Fenbendazole	Roundworms and their eggs
3.	Imidiothiazole	Levamisole	Roundworms
4.	Salicylanilides	Rafoxinide Closantel Resorantel Niclosamide Oxclosanide	Liver flukes, nasal worms and roundworms Tapeworms and conical flukes Liver flukes
5.	Phenols	Nitroxynil Disophenol	Roundworms
6.	Sulphonamides	Clorsulon	Flukes
7.	Organophosphates	Haloxon Trichlorfon Napthalophos	Roundworms
8.	Isoquinaline	Praziquantel	Tapeworms
9.	Other e.g. tetrahydropyrimidine	Morantel Pyrantel	Roundworms
10.	Amino acetonile derivatives	Monepantel (in registration)	Resistant roundworms

* The number refers to the numbering system on the labels of products

ROUNDWORM RESISTANCE

Worm resistance or, more correctly, anthelmintic resistance in roundworms refers to the resistance worms are able to develop to the chemicals used for their control. In South Africa currently resistance is a problem mainly in wire worm (*Haemonchus contortus*) with some seen in the brown stomach worm (*Telodorsagia*) and the intestinal bankrupt worms of the *Trichostrongylus* spp. In wire worms, resistance has been encountered to almost all anthelmintic groups. Benzimidazole resistance is common, followed by the salicylanilides (especially closantel); there is resistance, to a lesser extent, to macrocyclic lactones and less, in turn, to levamisole. Organophosphate resistance is seldom encountered, but does sometimes occur.

The ability of worms to resist chemicals is a genetic characteristic. Under natural conditions genetically-resistant worms occur at very low levels in worm populations. These resistant individuals are then selected when chemicals are used, since the susceptible worms are eliminated and the resistant individuals survive to reproduce and increase their numbers. These resistance genes then become prevalent on specific farms and are spread all over the country when animals are sold to other farmers. Once resistance develops, farmers switch to the next available group to which resistance then gradually develops, and so on. Eventually, the roundworms become multi-resistant and are very difficult to control.

One of the major causes of the spread of resistance is the introduction of resistant worms onto a farm, usually via stud animals; this spread of resistance is preventable by quarantine treatment of newly introduced animals (see Preventing worm resistance).

Another cause of resistance is frequent and prolonged treatment with the same chemical group. It is also postulated that remedies which have a prolonged (residual) effect may contribute to the development of resistance. Underdosing is also suspected of causing resistance.

FAMACHA© chart

Testing for resistance

The most effective way to determine whether resistance to a certain remedy has developed on the farm, is to use the faecal egg reduction count (FECRT). It should be performed under supervision of a competent person, preferably a veterinarian since the interpretation of the test is critical. To perform the FECRT, one group of animals is treated with the remedy under investigation, while another is is treated with a remedy group not used recently on the farm. A third group of animals remains as untreated controls. Faecal samples are collected before treatment, then 10 days after dosing, from all groups. For resistance to be suspected, egg counts before and after treatment shouldn't change significantly. The control sample will establish whether the results are valid.

Preventing worm resistance

Resistance to dewormers is seen mainly with *Haemonchus contortus* but also to some degree with *Telodorsagia* and the bankrupt worms of the small intestine (*Trichostrongylus* spp). Potentially, however, all worm species can develop resistance so there are several management principles that should be applied to prevent the dominance of resistant strains:

Quarantine dosing Carrying out quarantine dosing, using two successive treatments with two different groups of chemicals, can prevent the introduction of resistant worms onto a farm.

Optimal application Dosing to achieve maximal effect; e g before lambing and prior to weaning, rather than random dosing will limit the need for frequent treatments. Monitoring the effect of dosing by performing faecal egg counts will identify resistance and prevent unnecessary treatments.

Pasture management Practise camp management by rotating camps to reduce the survival of worm larvae. Reduce the egg loads on pastures with pre-lambing dosing. Cattle and older small stock can be used to reduce the level of infestation on pastures.

In refugia Worm experts recommend that stock should not be dosed when the larvae are absent from pastures; in other words, the entire worm population is inside the animal, since a large population of worms are being treated and therefore being selected for resistance. It's preferable to

dose when the larvae are present on the pasture (in refugia), which is during the rainy season. This leaves a portion of the worm population untreated and therefore non-resistant. The old practice of dosing and then placing animals on clean pastures should therefore be discontinued, as this promotes the survival of resistant worms only. Consult a veterinarian about the timing of dosing to ensure that dosing programmes address this issue.

FAMACHA© This system identifies animals that need treatment for the wire worm (*Haemonchus contortus*) rather than dosing every animal. The system uses a colour card to measure the colour of the mucous membrane of the eyes and therefore the degree of anaemia. Depending on the colour of the mucous membrane, the farmer will know whether to dose for wireworm or not.

The advantage of this system is that fewer animals need to be treated; some animals are most resistant to the effects of wire worm, since resistance in small stock to worm infestation and resilience (the ability to withstand the effects of parasites) have been shown to be moderately heritable. This means that sheep and goats can be either culled or selected for these traits.

The process of inspecting the eyes is quick and can readily be integrated into other activities like vaccination, weighing, condition scoring or counting. On average, up to 250 sheep can be inspected per hour, with practice and good facilities. A significant drop in the amount and frequency of deworming can be expected for the majority of the flock. Because fewer animals are treated, the development of resistance in worm populations will be slowed down. In the long term, elimination of non-resistant animals will allow for the breeding of better adapted animals.

Note that the FAMACHA© system is only applicable to the control of wire worm, so farms having other worm problems will need to implement other control measures. The FAMACHA© system is just one component of a good management programme and cannot be used on its own. A good, integrated control programme using smart drenching principles has still to be used.

Ineffective dosing

It is important not to confuse resistance with ineffective dosing. Ineffective dosing can occur due to a number of factors: Wrong remedy for the specific worm (check on the label), incorrect dose, some animals were untreated, animals were able to spit out the drench (poor dosing technique), faulty calibration of the drenching gun, the drench had expired or had a batch problem.

DOSING PROGRAMMES

The emphasis, for modern farming, has shifted from the straightforward control of worms to sustainable control that addresses the problem of the effects of worms on stock and at the same time preventing resistance. This is done by drawing up a programme for a specific farm, in consultation with a veterinarian. The important steps for such a programme will be to:

- Identify which worms are a problem in the area; this can be done by examining faecal or intestinal samples
- Select a suitable remedy (on farms where there is resistance, this will be very important and will need a FECRT, if possible)
- Identify other internal parasites which need to be controlled (e g fluke, nasal worm, tapeworms) and integrate them
- Integrate the internal parasite control programme with the production cycle eg treating ewes before lambing to reduce massive egg-shedding by wire worm
- Dose during the rainy season when worms are in refugia (larvae present on pasture)
- Prevent resistance, as discussed above, by quarantine dosing, good dosing practice and camp management.

TABLE 7. Example of dosing programme according to breeding cycle

GROUP	TIME	PARASITE
Rams	4 – 6 weeks before mating	Round- and tapeworms
Ewes	2 – 3 weeks before lambing	Round- and tapeworms
	30 days after lambing	Round- and tapeworms
Lambs	30 days after birth	Round- and tapeworms
	60 days after birth	Round- and tapeworms
	Weaning	Round- and tapeworms
	2 weeks before marketing	Roundworms and nasal worms

TAPEWORMS

Tapeworms are economically important in small stock, not only because of their effect on the animals but also because they have a public health implication. The adult tapeworm has a flattened, segmented, ribbon-like body which can vary in length depending on the species (from 1mm to 2m long). The head has suckers and hooks which help it attach to the host's intestine. The tapeworm has no digestive system but absorbs food through its body wall by diffusion.

Tapeworms have an indirect life cycle, which means they have two hosts, a temporary host in which the larva or cyst waits in a resting phase or cyst, and the final or definitive host in which the adult tapeworm develops. The general life cycle remains the same for most tapeworm species, but the intermediate and final hosts differ. The tapeworm sheds segments containing fertilised eggs, which can sometimes be seen in the faeces of the final host. When these egg-containing segments are ingested by an intermediate host, the embryo hatches and penetrates the intestinal wall. It is carried by the bloodstream to the tissues of the intermediate host for which it has an affinity (muscle, liver, brain). When this cyst or larval form − which occurs in the intermediate host − is eaten by the final or definitive host, it develops into the adult tapeworm in the host's intestine.

It's helpful to divide tapeworms of veterinary importance into two broad groups according to their final hosts: in small stock, the two important categories are ruminant and carnivore tapeworms.

Ruminant tapeworms (*Moniezia* spp)

The adult tapeworm of ruminants is found in the intestine of sheep, goats or cattle. Livestock pick up the infection when grazing, by ingesting a soil mite or a small louse; both these creatures are common in the soil or on the grazing in many areas. The mite or louse contains the larval or cyst stage of the tapeworm which then develops into a tapeworm once in the gut of the ruminant. Here it grows, increasing its segments, and eggs are then shed onto

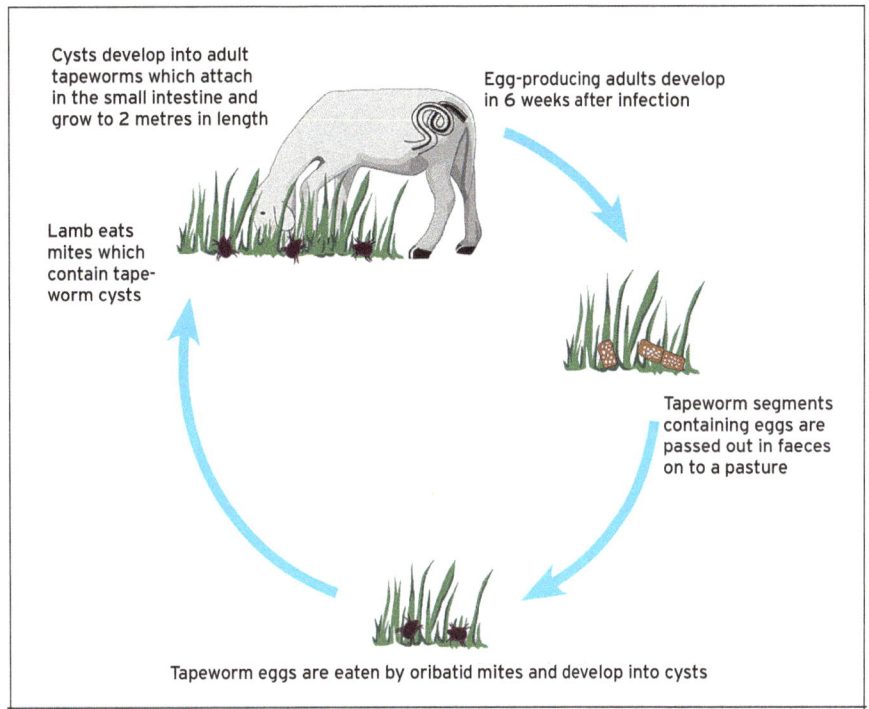

Life cycle of the ruminant tapeworm

Cysts develop into adult tapeworms which attach in the small intestine and grow to 2 metres in length

Egg-producing adults develop in 6 weeks after infection

Lamb eats mites which contain tapeworm cysts

Tapeworm segments containing eggs are passed out in faeces on to a pasture

Tapeworm eggs are eaten by oribatid mites and develop into cysts

The ruminant tapeworm *Moniezia* in the small intestine

pasture via the faeces. The soil mites or lice then become infected by eating the tapeworm eggs, released from the segments and so perpetuate the life cycle.

Moniezia tapeworms affect their hosts, especially young animals, because they compete for nutrition. Lambs become infested when they begin grazing and heavy

infestations retard their growth; they become pot-bellied, develop diarrhoea, may develop pneumonia and may even die. Occasionally, pregnant ewes on poor winter grazing die if they are heavily infested.

Ruminant tapeworms are widespread, but their presence in stock is seldom diagnosed unless clinical signs are seen or they are seen in the intestine on post-mortem. Dosing lambs or kids at critical times can prevent the adverse effects on growth. The most economical tapeworm remedies for small stock are those containing niclosamide and resorantel. On farms where niclosamide resistance is seen, remedies containing praziquantel should be used.

Carnivore tapeworms (*Taenia multiceps, Taenia hydatidgena, Taenia ovis, Echinococcus* spp)

Adult carnivore tapeworms occur in wild or domestic dogs and cats. The carnivores become infested when they eat the tissues of cattle, sheep or goats in which the larval forms occur.

These larval forms usually resemble bladder-like cysts. Herbivores become infected by ingesting the tapeworm eggs on pastures where dogs have defecated. Depending on the species of tapeworm, the cyst may be found in the brain, liver or lungs.

The larval cysts of *Taenia multiceps*, which occur in the brain of sheep, become large fluid-filled sacs and their presence gives rise to the condition called gid (malkopsiekte/draaisiekte, see Nervous conditions, page 54-55).

The cysts become so large that they affect brain function and, if large enough, they erode the bone of the skull by pressure necrosis. Humans, although not the usual intermediate hosts, can become accidentally infected, with serious consequences.

Taenia hydatigena cysts are found in the liver and lungs of small stock and other species at slaughter, and lead to the condemnation of these organs in abattoirs. Echinococcus granulosus cysts occur in the liver, lungs and brains of a number of species, including humans who develop hydatid disease. The most serious form is the infestation of the brain in which the

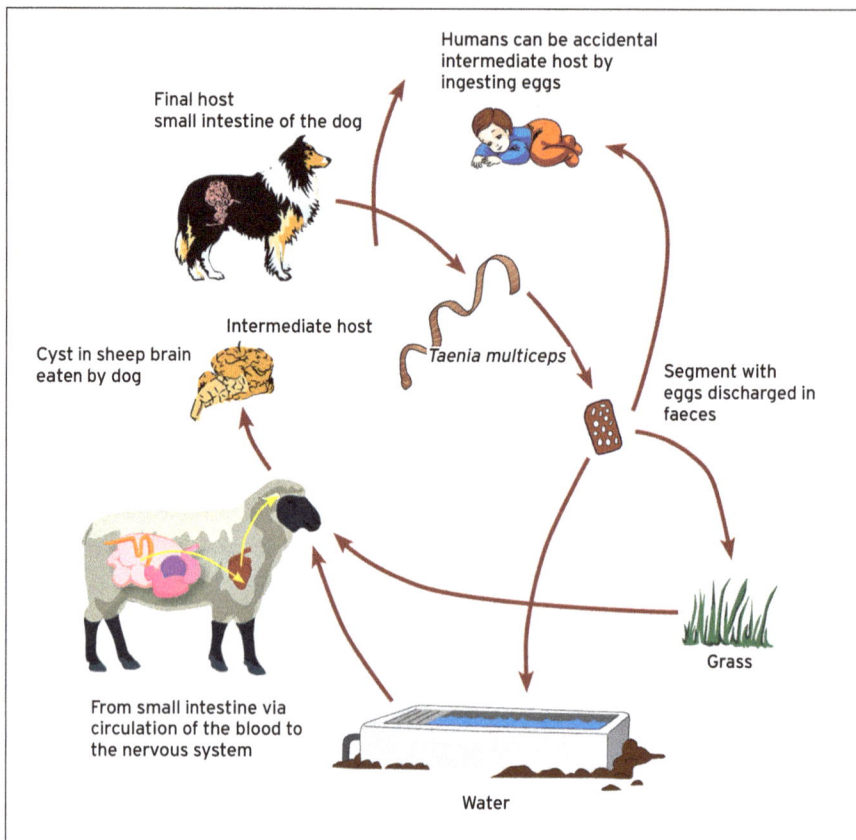

Life cycle of a carnivore tapeworm

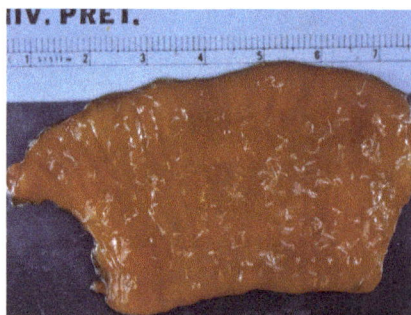

***Echinococcus* tapeworm in the gut of a canine**

***Taenia multiceps* cysts in the brain of a sheep**

cysts cause nervous symptoms and, occasionally, death.

On farms where carnivore tapeworms are identified as a cause of problems in small stock, all domestic dogs have to be dosed at three-monthly intervals, using a dewormer containing praziquantel (this is also available in combination with roundworm remedies). The dogs should not be fed raw offal, as this will reinfect them. Little can be done to control the disease if wild carnivores are the source of infestation.

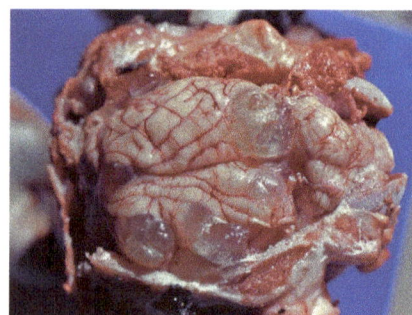

***Echinococcus* cysts in the liver of a sheep**

4

INTERNAL PARASITES

FLUKES

This group includes the liver flukes, conical flukes and bilharzia parasites. They all have an indirect life cycle, with various water snails as the intermediate hosts, and the final hosts being cattle, sheep or goats.

Fasciola hepatica (Liver fluke)
Fasciola gigantica (Giant liver fluke)

Adult liver flukes have a flattened leaf-like appearance. *F hepatica* grows up to 30mm in length, and *F gigantica* is considerably larger; the mature adults reaching 75mm. Liver flukes need wet conditions to survive because their intermediate hosts are small aquatic water snails (*Lymnaea* spp). These snails can live in permanent or semi-permanent water, either in dams, vleis or continually leaking troughs.

Animals become infected by the infective forms or cercariae, which are shed by the water snails. The cercariae swim through water searching for blades of grass onto which they climb and where they form resistant cysts while waiting for a passing host. If they're eaten by grazing animals, the cysts open once in contact with the gastric acid and release the young liver flukes, which penetrate the gut and migrate to the liver. These flukes then move through the liver tissue seeking out the bile ducts. The adult flukes lodge in the bile ducts where they suck blood. Female adult liver flukes lay eggs which are passed out via the bile into the faeces. The eggs hatch into a form called miracidium, which infects the water snail, completing the life cycle. The life cycle takes about three months to complete but can take considerably longer, depending on factors such as immunity of the host, degree of infestation as well as weather conditions.

Liver flukes cause scarring of the liver from the damage caused during their migration and the bile ducts become thickened, but heavy infestations can cause fatal haemorrhages in the liver. Sub-acute and chronic liver fluke infestation causes loss of condition, anaemia and bottlejaw. Sheep are more severely affected than cattle and rarely develop immunity.

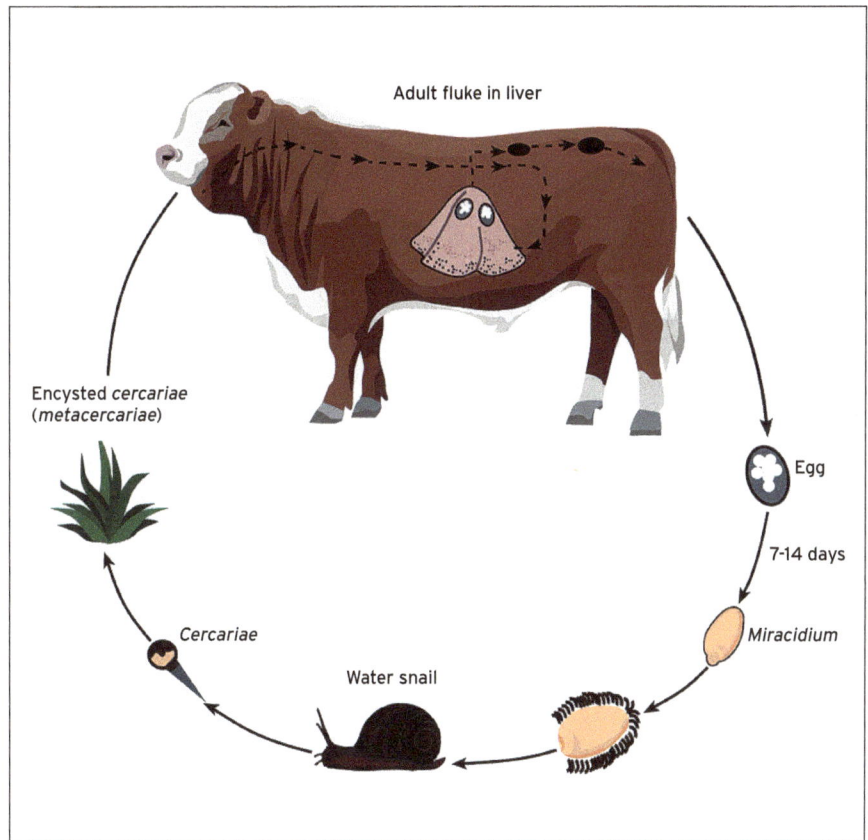

Life cycle of a fluke

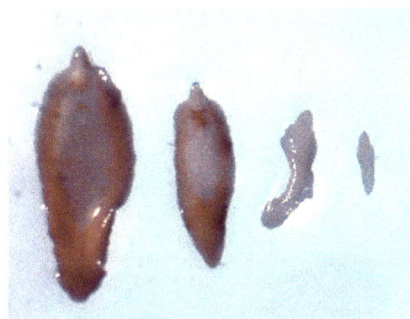

Liver flukes of various ages

Liver flukes in the liver

Although liver fluke eggs can be seen in faecal egg samples, the diagnosis of infestation is usually made when animals begin to show the symptoms described above, or deaths occur. Finding liver flukes or the damage they cause in the liver will confirm the diagnosis. Animals infested with liver flukes have to be dosed with one of the remedies registered for use (see **Table 8**, page 90).

Control

Integrated pasture management and an-

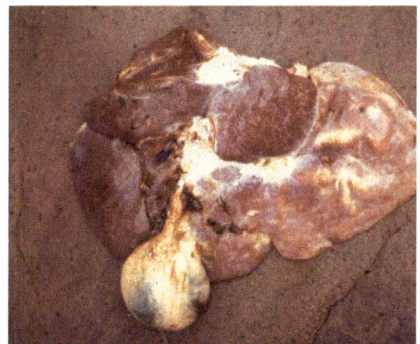

Fibrosis of the liver caused by liver flukes

thelmintic administration give the best control. Avoid grazing animals on infested pastures, if possible, and fence them off to prevent access. Snail control using molluscicides is not a long-term solution, as snails are easily reintroduced. Prevent the introduction of flukes onto farms where water snails may be present by treating newly introduced animals before they are turned out to pasture. Select the correct remedy for the problem (liver or conical).

To prevent liver fluke infestation when it cannot be avoided, it is important to use fluke remedies most effectively by considering the liver fluke life cycle:

The freshwater snails which are the reservoirs of liver fluke infestations are only active from late spring until the beginning of autumn. In winter, when the minimum temperature is below 10°C, these snails hide in the mud. During that time no infective cercariae are present. Once the temperature rises and the rains begin, the snails emerge again and can get infected with miracidia from stock infested with adult flukes from the previous year. After one month the infected snails start shedding cercariae which can infect grazing animals again.

To break the cycle and avoid a dramatic multiplication of the fluke population in the summer season, it is critical to treat the animals strategically when the intermediate host isn't active. There are two specific times when strategic treatment is practical:
- In autumn or early winter, about two weeks after the minimum temperature has dropped below 10°C
- The late winter treatment, just before the first rains. The selection of a suitable anthelmintic with the right spectrum of activity is crucial. Most fluke remedies (flukicides) are only effective against adult flukes, which is suitable for the late winter treatment. For strategic treatment in autumn and, more importantly, for any tactical treatment during summer a flukicide that can kill young liver flukes is needed.

Calicophoron (Paramphistomum) microbothrium (Conical fluke)

Conical flukes like liver flukes occur in wet areas where fresh water snails occur. However, conical fluke infestation is less common than liver fluke infestation.

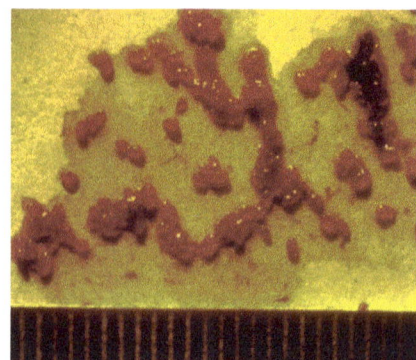

Conical flukes

Adult conical flukes are 5 – 13mm long and have a sucker with which they attach to the rumen mucosa. The flukes are pink in colour and the body is fleshier than that of the liver fluke, assuming a cone shape.

The life cycle of the conical fluke is similar to that of the liver fluke. Animals pick up conical fluke infestation from grazing on grass contaminated with cercarieae. Immature conical flukes, which are found in the first part of the small intestine, look like pink or white rice grains. These stages are responsible for most of the damage and the clinical effects. The immature conical flukes attach to the small intestine

TABLE 8. Remedies available for fluke control

REMEDY	LIVER FLUKE		CONICAL FLUKE	
	Immatures	Adults	Immatures	Adults
Closantel	-	X	X	-
Rafoxanide	-	X	-	-
Triclabendazole	X	X	-	-
Resorantel	-	-	X	X
Oxyclozanide	-	X	X	-
Albendazole	-	X	-	-
Niclosamide	-	-	X	-
X: controls (higher than 90% effective)				

by grasping a plug of mucosa. The swelling and strangulation of tissue causes severe discomfort and loss of appetite, resulting in progressive weight loss. Foul-smelling diarrhoea may occur due to the decomposition of intestinal contents. Massive infestation can cause swelling of the head or bottlejaw and death may occur. Adult flukes in the rumen, on the other hand, are well tolerated. Sheep are more severely affected than cattle.

When the condition is diagnosed, usually on post-mortem or when the eggs are detected in faecal samples, a suitable remedy must be selected. Conical fluke infestation can occur during winter and animals should be removed from infested pasture during this time. Treat outbreaks with remedies containing resorantel or oxyclozanide.

Schistosoma mattheei (Bilharzia worms)

Bilharzia infestation of livestock is not very common in South Africa and seems confined to warm, moist sub-tropical areas such as Mpumalanga.

The small (6 – 22mm), whitish male bilharzia worms have a thin groove in their bodies in which the long black female worm lives. Schistosomes have an indirect life cycle with various water snail species serving as intermediate hosts. The cercaria shed by the snails infect hosts by penetrating the skin when the host enters water. After penetrating the skin the young schistosome migrates to the lungs where it enters the bloodstream and travels to the liver, finally entering the mesenteric blood vessels which drain the small intestine. The worms live off the blood of the host, laying eggs which migrate out into the faeces by penetrating the intestinal wall.

Bilharzia parasites cause a number of syndromes in their host due to the progression of the life cycle. The presence of the worm in the blood vessel can cause inflammation of veins and those that die off are carried to the liver where they may cause thrombi. A typical sign of bilharzia

Typical grey lungs seen in bilharzia cases in small stock

in sheep is grey lungs, which are seen at post-mortem. The greatest damage is done by the eggs on their migration out of the blood vessels, when they cause severe irritation of the tissues. Sheep are more severely affected than cattle and show loss of weight, sunken eyes, diarrhoea and eventually death. If bilharzia infestation is identified on a property, a veterinarian must be contacted to advise on control.

NOTES

NOTES

5

External PARASITES

External parasites and their control

THE PARASITES

External parasites are the cause of millions of rands worth of losses to the small stock industry in southern Africa. The chief culprits are the parasites that damage fleece and cause loss of condition. In addition, there are external parasites that cause wounds, irritation and transmit infectious diseases which can be fatal. Chemical control is still the farmer's main weapon against external parasites, but the emergence of resistance in lice and blowflies has caused researchers to look more closely at additional factors such as management and alternative methods of control.

The public concern about residues in meat and environmental concerns about residues in wool will force farmers to minimise chemical use for certain markets. Judicious, minimal use of chemicals should be employed where possible to lengthen the useful life of available products since very few new products have emerged onto the market in the past two decades.

This section addresses, in sequence, the external parasites, the chemicals used for their control and the methods of application. Under external parasites reference is made to the chemicals and control methods so the reader may need to refer to the subsection on these later in the chapter.

Stages of the tick lifecycle

Engorged female tick laying eggs

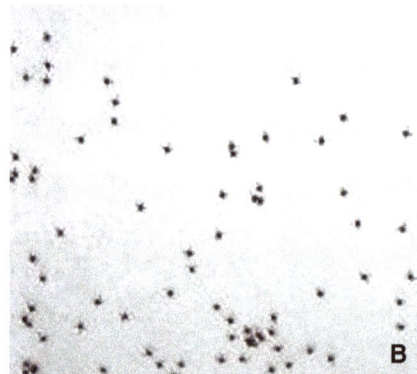

Tick larvae

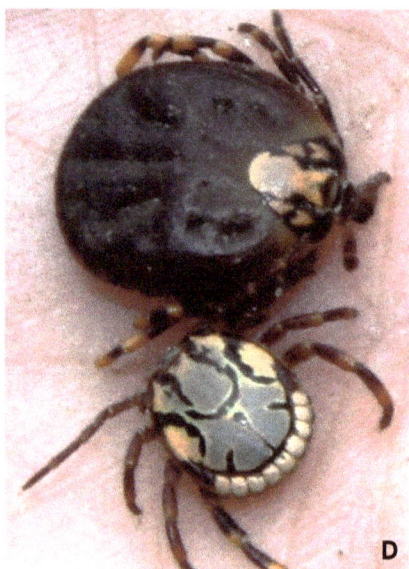

Adult ticks

Tick nymph

TICKS

Adult ticks are eight-legged, bloodsucking parasites related to mites, that have a fairly uncomplicated life cycle. When they hatch from eggs laid by the female they are tiny six-legged larvae, often referred to as pepper ticks or seed ticks.

They climb up grass stalks and sit there, waiting for a host. When a host brushes past, the tick climbs onto it and attaches at a preferred site on the body, where they feed by sucking blood. After their first feed on the host, larvae moult and become nymphae, slightly larger than larvae but having eight legs like adult ticks.

These, in turn, feed and moult to become adults. Adults then mate and the females engorge on a host and drop off to lay their sometimes massive (up to 20 000) numbers of eggs.

There are many tick species in South Africa but only a small percentage of these are found on small stock. Ticks are difficult to identify because the different stages of the life cycle of the varous species look very similar, even the engorged females. The distribution of tick species is determined by climate and rainfall, so most are limited to a certain area. Each species also

has a preferred site of attachment. Armed with this information, the farmer will be able to decide which tick species will be problematic on the farm.

The ticks that occur on small stock are two- or three-host ticks of which the immature stages feed on a variety of birds and wild animals. Adult and immature ticks may be found on small stock depending on the species.

Bont tick (*Amblyomma hebraeum*)
Important hosts Immature bont ticks are found on small game, sheep, goats and

TABLE 9. Important ticks of small stock

COMMON NAME	SCIENTIFIC NAME	DISEASE/ DAMAGE
Bont tick	*Amblyomma hebraeum*	Heartwater in sheep and goats Wounds, abscesses with secondary screw worm strike
Red-legged ticks	*Rhipecephalus evertsi*	Spring lamb paralysis
Foot ticks	*Rhipicephalus* species	Lameness Foot abscess
Brown paralysis tick	*Rhip warburtoni*	Angora goat paralysis
Bont-legged tick	*Hyalomma* spp	Lameness Abscesses
Karoo paralysis tick	*Ixodes rubicundus*	Tick paralysis
Sand tampan	*Ornithodoros savignyi*	Anaemia Toxicosis

cattle. Adult ticks tend to feed on large game, and cattle.

Distribution Bont ticks occur in the eastern parts of the country where the rainfall and the mean temperature are higher. The distribution of this tick extends from the Limpopo bushveld down the eastern coastal areas as far as Port Elizabeth and Mossel Bay. The bont tick needs the shelter of trees and bushes and so is absent from open grassland.

Description The males have the characteristic bont or coloured patterns on their shields or scutums (see photograph). The females are large, dull mustard colour ticks, with a patterned scutum which becomes more difficult to see once the female has engorged. Both males and female adult ticks have very long mouth parts and orange and brown-banded legs.

Life cycle The bont tick is a three-host tick with a long life cycle which can take from five months to three years to complete. The females lay as many as 18 000 eggs.

Season The larvae which occur on small mammals are active in late summer to autumn, with a peak in spring, the nymphae in winter and spring and the adults predominate in summer. However, in wet coastal areas, all three stages may be found together at any time of the year.

Site of attachment On sheep, the adults attach to the groin, armpit, sternum and peri-anal area. Goats tend to have adults on the underline and groin, with nymphae on the feet and legs, and larvae on the feet, legs and ears.

Importance Bont tick nymphae and adults are important as transmitters of *Erlichia* (*Cowdria*) *ruminantium*, the organism that causes heartwater. Their long mouth parts cause damage to hides and also abscesses. Adults tend to cluster in groups and can therefore cause serious damage to udders, teats and sheath of the penis. The wounds they cause are often secondarily infested with screw worm. Bont ticks transmit *Rickettsiae conori*, the organism that causes tick-bite fever in humans.

Control When bringing susceptible small stock into heartwater areas, bellybathing should be done with dips containing diazinon, deltamethrin or liquid formulations of amitraz, weekly for the first three weeks. For sustained control, dipping can be done every two to four weeks in summer. The dipping intervals can be extended in winter if tick challenge is low (for more detailed discussion see Heartwater, page 55-56). Bellybathing also controls wounds

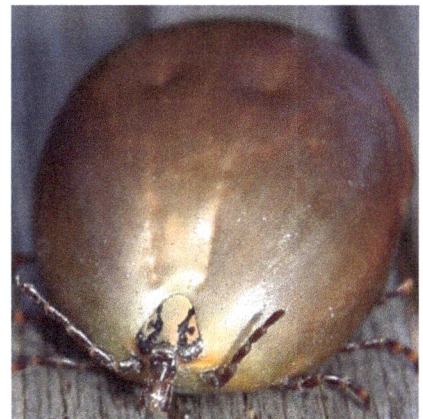

Amblyomma tick

and abscesses caused by the long mouthparts of the ticks.

Brown ticks

This group contains ticks of the genus *Rhipicephalus* – the red-legged tick, the brown paralysis tick and the glossy brown tick.

Red-legged tick
(*Rhipicephalus evertsi*)

Important hosts Cattle, horses, sheep and goats

Distribution The tick occurs in eastern

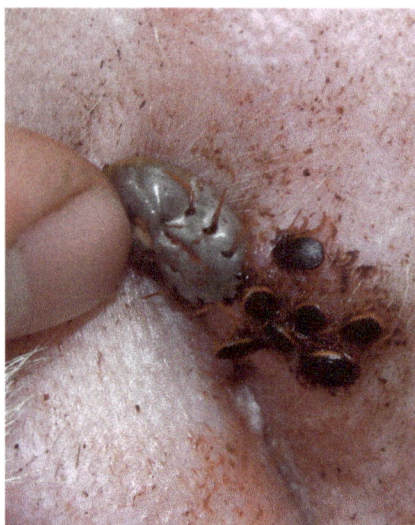

Red-legged ticks clustering around the anus

parts of the country.

Description This is a glossy brown tick but its red legs are a clear diagnostic feature. It has a thin red band along the rim of the body.

Life cycle These are two-host ticks.

Season The ticks are numerous during wet seasons.

Site of attachment Larvae and nymphae are found deep in the ear canal; the adults are seen around the anus.

Importance When there is a large population of these ticks, cases of spring lamb paralysis will be seen in young lambs.

Control When cases of spring lamb paralysis are seen, dipping of all animals should be done to reduce tick numbers. Plunge-dipping with amitraz, pyrethoid (deltamethrin) or organophosphate will control tick numbers. Patch treatment of ears and under the tail might be necessary if there was insufficient wetting to control infestations. Lambs with paralysis must be treated with amitraz which will cause rapid detachment.

Foot/claw ticks (*Rhipicephalus* spp)

Various *Rhipicephalus* tick species in different parts of the country have been shown to attach to the legs and between the claws of small stock.

Distribution

Rhipicephalus simus Eastern Cape
Rhipicephalus glabroscutatum southeast areas of the Eastern Cape

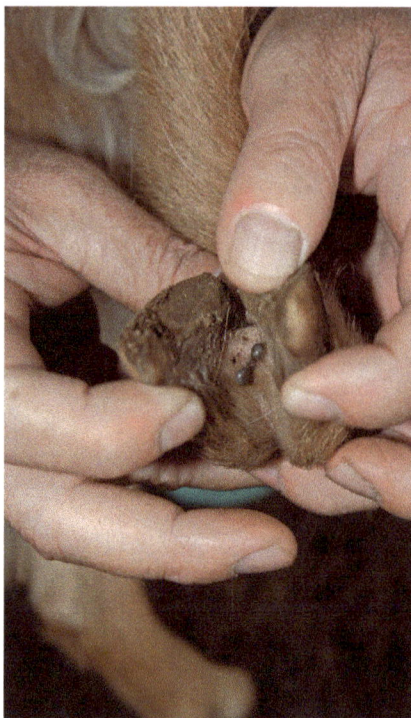

Certain tick species attach between the claws of the foot in small stock

Rhipicephalus lounsburyi the Eastern Cape, certain areas of KZN, the Swellendam area near the Bontebok Park and the Calvinia area in the Northern Cape.

Importance These ticks attach to the legs and in between the claws of small stock, initially causing acute lameness. The wounds caused by the tick bites may give entry to *Arcanobactreium* bacteria. These bacteria initially cause local swelling of the skin between the claws but then spread and lodge in the joints causing septic arthritis. The condition causes severe lameness, and eventually loss of weight. It is difficult to treat with antibiotics once the infection has become lodged in the joints.

Control Frequent dipping using foot-baths or applying pour-on remedies to the feet will control the problems caused by this tick and *Hyalomma* ticks which also attach to the feet.

Brown paralysis tick (*Rhipicephalus warburtoni*)

Hosts Adult ticks infest Angora goats
Distribution The ticks are confined to the Free State, the Northern Cape and the Barkly East area.

Life cycle These are three-host ticks. The immature stages are found on elephant shrews and all stages can be found on hares. The adults are also found on Angora goats.

Site of attachment The adult ticks creep into the ears of goat kids while they lie flat in the bush, resulting in heavy infestations. They also occur on adult Angoras, on the head, neck and brisket.

Importance These ticks cause heavy losses of Angora kids from paralysis. The goats may die in spite of the ticks being removed.

Control Treat heavily infested goat kids with amitraz dip to facilatute rapid detachment. Prevent cases during the danger period of September to February, by spot treatment with sprays or pour-on tick remedies, on head and ears to prevent attachment of these ticks.

Bont-legged ticks (*Hyalomma marginatum rufipes, H truncatum*)

Important hosts Cattle, sheep, goats and wildlife.

Distribution This is a tick of drier areas and other areas too, except in the winter rainfall areas and high-lying areas where snow falls during winter.

Description These ticks are medium to large, shiny brown with long mouthparts; they have banded red and white legs.

Life cycle The two-host life cycle takes a year to complete.

Season The larvae and nymphs are numerous during dry winters and the adults

Hyalomma **(bont-legged) tick**

during wetter summers.

Site of attachment These ticks attach around the anus but also along the underline, between the hooves and on the tip of the tail.

Importance The long mouthparts of this tick cause serious wounds which give rise to abscesses such as spinal abscesses in lambs, hypophyseal abscesses (goats) or foot abscesses. The tick wounds are sometimes secondarily infested by screw worm.

Control Bellybathing or footbaths can be used, depending on the type of abscess problems.

Karoo paralysis tick
(Ixodes rubicundus)

Important hosts Sheep and goats (antelope, elephant shrews and red hares).

Distribution This tick occurs sporadically in the Western Cape, widely in central and south-east Free State, sporadically in the Eastern Cape in the Queenstown area, with foci in Mpumalanga. The tick occurs where specific unpalatable vegetation grows, namely besembos (*Rhus erosa*) and tussocky grass or suurpolgras (*Danthonia disticha*) which occur on the southern slopes of mountainous areas. The vegetation serves as a shelter for red hares and elephant shrews, intermediate hosts of the immature ticks. Distribution has expanded due to overgrazing of farms which results in invasion of this unpalatable vegetation.

Description The ticks are small, reddish-brown, shiny and eyeless, with legs set far forward.

Life cycle This is a three-host tick with a two-year life cycle.

Season The adults begin to feed in late summer, usually after the first sudden cold, rain or snow, from February until May or June.

Site of attachment The ticks attach along the underline, on the neck, the legs and sometimes the cheeks and the lower jaw.

Importance Once the adult ticks begin feeding, a toxin in the saliva causes paralysis of varying severity, from slight lameness to total paralysis. One tick is sufficient to cause paralysis. Large numbers of animals can be affected during outbreaks. Affected animals will recover within 24 – 48 hours if the ticks are removed quickly enough.

Control If possible, remove animals from hill camps, especially the southern slopes from February until the danger period passes at the end of June. Otherwise, prevent attachment by using tick remedies registered for Karoo paralysis tick control. These can be administered in a bellybath or using pour-on remedies applied to the axillae (armpits). Note that only water-based pour-on remedies are suitable for woolled sheep and Angora goats. Most

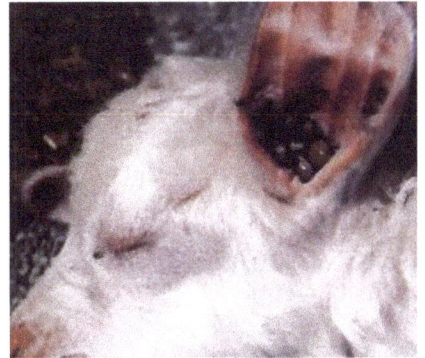

Rhip warburtoni causes paralysis in Angora kids

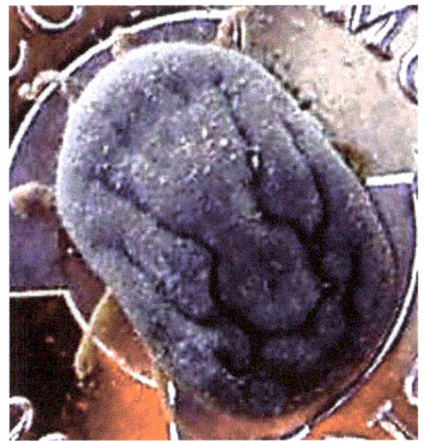

An example of a tampan

remedies have a longer residual action on wool sheep than on hairy sheep or goats.

Sand tampan
(Ornithodoros savignyi)

Hosts Sheep and goats (and humans).

Distribution Sand tampans occur in arid areas of the country such as the Kalahari.

Description Tampans belong to the group referred to as the soft-bodied ticks; these are ticks that have no scutum (the hard shield-like part behind the head). The legs are typically bent forward into little hooks. Unengorged tampans have a flat, wrinkled appearance.

Life cycle Sand tampans lay their eggs in the soil. These hatch into non-motile larvae which never feed but merely moult into nymphae, which in turn pass through several nymphal stages before becoming adults. These adults stay buried under the soil in the shade of trees, bushes or rocks and avoid sunlit places. However, they im-

A case of karoo paralysis in a sheep

mediately detect the carbon dioxide given off by resting animals or humans and they emerge to attach to these hosts. Sand tampans can literally survive for years without a meal but when they attach on an animals they feed rapidly, engorging within 20 minutes.

Season Sand tampans are most active in summer, especially during dry weather.

Site of attachment Tampans attach to any part of the body but especially the legs; they are commonly found around the hooves.

Importance The bites are painful and the tampans secrete a toxin in the saliva which can kill animals, especially young animals, with heavy infestations.

Control Weekly dipping or dipping every two weeks depending on the dip being used. However, chemical control may is not as effective as for ticks because the tampans feed so rapidly. It is also impractical to spray infested soil because of the wide areas that need to be treated. Bantams and ground birds are said to eat large quantities of tampans and are therefore considered useful for reducing tampan numbers.

NOTES

_____
_____
_____
_____
_____
_____
_____
_____
_____
_____
_____
_____
_____
_____
_____
_____
_____
_____
_____
_____
_____
_____
_____
_____
_____
_____
_____

5

EXTERNAL PARASITES

MITES

These small parasites have eight legs and are closely related to ticks. The largest of these parasites are 2mm long, which makes them difficult to see with the naked eye. They are permanent parasites that are only able to live for short periods off their hosts.

All mites are species-specific (adapted to a specific host species), with the exception of the Sarcoptes mite which is found on a wide species range including on humans, in whom it causes scabies. The life cycle of the mite takes roughly 14 days to complete, from the hatching from the egg to the maturing of the eight-legged adult. Mites are spread by contact between animals and also for short periods on inanimate objects.

The parasites feed on skin particles and serum, causing skin damage and inflammation (dermatitis). This gives rise to irritation, often with severe itching; animals rub the skin lesions against objects and sheep pluck vigorously at the wool, causing fleece disturbance. The mite lesions usually start as small focal areas but if the condition progresses untreated, these can become extensive. Mite infestations can be confirmed by examining hair/wool and skin scrapings microscopically.

Sheep scab (Psoroptes ovis)

Sheep scab is caused by the infestation of sheep with the mite *Psoroptes communis* ovis. It is regarded as the biggest threat to the wool industry in South Africa. The insidious nature of the infestation results from its slow and almost unnoticed initial spreading, which prevents its being noticed in the early stages. The irreversible damage done to the fleece and the dramatic effect on the overall condition of the animal lead to great economic losses. Because wool is such an important export commodity for the country it is important that outbreaks be declared and it is therefore a notifiable disease.

The sheep scab mite (*Psoroptes communis ovis*) is so small that it's almost invisible to the naked eye. The mite is a specific parasite of sheep, although it can be carried for short periods on the hair of

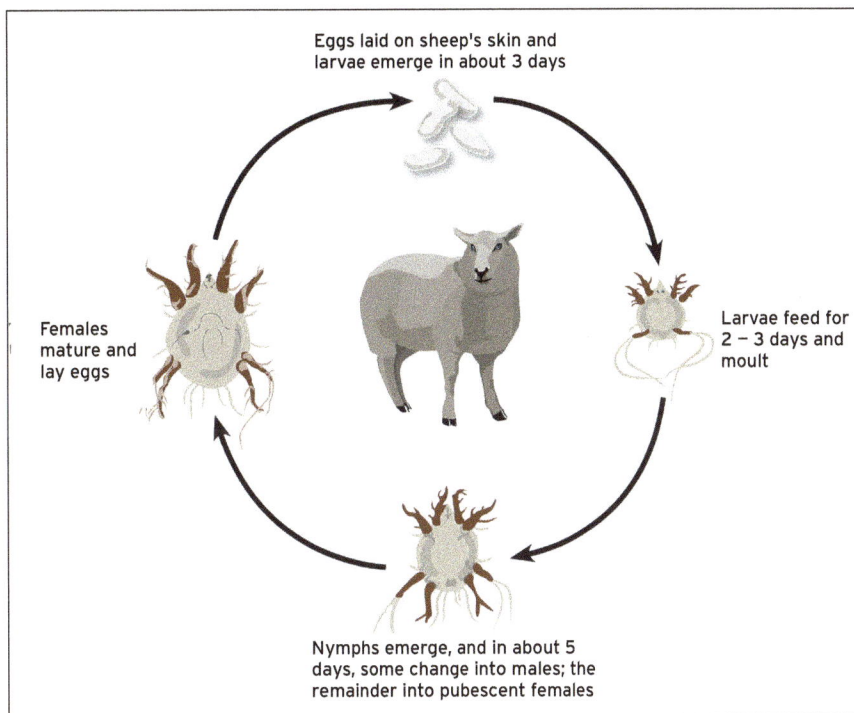

Life cycle of sheep scab mite

goats, as well as on clothing and implements. It can infest all sheep of any breed or age.

The sheep scab mite can only be identified by microscopic examination to distinguish it from other infestations, such as Australian itch mite, although there are some characteristic features of ectoparasites of the skin which can be used in absence of veterinary or laboratory help (see **Table 10** on page 101).

The sheep scab mite has impressive reproductive abilities: The female can lay eggs from the age of nine days. After mating, she lays eggs on the skin and these hatch within two to three days. Within three days, the larvae moult to become nymphs and six days later these become adult mites. The life cycle is therefore completed within 11 days.

The adult mite feeds on the sheep by piercing skin and feeding on the serum which seeps from the small wounds. The bites cause severe irritation and inflammation and after four days, scabs develop. The lesions enlarge by 2,5cm per month and the parasites move outwards to the edges.

The most common method of transmis-

sion is direct contact with infested sheep, but the mites can be transmitted over a period of 13 days by pieces of wool, overalls, implements, camps and vehicles. Outbreaks are usually noticed in winter, but sheep can have invisible infection during summer.

In hot weather, the mites creep away into places like the "ou oog", the armpit, and the base of the horn. In fat-tailed sheep, they hide in the folds of the tail. Infected sheep show signs of scratching, biting and plucking at the wool. They lose weight from the constant irritation; rams won't mate and ewes may refuse to feed their lambs due to their discomfort.

The diagnosis must be confirmed by a veterinarian identifying the parasite microscopically. This is important because it is a notifiable disease and can also be confused with other conditions. If a diagnosis of sheep scab is suspected, the outbreak must be reported to the nearest state veterinarian. The farm is immediately placed under quarantine, which means small stock may not be removed from the farm.

Sheep scab has spread in SA because of a number of factors, including itinerant

sheep shearers who don't practise good hygiene spreading the infestation, holding of sheep in auction yards, the use of under-strength dips, and extensive farming which makes regular dipping difficult. Lack of or ineffective fencing promotes the spread of the condition.

When sheep scab outbreaks are confirmed, all small stock on the farm have to be treated twice with remedies registered for sheep scab at an interval of eight to 10 days. There are various approved methods and remedies:

Dipping

The only acceptable dipping method for sheep scab control is plunge dipping, which allows for effective wetting of the whole animal.

Registered dips for sheep scab include the organophosphate diazinon, and deltamethrin (the only effective pyrethroid for scab). Amitraz-containing dips are very effective but has to be made up at a higher concentration than the dilution used for tick control. The animal must be submerged for 60 seconds, and the head submerged three times to ensure total wetting.

The dip must be correctly diluted and the replenishment calculated carefully. Constant replenishment is the most effective method of maintaining the concentration. Dipping must be repeated eight to 10 days later because not all dips kill the mite's eggs.

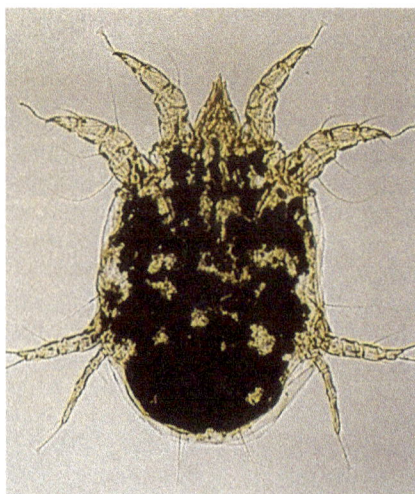

The sheep scab mite

A case of sheep scab

Injection

Injection with macrocyclic lactones (ivermectin, moxidectin, doramectin) is effective against sheep scab at the recommended dose and is a very convenient means of treatment. To be effective, all animals must be treated and the correct dose per weight must be given. All animals have to be treated twice with an interval of eight to 10 days, unless stated otherwise on the label.

The accuracy of automatic syringes is extremely important and should be checked before treating the flock. Not all injectable MLs are suitable for use on goats, so this must also be checked on the label.

Prevention

Because sheep scab mites are permanent parasites, prevention on the farm is very simple: It requires a single annual dipping or injection of sheep one month after shearing. Dipping has the advantage of controlling other infestations such as red or blue lice, sheep keds and itch mites. Newly introduced sheep should be given two treatments at an eight- to 10-day interval before being introduced to the rest of the flock. Visiting shearers should get clean overalls and must disinfect shearing equipment. Keep stray sheep off the

property by ensuring fences are in good condition.

Australian itch mite (*Psorogates ovis*)

This condition is a lot less common in South Africa than sheep scab but causes similar symptoms of itching, wool plucking and fleece disturbance. These mites are less numerous than sheep scab mites and a number of deep skin scrapings may be needed to find the parasite. This is not a notifiable condition. Treatment and prevention are as for sheep scab.

Scabies Sarcoptes infection

Sheep occasionally develop *Sarcoptes* infestations which cause severe itching, and can be transferred to humans and other animals. The mites are usually found on the face and head. Diagnosis and treatment are as for sheep scab.

Sheep scab and mange in goats

Although sheep scab mites can survive on goats for short periods, these animals are not permanent carriers. They do, however, suffer infestations of goat mange caused by *Sarcoptes* and *Psoroptes* which infest their ears, and *Chorioptes* which occur on the legs and fetlocks. Their control is as for sheep scab.

TABLE 10. Field guide to differentiating between skin infestations in small stock

SIGNS	SHEEP SCAB	AUSTRALIAN ITCH MITE	RED LICE	BLUE LICE
Itching	Intense	Yes	Yes	yes
Wool plucking	Yes	Yes	Yes	Yes
Disturbed fleece	Yes	Yes	Yes	Yes
Scabs	Yes	No	No	No
Discoloured fleece	No	Yellow	No	No
Deposits on skin	No	Yellow pasty deposit	No	No
Parasites visible	Tiny mites sometimes seen on wool held up to the light	Too few and too small to see	Very mobile pink lice seen scurrying when fleece opened	Sluggish blue lice seen where wool is short

NOTES

_____
_____
_____
_____
_____
_____
_____
_____
_____
_____
_____
_____
_____
_____
_____
_____
_____
_____
_____
_____
_____
_____
_____

LICE

Lice are small, flattened, wingless insects with a simple life cycle. They hatch from the eggs or nits within seven to 14 days in the form of nymphs, which moult three times before they become adults. The life cycle is completed within two to three weeks.

Lice vary in size from 1 – 10mm, so some species can be seen with the naked eye. They are permanent obligate parasites on animals and are species-specific, which makes them easy to eliminate. Lice proliferate in winter when the condition of animals deteriorates, and in certain hosts, long hair or wool gives them better protection against the elements, since high temperatures and exposure to sunlight can kill the lice and their eggs. Infestations are most common in young animals, those under stress and those suffering from malnutrition. Infested animals are restless, eat poorly, scratch and bite at the lesions. The hair is worn off and occasionally the nits or eggs can be seen on the hair around the lesion.

There are two main groups of lice: biting (red) lice and sucking (blue) lice, and distinguishing them is important for choosing the correct remedy for treatment.

Biting or red lice have chewing mouthparts with which they feed on the superficial layers of the skin, causing severe irritation. They are active and may be seen scuttling for cover if the fleece or hair is opened, but light infestations may not be detected without thorough examination of the fleece. Red lice of sheep (*Damalinia ovis*) are becoming more common due to the reliance on macrocyclic lactone injection for sheep scab control. They were formerly well controlled by the single annual dip for sheep scab prevention. Red lice can cause severe irritation which results in fleece disturbance due to the animals rubbing, and plucking at the wool. They spend less time eating and lose weight. Red lice of goats include the species *Damalinia capra* and *Damalinia limbata*. Red lice on Angoras (*D limbata*) are a serious threat to the mohair industry because of the irritation and the loss in condition caused by these lice. The infestation occurs all of the

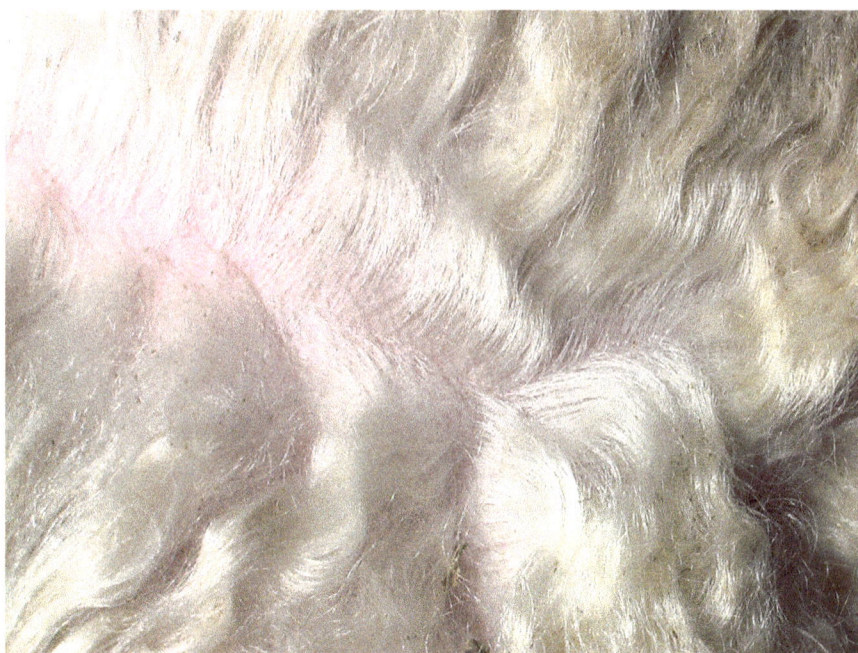

Louse infestation on an Angora goat

body and causes severe irritation which is manifested by fleece pulling.

Treatment and control of red lice

Red lice infestations in small stock can be treated effectively with organophosphate (OP) dips, or pyrethroid dips or pour-ons. Because sheep and goats with long fleece cannot be dipped, pyrethoid pour-ons have to be used, but this may not eliminate infestation completely and treatment has to be repeated one month after shearing, using OPs, pyrethroids or IGRs (see Chemicals for external parasites, page 108-110). The latter don't kill red lice but work by inhibiting the life cycle, so signs of control will only be seen after two to three weeks. Alternatively, spinosyn jetting fluid or IGRs can be applied to the fleece by spraying for red lice control, especially in flocks where there is pyrethroid resistance. Macrocyclic lactone (ML) injections, although registered for red lice control, don't always give complete control.

The prevention of red lice infestation is best achieved by implementing biosecurity, including quarantine and treating newly introduced animals, keeping fences intact and controlling shearers' hygiene practices, such as using clean overalls and disinfecting equipment. Annual post-shearing

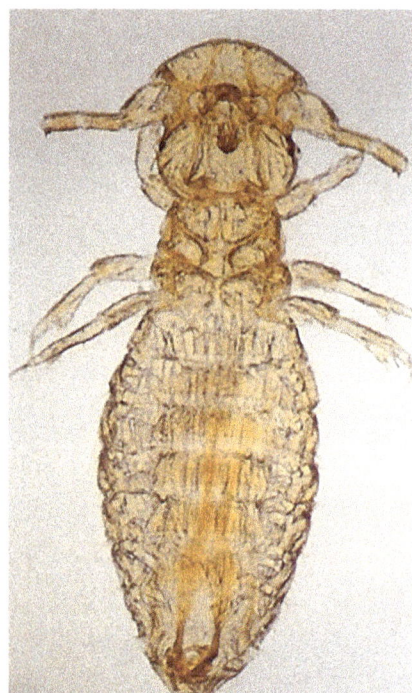

***Damilinia ovis*, the biting louse of sheep**

dipping, as for wool sheep and angora goats, will also help prevent infestations.

Sucking or blue lice have piercing mouthparts for sucking blood, which gives them a blue colour. Sucking lice are not very active and are confined to certain areas of the body. Heavy infestations cause severe anaemia in young animals. Their presence is indicated by hairless patches on various parts of the body, depending on the species of louse. Both sheep and goats are prone to sucking lice and, in the Eastern Cape, a blue louse species (*Linognathus africanus*) occurs on Angora goats, which damages mohair. Heavy infestations cause anaemia, oedema and stunting or death of young animals.

Treatment and control of sucking lice

Sucking lice are very effectively treated with injectable macrocyclic lactones such as ivermectin. Two treatments should be given at eight- to 10-day intervals, to ensure that lice hatching after treatment are also killed. All animals in the flock have to be treated. Post-shearing dipping with OPs, pyrethroids or IGRs or an annual ML injection for preventing sheep scab will avoid infestation, provided that biosecurity is practised to prevent reinfestation.

Note that only certain injectable ML products can be used for goats. Alternatively, dipping – as discussed above – is suitable. Although some pyrethroid pour-ons are registered against blue lice, they don't always control them very well because blue lice are not very active.

NOTES

FLIES

Nasal bot fly of sheep (*Oestrus ovis*)

The nasal bot fly occurs widely in South Africa and parasitises both sheep and goats. The female fly seeks out an animal and lays tiny larvae around the nostrils. These worm-like larvae migrate up the nasal passages and lodge in the sinuses where they live off the secretions. They cause severe irritation, and infested animals sneeze and shake their heads. There may be a severe discharge from the nose, which could lead to confusion with other diseases such as Pasteurella and blue tongue. Heavy infestations cause loss of weight, especially in lambs.

When the larvae have matured, they emerge from the sinuses into the nostrils and are sneezed out onto the ground where they burrow into the soil and develop into pupae. After a month or more, the adult fly emerges from the pupa. Treatment with macrocyclic lactones, such as ivermectin, will kill off the larval stages in the sinuses, but it may take some weeks for the nasal discharge to disappear. Treatment should be administered in summer, when the flies are actively laying larvae, but an additional single treatment at the height of winter will kill overwintering larvae which makes a significant impact on the fly population. Remedies containing rafoxanide or closantel can also be used for treatment.

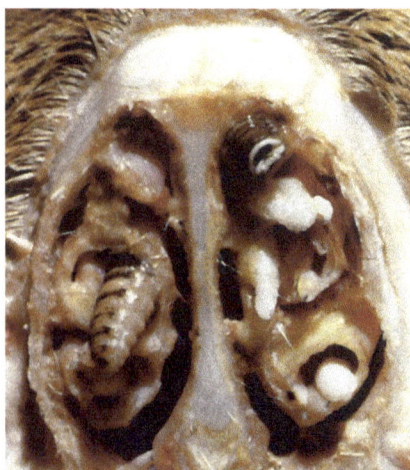

***Oestrus ovis* fly larvae in the nasal sinuses**

The blowfly *Lucilia cuprina*

Sheep ocular fly (*Gedoelstia hassleri* and *G cristata*)

The usual hosts of these parasites are the alcelaphine antelope such as wildebeest, hartebeest and blesbok. In sheep, the larvae are deposited on the eye by the female fly and from here they migrate through the eye to the circulatory system and to the brain. During their migration, they cause severe inflammation of the conjunctiva, and later haemorrhages and swelling of the eye develop. The resulting bulging of the eyeballs has given rise to the Afrikaans name for the condition, uitpeuloog. These animals become blind as a result of damage to the eyes. The condition is often seen in Karakul, Persian and Afrikaner sheep. Treatment with injectable insecticides such as macrocyclic lactones and closantel will kill the parasites but won't reverse serious damage to eyes.

Blowflies

European green blowfly (*Lucilia cuprina*)
Banded blowfly (*Chrysomyia albiceps*)
Copper-tailed blowfly (*Chrysomyia chloropyga*)
Regal blowfly (*Chrysomyia marginalis*)

Blowflies are large metallic flies that lay their eggs on carrion, on which their larvae feed and develop into pupae. With the advent of wool sheep farming in South Africa, some species of blowflies adapted their breeding habits, laying their eggs on the skin of wooled sheep, especially fine-wooled merinos.

Biology There are four main flies involved in blowfly strike of sheep, and *Lucilia cuprina* is the primary attacker. The other three blowfly species lay their eggs once *L cuprina* has caused wounds on the skin. *L cuprina* lays its eggs on the skin of sheep under certain conditions, specifically when the fleece becomes wet from rain, scouring or urine. In fine-wooled sheep, in particular, this wetting of the wool causes fleece rot, a bacterial infection that leads to a breakdown of the wool fibre. It gives off a typical smell that attracts blowflies.

The flies lay their eggs on the areas of fleece rot and within 72 hours the larvae hatch and begin to feed on the skin with their strong mouthparts. As the larvae feed, they cause wounds and the smell attracts the secondary blowflies, which in turn lay their eggs on the wounds. The larvae feed for three to five days and then drop off to pupate in the soil. The adult flies hatch out some days later. Blowflies emerge in spring and are numerous until autumn; they then hibernate in the soil as pupae.

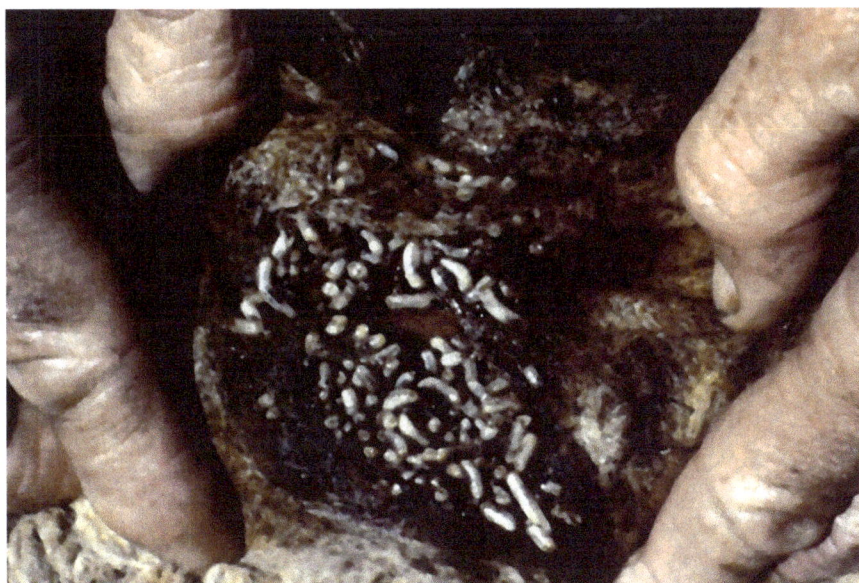

Blowfly infestation (fly strike) in a wooled sheep

The Lucitrap

Symptoms Blowfly strike can occur on various parts of the body; in the breech area, between the shoulders, around the horns of rams, around the urethral opening of rams, or on the body. The condition is difficult to detect initially because the wounds may be concealed by the fleece, but sheep show signs of lameness, biting and nibbling at their lesions, stamping and constant tail wagging. They may die within a week if their infestations are not treated.

Treatment Blow fly strike is treated by clipping the fleece around the wound which encourages drying out of the skin, and the larvae or maggots are then be killed by local application of a registered insecticide, either an organophosphate or deltamethrin solution, sprayed or poured onto the lesions at the recommended dilutions. Wound oil that contains insecticides

such as deltamethrin may also be used.

Prevention Blowfly strike can be prevented by using a combination of chemical and other factors (Integrated Pest Management).

Chemical Various remedies are registered for preventing blowfly strike (insect growth regulators, organosphosphates or the newly registered spinosyn). These are applied as required, either locally or as full body treatment, depending on the type of fly strike being experienced. Sheep can be dipped or jetted for up to a month after shearing, but as the wool grows longer, jetting is the method of choice. When jetting is done the fleece has to be thoroughly wetted to make sure the skin also gets thoroughly wetted. Treatments should be repeated as recommended for the specific product, throughout the blowfly season. Note that some resistance to organophosphates has been seen. Residues from OPs in wool are also of concern. The withdrawal times of products should be observed to prevent shearing treated wool.

Other control methods Other measures may be used in conjunction with chemicals to minimise the use of chemicals. Biological control, by trapping the adult flies, reduces the blowfly population. Lucitraps are commercially available traps which one baits with a scent specifically intended to lure *L cuprina* (the blowfly responsible

for primary strike). For more information about Lucitraps see www.bioinsectsa.com

Management factors are very important in reducing blowfly strike, including trimming the fleece around the crutch (crutching) to prevent soiling with faeces and urine, which attracts blowflies. The Mule's operation, which removes skin folds from the crutch area, was developed in Australia to prevent fly strike on very extensive farms. This drastic operation is not done much in South Africa, and the need has hopefully been eliminated by the breeding of smooth-bodied merinos, less susceptible to blowfly strike. Prevent scours by managing the diet correctly and regular dosing with anthelminthics. Tails should be docked to the correct length – only one to two vertebrae should be removed; in females, the tail should be just long enough to cover the vulva and prevent breech soiling. If the tail is docked too short, the ewes don't squat during elimination, and consequently soil the hindquarters. If the tail is left too long, the hindquarters and tail become soiled.

Integrated Pest Management (IPM)

This means using other control measures in conjunction with chemicals for controlling external parasites in animals. An example is the use of management, genetic, and biological means in addition to the application of chemicals for the control of blowflies in sheep. IPM reduces the quantity of chemical used and therefore the residues left in wool, and reduces the risk of resistance to chemicals developing.

Cattle blowfly (*Chrysomyia bezziana*)

This fly occurs in the northern and eastern parts of the country, namely Limpopo, Mpumalanga, KwaZulu-Natal and the Eastern Cape. These blowflies only attack existing wounds. They favour cattle, although they do attack sheep and goats as well. The flies lay their eggs on wounds of various types, especially operation wounds, abscesses, bruises and dip scalds, as well as small wounds such as tick bites on the ears, under the tail, perineum and the udder. In the Eastern Cape, the flies attack

bites caused by red lice. The larvae hatch and begin to feed on the wounds which, as they enlarge, suffer more strikes.

Infested wounds should be treated with wound oils containing insecticides such as deltamethrin or organophosphate, or diluted dips containing these active ingredients. Wound oils can also be used to treat wounds prophylactically to prevent blowfly strike. In areas where these flies occur, surgery should be carried out during winter months when the flies are inactive.

Midges

Midges (muggies), also known as gnats, are a group of small blood-sucking flies. These include *Culicoides*, *Simulium* and *Leptoconops*.

Culicoides spp are plentiful during the summer months in most areas of the country. They breed in manure or other organic matter and are active from sundown until daybreak. Midges frequent moist, low-lying areas such as vleis, feeding preferably on cattle but also on sheep and horses. In wet, warm summers they occur in truly enormous numbers − a single night's trapping in horse stables has produced 1 million *Culicoides* midges. As a result, the animals on which they feed suffer heavy attacks during summer nights. The midges transmit blue tongue to sheep so vaccinating annually is essential (see Blue tongue page 58).

Simulium (blackflies) breed in fast-flowing rivers, and build their larval cocoons under the surface of the water. They breed in vast numbers and can be a particular problem along the banks of the Gariep and Great Fish rivers. Blackflies bite and suck the blood of stock on hairless areas, and in the process cause severe irritation and crusty, wart-like lesions develop on the face and ears.

Controlling them on sheep is difficult because the application of fly repellents is tricky. In severe outbreaks, one can apply pyrethroid pour-ons to the head, nose and ears to repel the flies. Usually, the authorities are approached to lower the river level for a few days, which exposes and dries out the larval stages.

Leptoconops (Day-biting midges) breed in seasonal watercourses in arid areas, es-

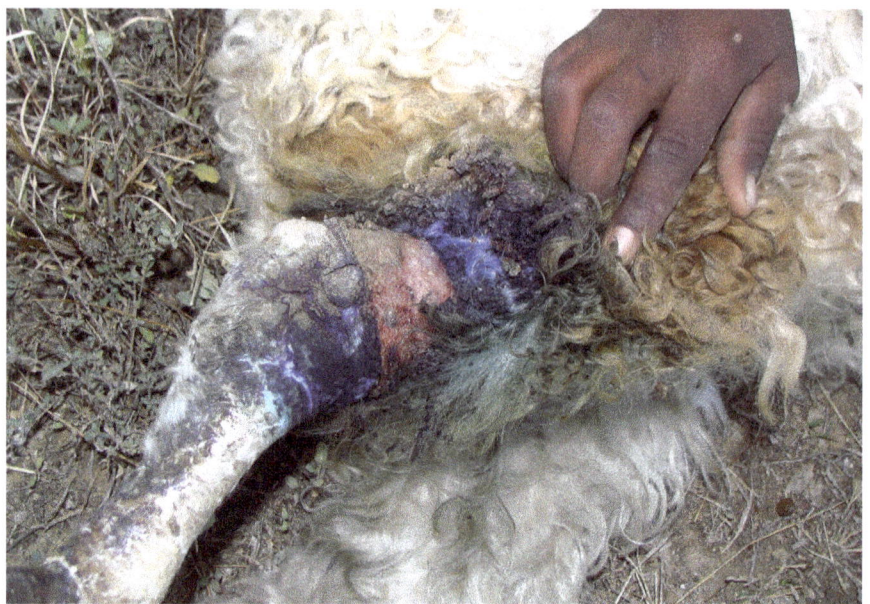

Wound caused by cattle screw worm

pecially those that have high levels of salt in the soil. In South Africa, midges are a problem around Aliwal North, De Aar and Williston. In Namibia, they're a problem around Walvis Bay.

These midges attack humans and animals in swarms during the summer months, and inflict painful bites. Control is aimed at draining or treating seasonal watercourses during problem periods. Pyrethroid dips or pour-ons help repel day-biting midges and greatly reduce the irritation and production loss.

Mosquitoes
(*Aedes* spp *Culex* spp)

All mosquito species need water in which to breed because their eggs and the immature stages are aquatic. Certain mosquito species, which show a preference for livestock, breed in their millions during very heavy summer rainy seasons, particularly when pan formation results. This creates ideal conditions for outbreaks of the viral disease Rift Valley fever (RVF), which is transmitted by these mosquitoes.

RVF is a disease of cattle, sheep and goats and causes abortion storms of 40 − 100%, and acute (sudden) deaths of lambs and kids (30%). The most practical control measure for RVF is annual vaccination with a live vaccine. During outbreaks, unvaccinated animals can be protected by

The *Culicoides* midge which transmits blue tongue

regular application of pyrethroid dip, spray or pour-ons. (See also Reproductive diseases page 52.)

Sheep ked (louse fly)
(*Melophagus ovinus*)

Sheep keds are large flightless parasitic flies, easily seen when the fleece is opened. They are totally dependent on sheep, as they can only survive for a few days away from the host.

They are now seldom seen because they're very well controlled by sheep dips. Sheep keds are transmitted by contact between sheep. Heavy infestations cause anaemia, loss of weight, scratching and biting of the fleece. Keds cause fleece damage and staining, which lowers the value of the wool. Organophosphate or pyrethroid dips are effective. Infestations can also be treated with injectable macrocyclic lactones.

CHEMICALS USED FOR EXTERNAL PARASITE CONTROL

Six main groups of remedies are registered for the control of ectoparasites in South Africa.

Table 11 summarises the groups, their members, activity against various parasites, safety and toxicity for the environment. This is discussed in more detail after the table. It's recommended that chemical use be minimised by using Integrated Pest Management (see above) to reduce the development of resistance and residues in wool.

Pyrethroids

Examples Deltamethrin, flumethrin and cypermethrin

Action Pyrethroids act on the nervous system of ectoparasites, causing paralysis and death

Spectrum Pyrethroids kill ticks, repel flies and − with the exception of flumethrin − have a knock-down effect on them. They provide effective control against biting and sucking lice

Formulations Pyrethroids are available as liquid concentrates which have to be diluted before applying as dips or sprays. They are included in many pour-ons and some wound oils

Advantages They generally have a broad spectrum

Disadvantages Pyrethroid pour-ons for red louse control take time to work

Safety Pyrethroids are safe for mammals and birds, including oxpeckers

Environmental effects Although pyrethroids are fairly safe, they shouldn't be discarded in rivers or dams as they are toxic to fish and crustacea

Resistance This has been seen in red lice, flies and ticks

Amidines/formamidines

Examples Amitraz is the only member of the group used for small stock

Action This group has a dual effect on the nervous system of ticks, including detachment and hotfooting − aimless wandering around until the ticks die

Spectrum Amidines are effective against all tick species and are very effective against mites, including sheep scab. They are generally not effective against the insect groups (lice and flies)

Formulations Amitraz liquid concentrates are registered for use in dips for small stock

Advantages They are safe and there's less resistance to amidines than to pyrethroids

Disadvantages The amidines have a narrow activity spectrum compared to some other groups because they're not very effective against the insects (lice and flies)

Safety Amidines are very safe for livestock and for humans. Overdosing causes sleepiness which wears off eventually. They shouldn't be used on horses, certain dog breeds or cats

Ecological effect Amidines are safe for the environment, particularly for birds and mammals. They degrade rapidly, but shouldn't be discarded into water bodies such as dams or rivers

Resistance Some resistance has been seen in ticks in the Eastern Cape

Organophosphates (OPs)

Examples Chlorphenfinvos and diazinon are the commonly used OPs in stock

Action OPs cause overstimulation of the nervous system which leads to its malfunction. In the early stages, poisoning can be reversed if atropine is administered

Spectrum OPs have a broad spectrum of activity as they are effective against ticks, blowflies, mites, lice and maggots, and they kill all species of ticks. In sheep, OPs are effective against sheep scab, ticks, lice and blowfly maggots. Certain formulations prevent blowfly strike for a few weeks

Formulations OPs are available as plunge dips and sprays

Advantages They are effective again after a long period of minimal use, due to the development of resistance and the use of newer chemicals

Disadvantages This is a highly toxic group. Resistance has been seen in lice in South Africa

Safety Organophosphates are the most toxic of the dips and have to be diluted, used and disposed of with extreme care. Do not use in areas where oxpeckers occur

Environmental This group is the most destructive to the environment

Resistance Resistance has been seen in blowflies and red lice

Macrocyclic lactones (MLs)

Examples This group includes ivermectin, moxidectin, doramectin and cydectin

Action MLs affect neural transmission and cause paralysis

Spectrum They are registered for the treatment of nasal worm in sheep and goats, to control sheep scab and treat blue lice

Formulations MLs are used mainly as injectables, in which form they affect parasites that suck blood or serum, such as blue lice and nasal worm larvae. Pour-on formulations are also available

Advantages They are useful for the treatment and prevention of sheep scab and other mites. MLs are also active against blue lice and nasal worm infestations

Disadvantages Although their use in sheep has almost made dipping redundant, other sheep parasites, such as red lice, aren't controlled well by MLs

Safety MLs have a high safety margin in most livestock, but not all can be used in goats or animals in poor condition

Environment Some MLs may have a negative impact on the biology of dung beetles, and if this is a concern the label should be checked for the extent of the effect. They can be used in winter when dung beetles are not active

Resistance No resistance has yet been seen in SA

Growth regulators (chitin synthesis inhibitors)

Examples Diflubenzuron, triflumuron, cyromazine and novaluron

Action Growth regulators don't kill parasites; they inhibit the development of immature stages into adults

Spectrum Diflubenzuron, triflumuron and cyromazine control the life cycles of blowflies, house and stable flies and lice and are known as insect growth regulators. Novaluron is highly effective against flies

Formulations Insect growth regulators are available in dips, sprays or − in some cases − pour-ons for sheep, for the con-

trol of blowfly strike and lice. They can be sprayed on compost heaps and manure for the control of house and stable flies

Advantages They are non-toxic to warm-blooded animals and can be used as alternative control measures on farms where there's resistance to conventional dips

Disadvantages Because they don't directly kill parasites, growth regulators will take a while to reduce the parasite population

Safety Growth regulators are non-toxic to hosts and operators

Environment Growth regulators break down rapidly in the environment but should not be disposed of in natural watercourses

Resistance None has yet been seen in South Africa

TABLE 11. Chemical groups for external parasite control and their activity

PARASITE		TICKS		MITES	FLIES		MIDGES	LICE		TOXICITY	
		Blue	Multi-host		Adult	Larvae – maggots		Biting (red)	Sucking (blue)	Host	Environment
ACTIVE											
Organophosphates		++	++	+++	++	+++	++	+++	+++	3	4
Pyrethroids	Most	+++	+++	+	++++	++	++++	++++	++++	1	2
	Flumethrin	++++	++++	++	++	+	++	++	++	1	2
Amidines	Amitraz	++++	++++	++++	-	-	-	-	-	1	1
	Cymiazole	++	++	+++	-	-	-	-	-	1	1
Macrocyclic lactones	Ivermectin	+	-	+++	+	+	-	+	+++	1	2
	Cydectin	+	-	+++	+	+	-	-	++	2	2
	Doramectin	++	-	+++	+	+++	-	++	++++	1	2
Growth Regulators	Diflubezuron	-	-	-	-	++++	-	++++	++++	1	1
	Fluazuron	+++	-	-	-	-	-	-	-	1	1
Spinosyn	Spinosad	-	-	-	-	+++	-	+++	-	1	3
Footnote: These are general comparisons and activity can vary in different formulations.											

KEY:
-no effect
+ some
++ moderate
+++ good
++++ excellent

KEY:
1 = low toxicity
2 = moderately toxic
3 = toxic
4 = very toxic

Spinosyn

This newly registered chemical in South Africa is derived from the fermentation of soil bacteria

Example Spinosad

Action This remedy affects the nervous system of insects, causing a rapid knock-down effect on lice and maggots

Spectrum The products are registered for the treatment and prevention of blowfly strike and the control of red lice on long-wooled sheep

Formulations These are used as dips and pour-ons

Advantages The chemical is active against organophosphate-resistant blow-flies and lice. There is no wool-withholding period for this product

Disadvantages They have a relatively short period of action

Safety The chemical is safe for stock and operators

Environment Correct disposal of dipwash is critical as the chemical is very toxic to invertebrates

Resistance Not yet seen in South Africa as the product is new

NOTES

EXTERNAL PARASITE CONTROL

There are various ways of controlling ectoparasites in small stock. The method of choice depends on how many animals have to be treated, the cost and the ectoparasite to be controlled. The chemicals used for ectoparasite control are discussed at the end of the chapter. A summary of control methods is given in Table 12, and discussed in more detail under separate headings.

PLUNGE DIPPING

Plunge dipping of small stock is the only method suitable for sheep scab control, and one after-shear dip is sufficient for louse control. Effective plunge dipping can only be done effectively if the dip tank is correctly constructed and managed. The tank must be deep enough to cover the whole animal.

For small numbers of sheep, a 200 litre drum sunk into the ground is adequate, but for larger flocks, bigger tanks have to be built. For flocks of a thousand or more, the capacity should be 4 000 – 8 000 litres. The tank should be 0,7 – 1m wide and 1 – 1,5m deep. The whole length of the tank has to be accessible in case animals

Surface area measurement of the rectangular plunge dip.
Because the dip tank is not a simple rectangle, an average length and average width have to be calculated:

Measure A = length at full dipping level
Measure B = length of floor
Average length =A+B and divide by 2
Measure C = width of tank at full dipping level
Measure D = width of floor
Average width = C+D and divide by 2

Now calculate
Depth of tank (E) x average width x average length
= metres x 1 000
= capacity of tank in litres at normal dipping level

get into difficulties. Calibrate the tank carefully so that the capacity can be correctly determined. The volume of the tank can be calculated using the surface area measurements or other methods. Calibration of the tank is done using permanent marks or a measuring stick. Replenish the dipwash to replace the stripping or removal of the active ingredient by the dipped animals.

The replenishment method depends on the product used; the best method for small stock is constant replenishment. This method allows for a constant stream of replenishment solution to run into the dip and keeps the dip at a constant concentration.

If the dip wash is to be used for more than one day, zinc sulphate ($ZnSO_4$), at a rate of 1kg/400 litres of dip, has to be added to inhibit the growth of bacteria that cause lumpy wool and post-dipping lameness.

Round tanks
These are usually prefabricated tanks supplied by manufacturers with known volume, or their volume can be measured by using 200 litre drums.

Flow meter
Using a flow meter, add water and mark off at 1 000 litre intervals.

Manual measurement of volume
Using a 200 litre drum, add water to dip and mark at 1 000 litre intervals.

TABLE 12. A summary of ectoparasite control methods in sheep and goats

METHOD	SUITABILITY	ADVANTAGES	DISADVANTAGES	COST
Plunge dip	Only dipping method suitable for sheep scab treatment	Good wetting of whole body	Not suitable for sheep with long fleece	Low
Bellybathing	Karoo paralysis ticks, brown ticks and heart-water control	Applies product to belly, legs and feet	Not suitable for scab control	Very low
Foot baths	For brown ticks on feet	Applies product to feet	Only effective on feet	Cheaper than plunge dip and bellybath
ML injection	Sheep scab and blue lice	No dip tanks needed	Poor action on red lice and ticks	Relatively expensive
Spraying and jetting	Blowfly preparations, louse infestations	Full or focal application	Only suitable for blow-fly and lice	Low to moderate
Pour-on/patch	Various, except sheep scab	Don't need dip tank	Often not suitable for long-wooled sheep; labour intensive	Moderate to expensive

Round dip tank for small stock

Rectangular dip tank for small stock

Mixing the dip concentrate

The fresh filling of a dip tank must be done according to the capacity of the tank and the instructions on the label. Measure off the amount of concentrate required, pour it into a bucket and mix it with water to make a premix or cream. Stir it with a stick to mix well. Add the cream to the dip tank at the steps of the exit. The tank must now be stirred by sending at least 20 adult animals through the dip tank. These animals have to go through the dip again once it has been thoroughly stirred.

Replenishment methods

This varies with the product used; the product determines the method of replenishment.

• Conventional

Because wooled sheep, in particular, rapidly strip the active ingredient out of the dip wash, the concentration has to be replenished by adding more concentrate at regular intervals. The label instructions indicate at which stages replenishment should be done, usually after $1/_3$ of the dip volume has been removed. The conventional method is the most commonly used by farmers, because it is the most convenient, but it doesn't give as good a control as constant replenishment.

• Constant replenishment

Constant replenishment was developed

Bellybath

because the conventional method is inaccurate and causes the concentration of the active ingredient to fluctuate below the required level. It operates by allowing concentrate to run from a small holding tank into the dip tank at a constant rate and according to the quantity detailed on the product label.

Stock management at dip tanks

Animals must be brought in calmly and quietly. They should preferably be dipped in the morning before they become hot

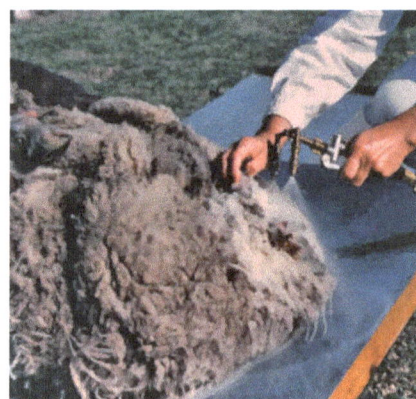

Jetting or spraying the crutch area

and thirsty and are tempted to drink dip wash. Rain will wash off dip. After dipping, record all details, such as the number of animals dipped, the lot number and the type of dip used, the quantity used and the replenishment rates. Plug the dip wash run-off hole to prevent rainwater entering.

Discarding dip

It's essential, when dip tanks are emptied, that the dip be discarded safely and without causing a potential hazard to humans, animals or wildlife.

This is done by running used dip wash out onto an allocated area of ground where the active ingredient will be broken down by the combined action of sunlight

Spot (local) treatment

and soil bacteria. Choose a level piece of ground near the dip tank and plough contour furrows to promote containment and prevent run-off.

Allow 600m² for a sheep dip tank. The disposal site has to be at least 100m from boreholes, streams, house/huts and public thoroughfares. The area has to be fenced off and marked DANGER SABS WW5 and KEEP AWAY in all local languages. There must be no run-off from this area into local watercourses.

BELLYBATHING
This method of dipping can be used to apply remedies for blowfly control in sheep, and for Karoo paralysis and brown tick control. The sheep walk through the dipwash rather than swimming through it, wetting their underline, breech area, legs and feet. The dipwash wets the underline and the breech area.

SPRAYING/JETTING
Jetting sheep using a semi-circular jet spray isn't commonly done in South Africa. Blowfly remedies are applied to the fleece using a pipe connected to a pump and a wide-mouthed nozzle which can deliver a stream rather than a fine spray of remedy, usually to the breech or other target areas. Operators have to ensure that the maximum pressure is not exceeded as this can

cause skin damage, irritation and poisoning, depending on which remedies are used.

POUR-ONS/SPOT TREATMENT
Pour-on remedies contain high concentrations of active ingredient suspended in a carrier substance that helps the spreading of the chemical over the skin. These products are available for sheep and goats for tick control, red louse infestation and for delivery of growth regulators for blowfly control.

The basic application principles are that the correct volume be applied, at the correct sites, either along the backline (for louse control), in the armpits (for Karoo paralysis tick), on the head (for infestations of the ears), or feet (for the control of foot ticks).

FOOTBATHS
These can be used to control the ticks that cause foot abscesses. Suitable dips are organophosphates, amitraz and pyrethroids.

CHEMICAL CONTROL PROBLEMS

The efficacy of chemical control can be affected by various factors. The most common chemical control problems encoun-

tered in small stock are summarised here:

Plunge dip
- If the dip tank isn't deep enough, control will be poor because the heads cannot be submerged.
- If animals used to stir the dipwash are not brought back to the tank they won't be treated properly.
- If some animals in the flock aren't dipped, the control of sheep scab, other mites and lice will be poor.
- the dipwash could be too weak as a result of incorrect dilution or replenishment – usually because the capacity of the dip tank was underestimated.

Spraying
The most common problem is inadequate wetting of the skin, which will lead to poor control.

Pour-ons
- Pyrethroids can take up to two days to kill off ticks and some stay attached even if they're dead – especially male bont ticks.
- Pour-ons could take two to three days to spread all over the animal, and their effect on the lower body (belly and legs) will be slower than on the head and neck.

Bellybaths and footbaths
Dip may be washed off when animals cross rivers or walk through long, wet grass.

Injectable products
Every animal must be treated, otherwise flock control will be poor.

General
- Poor control could result from damaged or faulty products; contact manufacturers if this is the case.
- All products have a shorter period of effective life on goats and hairy sheep than on wooled sheep, because chemicals bind better to wool fat than to hair. Treatments may, therefore, have to be given at shorter intervals.
- In the case of louse and blowfly control, resistance should be suspected if a product used for a long time suddenly doesn't work. Contact the manufacturers for help.

NOTES

POISONING

Poisoning of small stock

Sheep and goats are subject to poisoning from various sources, mainly from plants but agricultural products, feed, fertilisers and water are also potential sources of toxins.

PLANT POISONING

Plants use a variety of strategies to stop animals eating them, and producing toxic substances is just one of these protective mechanisms. In many cases, poisonous plants are unpalatable, so animals avoid them unless they are very hungry; for example, during droughts or if they've been introduced into the area and are unfamiliar with the plants. Some toxic plants are pioneers, which multiply when ground is disturbed by ploughing, or become dominant when other plants are overgrazed.

Many of the poisonous plants that kill small stock are ones that proliferate as a result of poor management, but there is a group of plants that only become toxic at certain times; when damaged in some way, or if they're infected with fungi or bacteria which produce poisonous substances.

Small stock eat poisonous plants for numerous reasons; for example, when the veld is overgrazed because it's overstocked. Under such conditions, especially in the Karoo, certain poisonous plants (such as kraalbos and tulp) predominate, and they can take years to disappear (see Karoo Veld, details in Bibliography). Animals may be exposed to poisonous plants that are the first to appear after veld fires, or when animals unfamiliar with the local plants are introduced to veld where poisonous plants predominate. Some exotic plants or weeds cause poisoning if livestock are kraaled next to gardens or camps adjoining farmyards. Planted pastures, which are otherwise good feed, may become toxic under various conditions, depending on the species.

Because there are very few specific antidotes for plant poisons, farmers should

Overgrazed veld, displaying a proliferation of tulp and kraalbos

rather avoid the problem. When specific antidotes aren't available for poisoned animals, they have to be given supportive treatment to salvage them, which is very expensive. Farmers should familiarise themselves with potentially poisonous plants and pastures, which will enable them to anticipate and avoid problems. Preventing overgrazing of the veld is a very important step in controlling stock poisoning. In addition, it's essential to monitor animals on planted pastures continuously during danger periods.

It's not possible to cover all the plants that cause small stock poisoning in this book, so only the most important ones are discussed here. For more complete references, consult the textbooks listed in the bibliography and speak to a local veterinarian about the poisonous plants in your area.

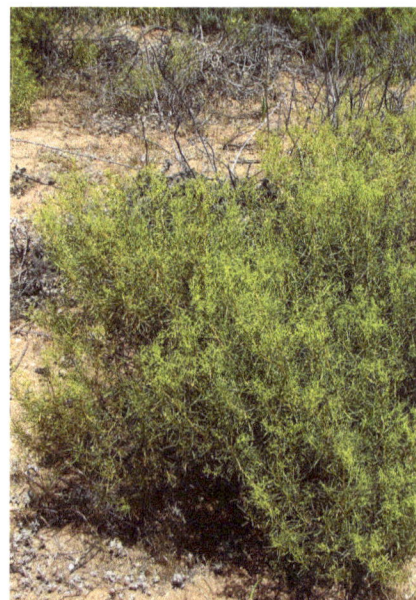

Kraalbos (*Galenia africana*) increases in the veld as a result of overgrazing

POISONING

6

LIVER POISONING

The liver is the organ most often affected by poisoning because it plays a role in detoxifying substances absorbed into the system. The plant poisons that affect the liver may cause an acute condition and sudden death, or a chronic condition displaying weight loss and jaundice. Some of those that cause liver damage also cause photosensitivity, a condition that causes sensitivity to light and inflammation of the skin (see Photosensitivity page 118-120).

Galenia africana
(Salt bush, Kraalbos)

Syndrome Waterpens

Poisoning resulting from ingesting kraalbos occurs in dry western parts, such as the Karoo, where it proliferates because of poor management practices like overstocking and overgrazing. It also colonises old lands. Although unpalatable, large quantities are often consumed, especially during droughts when no other food is available. Chronic intake of kraalbos causes fibrotic liver damage which manifests as fluid accumulation in the abdomen. The condition is known colloquially as waterpens.

At post-mortem, the liver is seen to be severely fibrous (cirrhotic). A diagnosis can usually be made based on evidence of large quantities of kraalbos being grazed, the typical symptoms of waterpens and signs of liver cirrhosis.

Eliminating these plants is problematic as large-scale mechanical or chemical clearing isn't recommended in arid areas, because doing so exposes the soil and the small kraalbos seeds often benefit from soil disturbance or burning. Clearing should be done in small strips rather than over large areas. Brush cutting when the bushes are in flower, before they set seed, may help to limit the spreading of the plants (for more information, see Karoo Veld, details in Bibliography).

Lupinus angustfolius (Lupins)

Syndrome Lupine poisoning

In some areas – especially in the Western Cape – lupins are cultivated for fodder. The plants and their pods become infested with

Damaged liver, resulting from acute *Senecio* poisoning

a fungus (*Phomopsis leptostromiformis*) during warm, wet periods. The fungus produces a poison which causes liver damage, jaundice and mild signs of photosensitivity.

Sheep sometimes die within a week after grazing on affected lupins. When weather conditions are favourable, use small numbers of animals to check if the pastures are safe. When sheep feed on bitter lupin seeds they sometimes develop poisoning, specifically an alkalosis. Symptoms may appear a few hours after ingestion and stimulation or exercise causes muscle tremors, staggering and paralysis. Death from asphyxiation occurs within a few hours. As for urea poisoning, using vinegar reverses the alkalosis.

Pteronia pallens (Scholtz bush)
Hertia pallens (springbokbos)

These Karoo bushes sporadically cause liver toxicity if they're eaten during dry periods, or when new sheep or goats are introduced onto farms.

Affected animals may show apathy, which could be confused with domsiekte, and jaundice may be seen as a result of liver damage. Damage to the kidneys and lungs may also be seen.

Senecio latifolius, Senecio retrorsus (Ragwort, dunsiektebossie)

Syndrome Seneciosis, dunsiekte

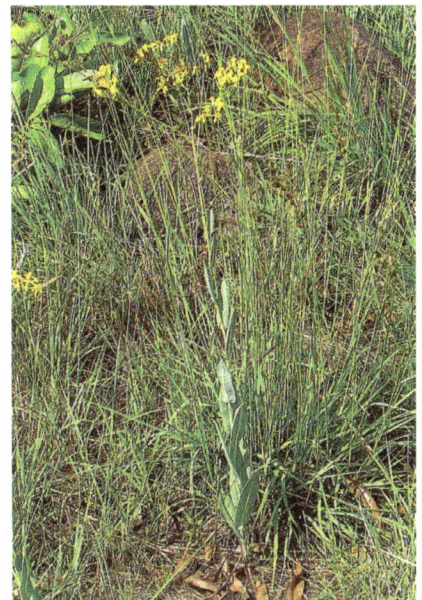

Senecio spp increase in areas of overgrazing

Acute and chronic seneciosis occur in small stock in regions where the plants grow abundantly, namely the central and eastern areas of the country, especially Queenstown in the Eastern Cape. It's estimated that the condition is responsible for 5% of all small stock deaths.

Senecio spp are typically found in open veld, on mountain slopes and in marshy areas. It's very invasive, especially after veld has been denuded by overgrazing, and infests camps heavily. The plants can

also cause poisoning if included in hay.

Acute seneciosis occurs when small stock eat large quantities of the plants; lambs die within 24 hours without showing any specific symptoms.

On post-mortem, extensive haemorrhages of many organs, pale mucous membranes and damage to the liver are seen.

Chronic intake causes gradual damage to the liver which results in progressive wasting. Sheep show depression, poor appetite, abdominal pain, constipation and jaundice. By the time the clinical signs are seen, liver damage is extensive and irreversible. There are various control strategies: Avoiding contaminated pastures, preventative dosing of animals with activated charcoal before grazing, or grazing the pastures in winter when the plant dies back.

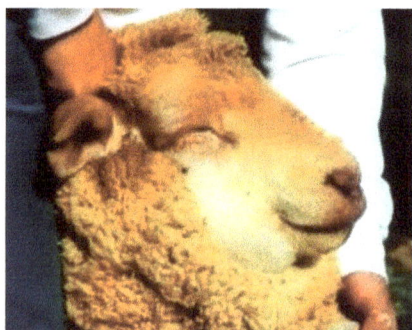

An early case of photosensitivity showing the swelling and inflammation of the head

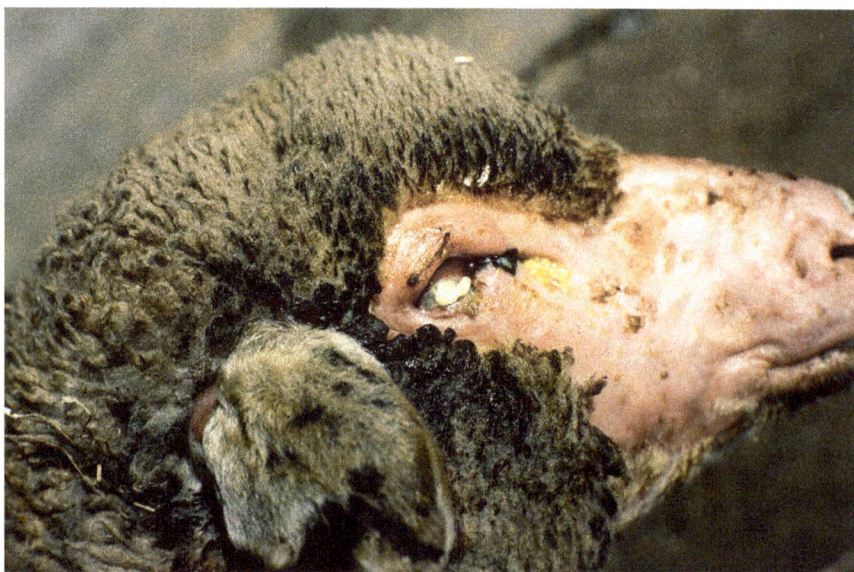

PLANTS CAUSING PHOTOSENSITIVITY

Photosensitivity is the inflammation of the skin when exposed to sunlight, caused by an accumulation of a breakdown product of chlorophyll called phylloerthryrin. This occurs because the chemicals in certain plants damage the liver. When phylloerthryrin reaches the bloodstream, it causes severe irritation if the skin is exposed to sunlight, especially on unprotected areas of the body such as the face and nose. This gives rise to severe inflammation and swelling of the skin, particularly on the head. The eyelids and lips may be so swollen that the animal is unable to feed. Since the primary damage takes place in the liver, some jaundice may be seen clinically.

Affected animals die from secondary infections and complications, if untreated. Liver damage will be seen on post-mortem examination. In most cases, irrespective of the plant involved, the symptoms and therefore the treatment are the same, as the pathogenesis (disease process) is similar (see Treating photosensitivity). Plants causing photosensitivity in small stock can cause millions of rands worth of losses, so farmers should familiarise themselves with the most important plants in their area that cause this syndrome. Geeldik-

kop and dikoor (see page 119) are the most important causes of small stock losses in South Africa; an estimated 74 000 deaths annually.

Athanasia minuta (formerly *Asaemia axillaris*) (Vuursiekte bossie) *Athanasia trifurcata* (Klaaslouwbos)

The genus *Athanasia* contains two species known to cause photosensitivity. Vuursiektebossie is a woody herb found in arid areas, where it grows near dams and pans. It becomes an invader, especially in overgrazed veld that's been inundated by flooding, and is eaten in spring only when no other food is available. The plant may cause acute (sudden) deaths or photosensitivity with liver damage and icterus. After a few days of grazing, sheep begin to seek shade and rub their ears and noses. Their ears, eyelids and lips swell and they may show jaundice because of liver damage. The swelling of the ears and the face may be mild or extreme. After 24 hours, the swelling subsides, the skin begins to ooze serum and it dries to form crusts on the skin. Affected animals lose condition dramatically and the damaged skin may peel off, exposing smooth pink skin areas.

Klaaslouwbos is an unpalatable bush commonly found on ploughed and disturbed lands in the south and south-eastern Cape. Regarded as a weed, it's only eaten when circumstances force sheep to do so. It causes a syndrome similar to those seen for vuursiektebossie and ganskweek.

Cyanobacteria (Microcystis) (Blue-green algae)

This is actually an aquatic bacterium that's widespread all over South Africa and flourishes during the warm summer months. It causes poisoning in Gauteng and the Free State, particularly around the Hartebeespoort and Vaal dams. The bacterium grows on the surface of dams or pans during hot weather when the water is full of nutrients, either as a result of evaporation or of eutrophication (increased nitrates in water). This favours the development of cyanobacteria, which form a scum-like

An advanced case of photosensitivity in which the damaged skin has peeled off. In this case, the eyes have also been infected

growth often on the leeward verge of the dam, but which may gradually cover the whole surface. As the bacteria begin to die off they release a toxin into the water which has an extremely unpleasant smell.

Animals drinking water containing cyanobacterial toxin develop either an acute case of liver failure which results in death or a sub-acute condition with photosensitivity, lack of appetite, constipation, weakness and jaundice. The diagnosis is based on a history of cyanobacterial blooms on drinking water sources, typical symptoms and liver damage seen at post-mortem.

Lasiospermum bipinnatum (Ganskweek)

These soft, herblike plants have white, daisy-type flowers. They occur in the eastern Karoo, especially around Graaff-Reinet, and certain areas in the Free State. The plant is unpalatable and eaten mainly when sheep are hungry or overcrowded. It's highly toxic to sheep and causes liver damage and photosensitivity, as well as damage to the lungs. Heavily infested pastures should be avoided as grazing for small stock.

Panicum spp (Small buffalo grass, Common buffalo grass)

Syndrome Dikoor

Buffalo grass pastures can cause the syndrome dikoor under conditions thought to be similar to those that precipitate geeldikkop. This grass is cultivated in the summer rainfall areas of the Gauteng Highveld and Free State. It becomes toxic when dry spells following summer rains cause the grass to wilt. Affected sheep show swollen red faces, and as the names suggest, very swollen ears. The skin then hardens and becomes crusty. The skin around the claws may also be affected and is sometimes confused with cases of blue tongue. Post-mortem examination reveals liver damage. Sheep on *Panicum* pastures in late summer should be supervised daily for symptoms and immediately removed when the first signs appear.

Pithomyces chartarum

Syndrome Facial eczema

Pithomyces chartarum is a fungus found throughout the country, but the poisoning

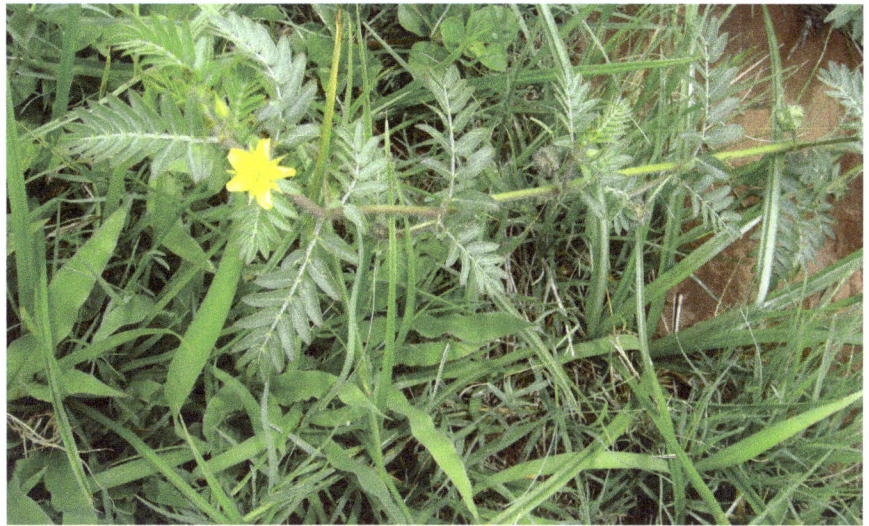

Tribulus terrestris (dubbeltjies) causes geeldikkop under certain conditions

has been seen only in the Karoo, the Highveld, Brandfort and coastal areas, specifically Humansdorp. Under conditions of high humidity and rainfall it infects certain types of pastures, mainly ryegrass (*Lolium* sp) and clover (*Medicago*). Toxigenic strains of the fungus cause poisoning of animals that graze on these pastures. The toxic compound sporidesmin causes photosensitivity known as facial eczema, with typical geeldikkop symptoms.

In New Zealand the condition is controlled on problem farms by spraying pastures with fungicides and administering zinc salts (see Kellerman et al). Selecting resistant animals has also been tried.

Tribulus terrestris (Devil's thorn; Dubbeltjies)

Syndrome Geeldikkop

Tribulus terrestris is a sprawling indigenous weed with yellow flowers which occurs all over the country, but extensively in overgrazed areas of the Karoo, where it's used as a grazing plant. Its characteristic thorns gave rise to the common names. The plant becomes sporadically toxic when early summer rainfall is followed by dry spells, resulting in the wilting of the leaves. This damage causes the plant to produce a toxin that causes photosensitivity.

Geeldikkop is the colloquial name used to describe the symptoms of swelling of the head and the jaundice that results from liver damage. Huge losses can be caused in sheep and goats, when the plants become toxic.

A few days after grazing on damaged plants, the skin starts swelling, particularly on the head, and the skin around the eyes and the mouth often bursts from the pressure. Affected animals avoid sunlight, scratch, rub and stamp their feet. Unpig-

TREATING PHOTOSENSITIVITY

The essential steps for treating photosensitivity cases are firstly removing the animals from the source of poisoning, then providing shelter from the sun, fresh water and good soft feed. If the skin lesions are mild and not extensive, apply a wound oil to prevent infection and soften hard, crusty areas. Severely affected animals may need injectable antibiotics to prevent secondary infections. If the eyelids are affected, use eye ointments to prevent infection and to soften the skin. Severely affected animals may need veterinary aid for liver support and cortisone to reduce the inflammation.

mented or unprotected skin areas are affected, showing reddening and swelling. The ears often hang and the lips swell. The skin may crack and ooze serum, which then crusts. The eyelids and lips become stiff and immobile, and skin may actually fall off. Black-headed sheep like Persians show swelling of the body rather than the head. Geeldikkop can easily be confused with other causes of photosensitivity and conditions such as the clostridial dikkop of rams, blue tongue and snakebite, which also cause a swollen head in sheep.

The diagnosis of geeldikkop is made based on the history of animals eating damaged or wilted dubbeltjies, the symptoms and the pathology, which shows a typical liver damage pattern.

NOTES

HEART POISONS

A wide range of plants in South Africa contain cardiac glycosides, and this group is one of the most important causes of stock poisoning. Most important are the tulp, slangkop and plakkie groups.

Cardiac glycosides affect three body systems: The heart, the gastrointestinal system and the nervous system. Generally speaking, the latter is a chronic, cumulative poisoning caused by the plakkie group of plants. It's discussed in Nervous system poisons (starting on this page).

Tulp and slangkop

The tulp group includes the bulbous plants of the *Homeria* and *Morea* spp. These plants are found in the central and western areas of the country, as well as in certain areas of the Eastern Cape. Tulp poisoning affects sheep and goats and most commonly occurs in animals either newly introduced into areas or hungry animals put on barren winter pastures where the only greenery is sprouting tulp bulbs. Animals familiar with the plant don't willingly eat tulp – even stabled animals offered the plants refuse them. In cases of acute tulp poisoning, animals may die suddenly of cardiac arrest after the slightest exertion. More chronically affected animals show apathy, stand with their heads hanging, groaning and grinding their teeth.

Control is by management of tulp-infested pastures, by camping off or eradication, which is difficult to do because the plants form corms or bulbs.

Slangkop plants include *Drimia* spp (formerly *Urginea*), *Ornithoglossum* (the Karoo slangkop), and *Merwilla* spp (formerly *Scilla* or blue squill). Animals eating slangkop show symptoms as described for tulp poisoning. Diagnosis is based on clinical symptoms, signs of the plants being grazed and general signs at post-mortem of heart failure; namely, congestion of the carcass, fluid accumulation in the lungs, thorax or abdomen, and subcutaneous haemorrhages.

Animals suspected of tulp or slangkop poisoning can be treated effectively with activated charcoal at a rate of 2g/kg body weight. Adding oils or other substances

An example of a tulp plant

is not recommended because doing so reduces the efficacy. Specific veterinary treatment can be sought for valuable animals.

The best control measure is to avoid introducing new animals onto heavily infested pastures. Eradication of the plant is just as difficult as for tulp, because the bulbs have to be dug out. Attempts at developing a vaccine against cardiac glycosides have so far been unsuccessful.

Other plants containing cardiac glycosides are the exotic oleander (*Nerium oleander*), poisonous rope (*Stropanthus* spp), milkweed (*Asclepias* spp) and Bushman's poison bush (*Ackocanthera*).

NERVOUS SYSTEM POISONS

Certain plants can affect the nervous system of small stock; the important ones are those which cause krimpsiekte, and pastures and feeds infected with fungi or bacteria. Some less important plants are also mentioned.

Cynanchum spp (Bobbejaantou, klimop)

These creepers grow in coastal areas from Namaqualand to Port Elizabeth, and also in wooded valleys in Limpopo province. They have bright green, succulent leaves which exude a milky latex when cut. Cases of poisoning have been described in sheep which show staggering, tremors and tetanic convulsions terminating in paralysis before either recovery or death, depending on the quantity eaten.

Cynodon dactylon (Couch grass, kweek)

Syndrome Kweek tremors

Couch grass is widespread in South Africa and is cultivated as a pasture. Occasionally these pastures become infected with fungi during the winter months, and may cause poisoning in sheep. The syndrome is characterised by muscular tremors, ataxia and paresis, but death is rarely seen. Although the symptoms can last for a few weeks, most animals recover with no ill effects and continue to eat and drink during their illness, so usually no treatment is necessary.

Dipcadi glaucum (Wild onion, Malkop-ui)

This perennial bulbous plant grows in focal areas in Limpopo province, the Northern Cape province near Griqualand West, and adjoining areas in the Free State. Sheep sometimes die from eating the bulb of this plant. The symptoms of poisoning are loss of appetite, diarrhoea, and typical head-pressing – which gives the plant its Afrikaans name.

Lolium spp (Annual ryegrass)

Syndrome Annual ryegrass toxicosis (ARGT)

Annual ryegrass (*Lolium* spp) is grazed widely in South Africa, either as a cultivated pasture or on stubble or fallow lands. Poisoning has, so far, only been reported in the Western Cape. When annual ryegrass becomes infested with tiny plant nematodes they sometimes bring with them bacteria that produce a corynetoxin, which poisons livestock when they eat the grass seeds.

Poisoned animals develop nervous signs, show abortion and a high percentage of mortality. The nervous symptoms include excitability, muscle twitching, abnormalities of gait, such as unsteadiness; terminally, convulsions are seen. The diagnosis of outbreaks can be made on microscopic examination of the ears of ryegrass at a veterinary laboratory experienced in such examination.

To control the condition, these lands should be grazed before the ryegrass develops seeds; burning the fields or using selective herbicides to control ryegrass growth. A single case of perennial ryegrass poisoning (*Neotyphodium lolii*) has been recorded in South Africa.

Paspalum dilatatum (Dallis grass)

Syndrome Paspalum staggers

A fungal infection of the seeds of *Paspalum dilatatum* (Dallis grass) causes non-fatal nervous symptoms in cattle and – less often – in sheep. This grass grows on clay and loam soils, mainly in the eastern and coastal areas of the country, either in cultivated lands, on roadsides or in marshes and vleis. After a few days of grazing on infected pastures, animals show hypersensi-

tivity, tremors and poor co-ordination. The grass should be grazed heavily in spring and summer to prevent the development of seed heads. Toxic pastures can also be made safe by mowing.

Phalaris spp (Canary grass)

Syndrome Phalaris staggers

Phalaris poisoning or staggers occurs on cultivated pastures of these exotic grasses when grazed predominantly. *Phalaris* poisoning can cause sudden death, an acute form manifested by collapse when excited, and difficult breathing. In this form death occurs mainly due to heart failure.

The other form of *Phalaris* poisoning is a chronic – and ultimately fatal – nervous condition in sheep which occurs two to three weeks after grazing the pastures. The number of animals affected varies from 5 – 50%. In this form, sheep show stiffness and unco-ordination, manifested by swaying of the back legs. Severely affected animals go down, lie on their sides and show convulsions, head nodding and eyes rolling back. At this stage, some animals may die but if left undisturbed, most will recover – provided they're not stressed in any way.

Remove all animals from the pasture as soon as the first signs of poisoning are seen. Dosing with cobalt bullets is said to prevent the condition.

Tylocodon (above) and *Cotyledon* (below) belong to the plakkie group of plants, which can cause krimpsiekte

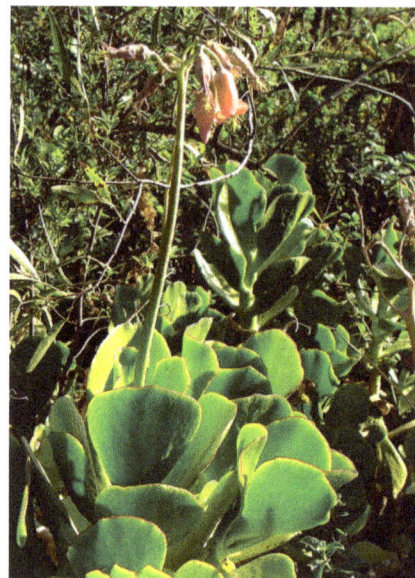

Plakkies (*Cotyledon, Kalanchoe, Tylocodon*)

Syndrome Krimpsiekte

This chronic poisoning is caused by certain cardiac-glycoside-containing plants, specifically the plakkie group, which includes *Cotyledon* spp, *Kalanchoe* and *Tylocodon*.

These plants occur mainly in the dry western areas of the country, the Little Karoo and the southern fringes of the

A case of krimpsiekte in an Angora goat, showing typical lip licking

Great Karoo. The incidence of krimpsiekte is highest in goats, but sheep are also affected.

Poisoning often affects newly introduced animals not familiar with the plants that cause krimpsiekte. It can occur throughout the year but is most common in spring during drought years, when animals are inclined to eat plants they would normally avoid.

Acute cases (opblaaskrimpsiekte) occur in animals that have ingested a large quantity of plakkies in a short time. They show sudden death or develop severe bloat and show regurgitation of rumen content.

Animals suffering from more severe, chronic krimpsiekte show various degrees of paralysis: in the early stages, the animals lag behind in the flock, tire when driven, lie down and tremble. Typical krimpsiekte symptoms can be seen; affected animals stand with their backs arched, feet held close together and the head hanging low, sometimes bent sideways.

There's no treatment for krimpsiekte. Note that the meat of animals that died from krimpsiekte is not suitable for eating as secondary poisoning can result.

Sarcostemma viminale (Caustic bush, Melktou)

This leafless succulent climber grows in trees all over South Africa, including the arid western areas. Sheep may eat the leaves when grazing is scarce, but Angora goats are especially partial to melktou. Poisoning causes animals to show hypersensitivity, tremors and unco-ordinated gait. They become recumbent and show tetanic spasms. More serious, chronic

Sarcostemma viminale is a favourite of Angora goats during periods of drought

cases may show paralysis which may last for weeks.

Stenocarpella maydis (formerly Diplodia maydis)

Syndrome Diplodiosis

The fungus *Stenocarpella maydis* grows on maize cobs (ear and stem rot) and is seen as a white growth. The fungus develops black spore-forming heads which distinguishes it from other fungi. This condition is seen mainly in livestock grazing maize lands in winter in the maize areas of the north-western Free State, Mpumalanga and KwaZulu-Natal, especially during cool wet weather. It's estimated that such poisoning is responsible for 2% of all the poisonings of small stock.

The symptoms are weakness, reluctance to move, a wide-legged gait, high stepping and paralysis. Stillbirths and neonatal deaths of lambs may result from poisoning.

If animals are removed from the fields, they could recover from these dramatic symptoms and the mortality rate is low. There's no specific treatment for the condition. Infected maize can be rendered less toxic by passing it through a hammer mill and feeding it mixed with other feed,

A maize cob infested with Stenocarpella maydis

which will dilute the toxin.

Fine clays used for adsorbing aflotoxins in feed can also be used to deactivate the toxin. Maize residues on infected lands should be burnt or ploughed into the land.

Trachyandra spp.

These low-growing plants have straplike leaves which grow in a rosette arrangement. They occur in the Western Cape and are eaten when the veld is overgrazed. Signs of poisoning are progressive ascending paralysis, difficult movement, knuckling over of the fetlocks, hypersensitivity and twitching. The animals finally lie down and die of starvation or secondary complications.

DIGESTIVE SYSTEM POISONS

Chrysocoma ciliata (tenuifolia) (Bitterbush)

Syndrome Kaalsiekte, valsiekte

This indigenous Karoo bush proliferates with overgrazing, especially during wet years, when it becomes palatable. The plant causes two conditions in small stock: Adult sheep and goats develop diarrhoea, weakness and death; and lactating ewes or does shed the toxin in the milk and this causes skin irritation in the suckling lambs or kids. These animals constantly lick the skin, causing hair loss and sometimes impaction resulting from hair balls. Lambs that have lost hair could die of exposure and lung infections. Older lambs – two to four months old – sometimes develop valsiekte, which produces the nervous symptoms of falling and dragging themselves around.

Geigeria spp (Vermeerbossies)

Syndrome Vermeersiekte

This is an important cause of sheep losses in the Griqualand West area, although the plants occur quite widely in various areas of South Africa and occasionally cause vermeersiekte. The plant is palatable and valuable grazing when eaten together with other plants, and only becomes a problem when it forms a large part of the diet. This situation arises when veld is degraded and the plant becomes dominant, replacing grass as the main plant being grazed. Merino and Karakul sheep appear to be more susceptible than other breeds.

In sheep, the toxin damages the muscles of the oesophagus causing it to widen and prevent swallowing. Affected animals regurgitate rumen contents and their lips and nose are usually smeared with it. The cud may collect in the cheeks. In addition to regurgitation, animals may cough, have diarrhoea, bloat and show stiffness and paralysis. Many animals die as a result of choking or developing foreign body pneumonia from inhaling the rumen contents. A post-mortem examination will reveal the dilatation of the oesophagus. Mildly affected animals recover if removed from

Geigeria (vermeersiekte) plants

the problem pastures. Goats are very susceptible, but they develop paralysis after feeding on this plant.

There's no economically viable treatment for badly affected animals. Where possible, pastures in which *Geigeria* spp dominate should be rested to allow grass and other herbs to re-establish themselves. If this isn't possible, infested pastures could be grazed non-selectively by large numbers of sheep, so that each animal receives a non-toxic dose of the plant. This is most effective if the pastures are grazed in the early stages, before the plants have had a chance to seed.

KIDNEY AND BLADDER POISONS

Oxalate-containing plants

A number of plants in SA contain oxalic acid, including suring (*Oxalis* spp), sorrel (*Rumex*), vygies (*Mesembryanthemum*), marog (*Amaranthus*), prickly pears (*Opuntia*), spekboom (*Portulacaria*) and garingboom (*Agave*), as well as certain vegetables; namely rhubarb, beetroot and spinach. Small stock are most commonly affected when they're forced to eat these plants, but whether or not poisoning de-

velops depends on the level of oxalic acid in the plants and how much is eaten. Oxalic acid forms insoluble oxalate crystals which accumulate in and damage the kidneys. In acute forms, there's a milk fever-like syndrome, reduced motility of the gut, depression, weakness, and coma. Chronic poisoning causes depression, lethargy, stiffness, lying down and death.

The diagnosis of oxalate poisoning is usually confirmed by doing histology on animals that have died or been slaughtered. Oxalate poisoning can be prevented by rotating pastures or, if this isn't possible, the animals can be fed a salt lick containing 25% dicalcium phosphate as a preventative measure.

REPRODUCTIVE SYSTEM POISONS

Salsola tuberculatiformis (Cauliflower, saltwort)

Syndrome Big lamb disease

This Karoo bush, if eaten by sheep in the last stages of pregnancy, delays lambing. This results in the foetus growing very large and sometimes not being able to be born naturally. This condition is discussed in more detail in Reproductive diseases (see page 46).

Trifolium spp (clover), Medicago (lucerne)

Clover pastures contain substances with oestrogenic effects and may cause reproductive disturbances such as vaginal prolapse in sheep (see Reproductive diseases, page ??). They are not often used in South Africa because of these potential problems. Lucerne pastures, which are more widely used in this country, may be implicated in low-grade fertility problems due to the production of oestrogens. Consult a veterinarian to establish the diagnosis if this is suspected.

BLOOD (circulatory) SYSTEM POISONS

Copper poisoning

Syndrome enzootic icterus, geelsiekte

The black discoloration of the kidneys seen with enzootic icterus or copper poisoning

Angora goats poisoned by prussic acid; note the severe bloating

Sheep are very susceptible to copper poisoning; they can get acute poisoning if they're fed poultry manure or are overdosed with copper sulphate as a remedy for copper deficiency. In such cases, the animals show abdominal pain and green mucoid diarrhoea. Affected animals usually die within 12 hours of ingesting the copper source.

The most common syndrome in sheep is a chronic toxicity, called enzootic icterus or geelsiekte. This syndrome is seen in certain areas in the Karoo, where it is suspected that either low levels of molybdenum or the ingestion of certain plants causes a high level of copper accumulation in the liver, since overgrazing of veld is said to increase the incidence of the condition. When these animals are stressed (usually by pregnancy or worm infestation) the copper stores in the liver are released into the blood, causing an acute haemolytic disease, with massive red blood cell breakdown. This results in anaemia, haemoglobinuria and jaundice. At post-mortem, the carcass is typically yellow and there is a black discoloration of the kidneys.

On farms where the problem occurs, animals can be supplemented (under veterinary supervision) with molybdenum in some form to prevent the increased copper uptake.

Prussic acid poisoning
Syndrome geilsiekte
Plants that contain substances called cyanogenic glycosides become toxic when trampled or damaged by frost, hail, or herbicide application; these processes cause the release of enzymes which then release hydrogen cyanide (prussic acid).

Examples of plants that can potentially cause this are sorghum (*Sorghum*), couch grass (*Cynodon dactylon*), Namaqua daisies (*Dimorphotheca* spp) and some of the acacias (*A caffra, erioloba, sieberiana*).

Symptoms of prussic acid poisoning are difficult breathing and convulsions, but most animals affected die acutely (suddenly) showing minimal signs. On post-mortem examination, these cases can be confused with pulpy kidney, as the kidneys decompose quickly. There's bloating, as well as a blue discoloration of the mucous membranes, subcutaneous haemorrhages and froth in the trachea. There may be a faint smell of bitter almonds from the gut in fresh cases. Confirming the diagnosis of prussic acid poisoning is difficult because it's volatile, and evaporates from the rumen content after 12 – 24 hours. In fresh cases, samples can be taken by a veterinarian for laboratory analysis. Preventing the formation of prussic acid can be achieved by feeding sulphur (flowers of sulphur) in a lick at 5 – 7 %, or hyposodium thiosulphate (hypo) in drinking water at a rate of 1kg/2 000 litres in summer, or 1kg /1 000 litres in winter.

Nitrate poisoning
Some plants accumulate nitrates, especially pigweed or marog (*Amaranthus*), *Brassica* spp, oats, ryegrass, sorghum and wheat, but these are less common causes of poisoning than pastures fertilised with nitrate-containing fertilisers. Nitrate fertilisation is becoming increasingly important as a source of low-grade poisoning, since it raises the nitrate level in plants. Chronic nitrate poisoning symptoms are the suppression of appetite, abortion and bloat.

Death due to nitrate poisoning often occurs when hungry animals are chased into nitrate-fertilised pastures. In goats, browsing on large quantities of *Acacia nilotica* pods cause a form of nitrate poisoning which results in abortion.

Acute nitrate poisoning causes difficult breathing, weakness, brown discoloration of the mucous membranes and diarrhoea. On post-mortem, the blood is a characteristic brown colour. Veterinary help should be sought if nitrate poisoning is suspected, to establish a correct diagnosis and give specific treatment to affected animals. Methylene blue can be administered by a veterinarian for treatment of clinical cases of nitrate poisoning. To prevent poisoning, avoid pastures for 21 days after they've received nitrate fertilisation.

CHEMICAL POISONS

Chemicals such as herbicides and insecticides are still an important cause of livestock poisoning. According to the Toxicology Department of Onderstepoort, the agricultural chemicals aldicarb, carbofuran, terbuphos, tetrachlorphinvos and endosulphan are the most common chemical causes of livestock poisoning. The most common animal health product involved in malicious or accidental poisoning is diazinon, an organophosphate.

The safe handling and storage of these chemicals is therefore of cardinal importance. Overdosing animals with dewormers and making up dips incorrectly or storing them in unlabelled containers are still an important cause of poisoning stock, and underlines the importance of reading labels carefully. Organophosphate poisoning can be treated with veterinary help if given timeously, but for most chemical toxins there are no specific antidotes.

Chemical poisons used as dips and rodenticides like arsensic and strychnine are still found in stores on South African farms, and sometimes attempts to dispose of them result in livestock deaths.

Urea poisoning
The use of urea as a non-protein source of

nitrogen for ruminants is useful but, if not properly managed, it causes poisoning. Urea should be introduced into the diet slowly, on a continuous daily basis, to allow rumen microbes to adapt It should never be given at more than 1% of the total feed intake. Lack of time to adapt, interruption in exposure or excess intake through licks will result in poisoning. Urea is also highly soluble in water, so if lick blocks dissolve in rain water and are drunk, they may cause poisoning.

Urea poisoning results in a generalised alkalosis (increased pH) of the system as a result of the accumulation of ammonia absorbed into the bloodstream. This causes nervous symptoms such as lack of balance, and signs of difficult breathing due to an accumulation of fluid in the lungs, and severe bloating. Death can occur rapidly if the animals are not treated promptly. Treat them with a litre of vinegar diluted in two litres of water, preferably directly into the rumen, since many of these animals are struggling to breathe and the vinegar solution dosed into the lungs will cause foreign body pneumonia. The treatment can be repeated a few hours later, if necessary.

Confirmation of the diagnosis is based on a history of feeding of urea, typical symptoms, severe bloating, a high rumen pH (8) and a response to the vinegar treatment. Prevent urea poisoning by proper feeding management and supervision of urea lick blocks.

Levamisole poisoning

This very effective worm remedy, which is administered as a drench or injection, has a narrow safety margin and will cause poisoning if dosed above the recommended level. This is most often due to the miscalculation of weight, usually in young animals, dosing animals twice or incorrect calibration of the dosing gun. Most commonly, poisoning occurs because the concentrate isn't diluted before being given.

The symptoms occur an hour after dosing. The animals show salivation, lip licking, muscle tremors, excitement and increased breathing rate. The tremors can become very severe and animals may die. The final symptoms are seen 24 – 36 hours after being administered.

The diagnosis of poisoning is made based on the history of dosing and the symptoms. There is no effective treatment, and the animals are best left alone in a shady place as they may recover if the overdose wasn't too high. Levamisole is a useful worm remedy, but must be used accurately to prevent poisoning.

WATER POISONING

The quality of drinking water given to livestock is often overlooked. Decreased water quality is becoming more common in South Africa, because of the contamination of ground water by mining and poor sewerage processing.

In arid areas, brackishness is a major water problem. It's caused by the presence of high levels of various salts in underground water, as a result of local geological conditions. The salts could be sodium chloride, magnesium chloride, sodium sulphate or magnesium sulphate.

Animals forced to drink brackish water show decreased water and food intake; they could also suffer from diarrhoea because of the high concentration of magnesium salts. The brackishness of water is aggravated when the water pumped into troughs evaporates during the day, increasing the concentration of salts. Regular cleaning of troughs will result in more palatable water. Not all boreholes in these areas are brackish, so one should look for the most palatable water for livestock drinking water, or use rain water.

Certain areas have high levels of nitrates in underground water, particularly areas like the Springbok Flats near Pretoria, certain parts of Limpopo, and the North-western Cape. Nitrate contamination of water sources such as streams, dams and underground water can result from run-off from fertilised lands or sewerage contamination. Chronic nitrate poisoning can result from high levels of contamination.

In general, the mineral content of water used for livestock is the same as that required for human consumption, but since the water sources used for animals on a farm are often different from those used by humans, it can be useful to have borehole or river water analysed for its suitability as a water source.

The table below contains rough guidelines for good-quality water.

TABLE 13. Specifications for water suitable for livestock

Parameter	Maximum permissible level
Solids	5 000 ppm*
pH	5,6 – 9
Sodium	2 000 ppm
Calcium	1 000 ppm
Magnesium	500 ppm
Chloride	3 000 ppm
Sulphate	1 000ppm
Fluoride	6 ppm
Nitrate	400 ppm
Adapted from Maree and Casey, 1998 * ppm = parts per million	

NOTES

NOTES

Afrivet's Plan A

Eleven years ago, in its Vision and Mission, Afrivet promised to concentrate its marketing efforts on "the provision of sound technical advice". This serious commitment is met through constant training of our agents, in our product literature, through the Afrivet helpline (0860VEEARTS) and in particular through a series of books on diseases and parasites of livestock for the farmer in southern Africa. This unique series of books specifically for the southern African farmer of which "Diseases and Parasites of Small Stock in South Africa" is the latest, was launched with much acclaim in 2006 and consists now of five books, viz:

- Diseases and Parasites of Cattle, Sheep and Goats.
- A Guide to Animal Diseases in South Africa: Horses, Donkeys and Mules.
- A Guide to Animal Diseases in South Africa: Dogs and Cats.
- A Guide to Animal Diseases in South Africa: Game (the latter three through Briza Publications).
- Diseases and Parasites of Sheep and Goats in South Africa (with Landbouweekblad).

But having technical information available is not enough. The stock owner must also be able to put this information to use and to use it in a scientifically planned way in his flock or herd management strategy. To this end Afrivet developed Plan A, using the country's leading veterinarians in their fields to create a comprehensive health and production management plan for the stock owner and manager.

The first Plan A, for beef cattle, was relatively easy to compile using the seasonality of the environmental challenges such as parasites and the annual breeding cycle of cattle. This is available in hard copy from any Afrivet agent and more details is available from our veterinarians at 0860VEEARTS.

Compiling a similar Plan A for Sheep and Goats proved to be a bigger challenge, due mainly to the fact that small stock can breed three times in two years. Eventually, after much hard thinking we were forced to turn to technology to assist and the electronic Plan A for small stock was born.

A long history of investment and development by various organizations in wool and mutton production means that much of the information, technologies and tools already exist which allow sheep producers to significantly increase productivity, profitability and sustainability – but the information is scattered and often difficult to find. The electronic version of Plan A for Small Stock will help the producer to develop a full flock health programme for a specific flock rather than focusing on a single component such as a vaccination programme. A flock health programme integrates specialised veterinary knowledge with the stock farmer's knowledge of climate, the production cycle of the flock and pasture management of the specific farm.

Plan A for Small Stock captures, in on one handy reference site, useful information about the management of a successful sheep and/or wool enterprise. Leading sheep producers and technical experts helped develop the plan which covers various parasite management and animal health issues.

Plan A will help small stock producers decide on what to focus first to maximise production and profitability. For readers who want to delve deeper into a particular animal health subject or issue, the sheep disease and parasite book comes in very handy. Plan A is not designed as a stand-alone reference but must be supported by your local veterinarian, animal health representative, workshops and other producer learning activities.

Afrivet has produced this electronic plan as part of our continuing efforts to deliver on-farm knowledge and technology to help sheep producers increase the long-term profitability and sustainability of sheep and wool production, and pave the way for a successful industry for the next generation.

Through Plan A all management, vaccination and parasite control measures required for the season are planned for each quarter and useful products for each procedure are detailed.

To register to use Plan A for small stock visit the following website: www.afrivetplana.co.za or enter via www.afrivet.co.za and follow the links to Plan A.

THE PLAN A IS SUPPORTED BY:

- Sound technical advice from any one of Afrivet's fulltime and consultant veterinarians. They can be reached on the Afrivet helpline: 0860VEEARTS.
- Well laid-out technical brochures.
- The Veld Talk technical bulletins on the Afrivet website, www.afrivet.co.za
- One of the largest, technically trained and equipped sales forces in Southern Africa.

For further information contact your nearest Afrivet agent (see the website) or call 0860VEEARTS.

BIBLIOGRAPHY

Bath, G.F. & de Wet, J.A.L. 1994. *Small Stock Diseases*. Tafelberg, Cape Town.

Brightling, A. 2006. *Livestock Diseases in Australia*. C.H. Jerram & Associates – Science Publishers.

Coetzer, J.A.W. & Tustin, R.C. 2004. *Infectious Diseases of Livestock with special reference to Southern Africa*. Oxford University Press, Cape Town.

Esler, K.J., Milton, S.J. & Dean, W.R., 2006. *Karoo Veld – Ecology and Management*. Briza Publications, Pretoria.

Hodkinson, C., Komen H., Snow T. & Davies-Mostert, H. 2007. *Predators and Farmers*. Endangered Wildlife Trust, Johannesburg.

Kellerman, F., Coetzer, J.A.W. & Naude, T.M. 20 *Plant Poisonings and Mycotoxicoses of Livestock in Southern Africa*. Oxford University Press, Cape Town.

Maree, C. & Casey, N. 1998. *Livestock Production Systems*. Agri Development.

Reinecke, R.K. 1983. *Veterinary Helminthology*. Butterworth Publishers, Durban.

Van Oudtshoorn, F.P. 1999. *Guide to Grasses of South Africa*. Briza Publications, Pretoria.

Van Wyk, B., van Heerden, F. & van Oudtshoorn, F.P.) 2002. *Poisonous Plants of South Africa*. Briza Publications, Pretoria.

Key to general symptoms of disease

Diarrhoea

Roundworm infestation
Fluke infestation
Lamb dysentery (lambs)
E. coli (lambs)
Coccidiosis (lambs)
Salmonellosis
Acidosis
Plant poisonings
Water quality

Nasal discharge

Nasal worm
Pneumonia
Jaagsiekte
Vermeersiekte
Blue tongue

Coughing

Jaagsiekte
Lungworm
Lung abscess
Pneumonia
Vermeersiekte

Emaciation

Inadequate nutrition
Roundworm or fluke infestation
Johne's disease
Ketosis (domsiekte)
Tooth problems
Mineral deficiencies (Co, Mb)
Wooden tongue
Chronic wasting (E. Cape)
Seneciosis

Hair/wool loss

Sheep scab (sheep only)
Louse infestation
Lumpy wool
Bolo disease
Copper deficiency
Iodine deficiency (newborn lambs)
Ringworm (goats)
Photo sensitivity
Break in wool (blue tongue)
Plant poisoning (kaalsiekte)

Weakness (adults)

Staggers (poisoning)
Botulism
Starvation
Milk fever
Worn teeth

Weak lambs

Low birth weight
Mismothering/starvation
Enzootic abortion
Congenital defects
Tapeworm infestation
Iodine deficiency

Lameness

(see page 57)

Blindness

Congenital blindness
Ketosis
Eye infections
Injury
Vitamin A deficiency
Acidosis

Abortions
Genetic defects of lambs
Chlamydiophilia (enzootic abortion)
Nutrition (especially Angora goats)
Rift Valley fever
B. melitensis
Fever reactions
Listeriosis
Flavi virus
Ketosis (goats)
Stenocarpella poisoning
Nitrate poisoning

Abdominal distension
Bloat (free gas or frothy)
Big lamb disease
Galenia africana poisoning
Opblaaskrimpsiekte (plant poisoning)
Prussic acid poisoning

Swelling of head/neck
Clostridial infection (dikkop)
Photosensitivity (geel dikkop)
Blue tongue
Snakebite
Bottlejaw (roundworms or Johne's disease)
Goitre

Sudden death
Anthrax
Black quarter (sponssiekte)
Redgut
Plant poisons (heart)
Prussic acid poisoning
Septicaemic pasteurellosis
Trauma (haemorrhage)
Exposure (cold)

Difficult breathing
Pneumonia
Lung abscess
Levamisole poisoning
Jaagsiekte
Nasal worm
Plant poisons
Urea poisoning

Abnormal behaviour
Gid
Heartwater
Rabies
Plant poisons
Ketosis
Milk fever
Botulism

Low lambing percentage
Management problems
Brucella ovis

Jaundice
Plant and fungal poisonings
Copper poisoning

Index

NOTES

NOTES

NOTES

NOTES

www.ingramcontent.com/pod-product-compliance
Lightning Source LLC
Chambersburg PA
CBHW060959030426
42334CB00033B/3294